On 6 August 2003 a former colleague, the Revd Merfyn Temple, at the age of 84, got on to a plane bound for Harare. He had a letter in his pocket which he proposed delivering personally to President Mugabe.

It was a crackpot idea, but Merfyn Temple had always been slightly crazy - crazy like Isaiah, Amos, Jeremiah and Jesus.

He was stopped, surrounded, questioned and intimidated by the soldiers . . . locked up for several days in Harare's Central Police Station. After further traumas, interrogations and conversations with other incarcerated victims he was released and deported.

There were interesting reactions from church members in Britain when his exploits appeared in the press. Official comment suggested that his actions were counter-productive . . . Those, however, who had been on the inside of Mugabe's jails hoped that the Church might produce more people like Merfyn.

Merfyn is one of God's crazy people and 'solid church' has no idea what to do with them. They appear from time to time like comets in the sky. . .

from Beyond the Box, *Tom Stuckey*

Having worked with you in Zambia Government service and in church and community work, I can assure you that you can be an impossible colleague! I once had to pressurise you (successfully) into giving up a hunger strike—but I value your zest for life, your truly prophetic witness, your outrageous courage and your persistence.

email to Merfyn, from Lawrence Taylor

Prophets have occupied this pulpit. I know of at least one, though I don't know him personally. His name is Merfyn Temple. What I hear, and what I have read, convinces me that he was and is, much more of a prophet than a priest. He appears to have been in a direct line of descent, spiritually speaking, from the prophet Amos.

I guess I would have found Merfyn well-nigh impossible to work with as a circuit colleague. But from everything t˙
from people here at All Saints, his was a prc

from Touching the Hem, *Rev. John St*

Visions for Peace

Volume Two

of the memoirs of

Merfyn Temple

edited by

Roland Lubett

millipede books

Published by
Millipede Books,
41a Portnall Road,
London W9 3BA

Copyright © Merfyn Temple, 2012

ISBN-10: 0-9530369-2-8
ISBN-13: 978-0-9530369-2-9
EAN: 9780953036929

Portions of the text have previously appeared in the following publications:
Angelus for Peace in the South Atlantic (1982)
Elephants and Millipedes (Millipede Books, 1997)
New Hope for Africa (Taurus Books, 1991)

The editors also gratefully acknowledge permission from the following to reproduce extracts of copyright material:

Interview with Rev Merfyn Temple by John Pritchard, 2006, The British Library's Sound Archive, Methodist Church Oral Archive project, British Library reference C640/146 © Trustees for Methodist Church Purposes on behalf of the Methodist Church Oral Archive project

Newspaper articles:
Sidmouth Midweek Herald
Brighton Evening Argus

Cover design: Tania Lubett
Set in Dante MT Standard
Printed by Lightning Source

Contents

Illustrations

Photographs and drawings

Newspaper articles

Maps

Broadsheets (publicity flyers and proposals)

Foreword

I FIRST MET Merfyn Temple when we both returned from Africa in 1975. I had spent a mere nine years in Côte d'Ivoire; he had worked in Zambia since 1943. He belonged to a generation of missionaries who expected to devote their working lifetime to overseas service, as had his parents and his father-in-law. But he was persuaded of the case for a moratorium on missionaries, which was advanced by a handful of African and Asian church leaders. They were grateful for the pioneers who had planted, built up and shaped the church. But, they argued, the indigenous leaders now at the helm needed space to reshape the church, its polity and liturgy, with African or Asian characteristics. They felt that they would not attain mature selfhood until their expatriate colleagues withdrew and left them to it.

The view was not widely shared, and the moratorium did not happen, but Merfyn was convinced. And for Merfyn Temple, conviction always produced action. He had played his part in bringing the Zambian nation and the United Church of Zambia to birth. This book is a sequel to *Zambia Stole my Heart*, where that story is told. But, although Zambia had stolen his heart, it was time to go. Some thought his departure was an extravagant gesture, but it was not a gesture at all; it was the extravagance of a woman in Bethany who braved her critics to honour Jesus. Like her, Merfyn often acted on impulse, and like her he was often subjected to sharp criticism, but he had the courage of his convictions.

Visions for Peace tells of Merfyn's life after Zambia, and of a series of return visits in his retirement to the land and people that stole his heart. There were to be plenty more mad impulses and rash actions. Back in Britain, I did the expected thing and went to minister in Sheffield. He took a job as a milkman. For the previous eighteen years he had not been on the Methodist payroll; he had worked as a publisher and then for the Zambian government. He wanted to go on serving his Lord from a secular base. He found he could not do it. The milkman's 3 am start left plenty of hours in the day to be a minister, but he was too weary to use them well. The spirit was willing, enthusiastic, impatient as ever, but the flesh was no longer youthful.

Merfyn was not afraid to admit his mistakes. He returned to full-time ministry in Abingdon, where he was loved for—not in spite of—his quirkiness and passion. He did not regret the extravagant gestures that drove his family wild: his impulsive flight to Chile in the forlorn hope of chartering a boat to sail into the middle of the Falklands/Malvinas war, his round-Britain cycle ride praying for peace at noon each day, even sneaking off to Harare at the age of 84 to deliver a blunt letter to Robert Mugabe charging him with crimes against humanity—an escapade which landed him in a fetid prison cell for three days.

His big mistake, he reckoned, was made in Chipapa, his Zambian village, in 1965 when he was bedazzled by the prospects of the Green Revolution. He made small loans to some of his neighbours so that they could buy 'miracle seed' and fertilizers. In the first year, the results were spectacular, harvests as much as ten times the norm. But in the second year the rains failed, the crops withered, and the farmers were left deep in debt. "Perhaps," he mused in his 1991 book *New Hope for Africa*, "if the benefit of chemical fertilizers had been introduced gradually and selectively, in conjunction with careful measures for soil conservation, rotation of crops, and liberal manuring, little damage need have been done to fragile African soils."

Realising the error of his ways, he became a convert to organic farming. With the courage of his convictions once again, he devoted eight years of retirement to a two-acre organic market garden near Reading; between his 70th birthday in 1989 and 1996 he returned almost annually to his beloved Zambia to encourage organic farming there, and he served with me on the advisory group of the West Africa Agro-Forestry Programme set up by the Methodist Relief and Development Fund.

Our paths kept crossing. The last time was when I recorded a five-hour conversation about his life and passions which is now in the Sound Archive of the British Library. I hear his voice as I read this book. It is the authentic voice of a man with a mission, a servant of God whose vision for peace spurred him on to his dying day.

John Pritchard

A word from the editor

MY PROFOUND THANKS and congratulations go to Ruth Quine. Ruth started work on Merfyn's memoirs in 2008, and has been the chief archivist, co-ordinator, and instigator, diggng through Merfyn's correspondence to find the gems that reveal his mind and vision. Her memory, patience, wisdom, thoroughness and organisation have been at the heart of both volumes of this, her father's memoir.

Thanks too, to Jane, Robin and Patricia for vital details and memories; to Colin Quine for the chronology; to Paul Williams for the account of Merfyn's appointment to All Saints, Abingdon; to Peter Bennett for photographs and information about All Saints and the Peachcroft Centre; to Self Help Africa for updates on their initiatives in Zambia; to Mary Stewart and Ian Rawes at the British Library; to John Pritchard for his foreword, and for the interview with Merfyn; and to Tania for the cover design.

To those who have read *New Hope for Africa*, we beg forgiveness for repeating a condensed version of Merfyn's African odyssey. I also have to confess to a little self-promotion, as I have included my family's and my part in Merfyn's journey, as he celebrated his seventieth birthday with us in Iringa, Tanzania.

This memoir must have its share of mistakes and inaccuracies, for which I take full responsibility. Apologies to the many who feature in this account, whom we did not contact in advance. Many other characters and anecdotes have not made it into the book at all. In particular we have had to leave out much material from the *Methodist Recorder*, as it is not indexed, and none of us had the time to sift through 40 years of the *MR*. I also apologise for the almost three-year gap between Volume One, *Zambia Stole my Heart*, and this volume. Sadly Merfyn did not live to see the job finished; however he knew that his values and his principles would be spread through a Foundation set up in his name.

Roland Lubett

Prologue:
Out of Africa

In August 1974 I said a sad goodbye to my friends in Chipapa, Zambia. For 31 years I had lived and worked in the former Northern Rhodesia, now Zambia, including the last seven as a villager in Chipapa. As a parting present they collected enough money to buy me a copy of Thompson's Chain Reference Bible.

Then I went to State House to say goodbye to President Kenneth Kaunda, whom I had come to know through a Bible study in our home. He gave me a copper tray inscribed with the words:

Reverend Merfyn Temple and Mrs Temple
FOR ALL YOU HAVE DONE IN ZAMBIA WE ARE MOST GRATEFUL
GOD'S BLESSINGS
from His Excellency the President and Mrs Kaunda. August 1974

I had a lump in my throat. For thirty years I had lived in Africa's 'third world' and now I was going to be wrenched back into life in the 'first world'. The thought filled me with trepidation, but one thing gave me joy: I would be back with my family again. No more letters, no more nights when only the light from a flickering candle kept my fears at bay. Now we would touch one another again, and I would somehow find a way back into my children's lives. Ruth was now 28, Jane 26, Robin 24, and Patricia 23.

Living with the people of Chipapa had changed my life. I had not become poor myself, but I had lived alongside them in their poverty. They had taught me so many things: for example, that you don't have to be rich to be happy; that the land if properly used can supply nearly all your food, and give you a little extra to buy your clothes and a little bit of sugar for your tea; that God is not far away, and will stand beside you even when your dearest four-year-old grandchild has been killed by a cobra.

Part One
The Minister

Abingdon ministry: relaxed and stressful moments

Re-Entry

Failure of my 'tent-making' attempt

ON MY RETURN TO BRITAIN, I must have presented something of a problem to the Methodist Church who had originally sent me out as a missionary. Fortunately my old friend Colin Morris was now the General Secretary of the Methodist Missionary Society, and he gave me a couple of years to settle down. He was wise enough to allow me to get rid of a few bees in my bonnet, such as my idea that it was a luxury to have 'full-time ministers'. Having lived for so long without depending on the Church to pay my salary, I was reluctant to return to a situation in which I would have to depend on a congregation. I had been paid for the first 14 years of my ministry by the Methodist Missionary Society, then successively for the next 17 years by the United Society for Christian Literature, the Zambia Youth Service, and the Government of Zambia as a civil servant.

I could not escape the fact that I was a minister of the Gospel, but I wanted to find some way of earning a living, while at the same time preaching. After all St Paul, the original missionary, earned his living as a tent-maker. If he could do it, why couldn't I? What I needed was a job that finished at ten o'clock in the morning so that I could be in the pulpit by eleven. A milkman's job would be just the one for me.

So I signed on as a milkman in the Oxford Milk Co-operative. I used to leave home at 3.00 am on my bicycle, pick up my electric milk float to load dozens of heavy milk crates—1000 bottles—onto my electrically powered milk cart, and finish my round by 10.00 am. For the first week I travelled on a float driven by an intelligent young man just out of school.

He believed in getting the job done quickly, delivering his bottles at the run. Some houses were at the end of a long drive, and I often failed to keep up with him. Living in Africa had kept me looking younger than I was. Once he asked me "How old are you?"

"Fifty-five," I replied.

"What!" he said. "Fifty f***ing five?!"

When I started the rounds on my own, I was unable to get home till after 1 pm. Then Audrey said she would come out to help me. At 6 every morning she would drive out in our little VW Beetle to find me on my milk round[1].

But although I did finish earlier, in the afternoons and evenings when I should have been visiting my parishioners or conducting Church meetings, I became bleary-eyed from lack of sleep.

Everyone on the round was kind to me, one customer leaving me a hot cross bun on Good Friday morning. But I was not a very good milkman. I was too forgetful, not remembering whether a bottle should be green or silver-topped, and being dyslexic I could never tally the numbers with my milk record book at the end of the day. I was in despair, but the Lord intervened and I was crippled with a hernia, for I had been lifting too many crates of full bottles too often. I had to resign and admit that I was, at 'fifty f***ing five', too old to do two jobs at the same time.

For some reason I happened to look in on the annual Methodist Conference, which was meeting somewhere in the Midlands. I knew nobody, and nobody knew me, so I went down to the refectory to get myself a cup of tea. It was a dreary room, and sitting there amongst the empty teacups, I was in a dreary mood. *What is the point,* I said to myself, *of pretending that*

---

1 "Between us we have walked up 350 garden paths and struggled with nearly as many garden gates before we finish [the round] . . Audrey and I are developing such appetites that we get through a loaf of brown bread as fast as an elephant can eat a hand of Fyffes bananas . ."
   Letter to his mother, March 1975

I am a minister, when I seem to have spent my life doing all sorts of jobs that any layman could do, probably a lot better than me?

Then there came into that room a man I had not seen since we were at school together. He was an up-and-coming minister, later to become principal of the top Methodist ministerial training college in Cambridge.

"Michael," I said, "it's no good. I'm no minister. What has happened to my calling? I'm going to resign from the ministry."

"Oh no, you're not," he said. "Our calling is a two-way thing. It is not just God calling us; after all, we have both been ordained by the Methodist Church. When our Church tells us that they don't need us any more, that is when you can start talking about resignation. Stop worrying; just get on with the job."

The allotment

The other step that I took in my search for self-sufficiency, was to find myself an allotment in Oxford. At first I was told there were none to spare; then the secretary of the allotment association said, "Wait a minute. There are two allotments on the land we rent from Pergamon Press, which have never been used, because they were reserved for a parking lot which we have never had planning permission to use. They are yours for the asking."

It was only seven minutes' walk from the house, so I went to see. The plot was covered with ten-foot-high bushes—elderberry and hawthorn—amongst which the local populace had thrown anything from mattresses to bicycle frames and broken concrete. It was a challenge, but no harder than stumping trees at Nambala. Someone had told me that you get the best results for vegetables if you dig trenches two feet deep, which I proceeded to do. But then I discovered that even at two 'spits' deep, there was no gravel or clay. It was deep, rich earth like chocolate cake. I later found out that long ago the owners of the big house, which is now Pergamon Press, had dumped the manure from their stables on this bit of land. Also, less than a quarter of a mile away was a huge pile of leaf mould made up from years of sweeping up millions upon millions of leaves from the local park.

New openings: Abingdon and the Grubb Institute

I took on a part-time job with the Grubb Institute of Behavioural Studies, and also worked part-time as a Methodist minister in Abingdon, south of Oxford. I was on the doorstep of the Atomic Energy Commission at Harwell, and many of my congregation were high-powered scientists there. Looking back, it seems like one of God's jokes that he should put a rough-and-ready missionary in charge of such a highly intelligent and sophisticated bunch of people. I think I had more scientists per metre of pew than any other church in Britain.[2]

The Grubb Institute did not work out well, but the people of Abingdon seemed to like me, and I began to love them. All my ideas of being a self-sufficient tent-maker had to go out of the window.

> I have had such a warm and enthusiastic welcome in the Abingdon Circuit that it seems almost too good to be true . . . John Dolling is a good 'organisation man' so all that side of the church's activity I can confidently leave to him, and myself get on with the pastoral and preaching work. The Church Stewards have spent £800 on re-decorating and furnishing the old Caretaker's cottage as a study for me and a church 'office' which will be 'personed' (not manned) by a rota of lay folk to answer the telephone, type church notices, etc.
>
> There is often a service to take on Sunday afternoon at one of the villages—we have three villages besides the two main churches in Abingdon. Some Sundays of course I go to other churches in the Circuit, Wantage, Didcot or Wallingford. The fact that you know where I am preaching and that you are praying is a great 'comfort'—using that word in the proper Biblical way. This whole ministry of intercession becomes more and more important as one realises how, humanly speaking, the task you have to do is utterly impossible: with only two afternoons a week, how can I possibly visit everyone in need? and how can I possibly satisfy the unique hunger of every soul in the congregation?
>
> The work for the Grubb Institute begins to take shape. I do not move easily in the company of sociologists and psychologists, and a busy London office full of Bright Young Men who talk a language I don't easily understand keeps me in a state of nervous tension; but I only go to London one

---

2 In his first years in Abingdon, Merfyn worked with two congregations: Trinity, the older town-centre church, and All Saints, planted in 1959 to serve the town's growing northern suburbs. By late 1977 Merfyn was giving most of his time to All Saints, and became their full-time minister the following year.

day a week, and on the other two days I manage to do my work in my own rather laborious and cumbersome way. However I am getting into touch with all kinds of interesting people and there are great possibilities.

Letter to mother, September 1976

Peachcroft

One day I went to see what was happening on the new half-built Peachcroft Estate in Abingdon. Houses of every shape and size were going up all over the place, but there was no sign of shops or a church or community centre.

The next day I went to visit the Planning Office in town. They said they had made provision for an acre of land for a church, but no one had been interested. "If you are interested," they said, "you had better get a move on. We can't keep the option open indefinitely."

Then a strange thing happened. I was in Wantage at a big Methodist Circuit meeting. On the other side of the room was an elderly lady I hardly knew. Later she told me that she had looked across the room and said to herself, *That young man* (I was fifty-eight years old) *looks as though he needs money.* So she came over and joined our little group.

"So you want money to buy a site for a church?" she said. "I'm on. But how much will it cost?"

"I don't have the faintest idea," I said.

"Well, you had better find out."

A few days later I went back to her and said somewhat diffidently, "It will be £20,000." She hesitated only a moment and then said, "When I say something I mean it. There will be a cheque in the post tomorrow, but remember, this is an anonymous gift."

I don't think this lady had any idea exactly where Peachcroft Estate was, and as far as she was concerned, a 'church' would be another Methodist church. There was nothing in writing, and I knew there was no chance of building another Methodist church within spitting distance of All Saints Methodist Church. So I went to the next meeting of a group which called itself 'All Churches Together in Abingdon' and announced brazenly that I had in the bank under my own name £20,000 for a church in Peachcroft, and it would have to be an ecumenical church.

They were all ministers of religion in that meeting, each with their own ecclesiastical corner to defend. They thought about it for a while, and then the Chairman said, with a sense of relief in his voice, "I am sure

Peachcroft: the 'tent of meeting', February 1986

Peachcroft: the first church, 1987

we are all greatly humbled by this magnificent gift, but of course it will be necessary to set up an L.E.P. (Local Ecumenical Project). I will get in touch with our local Ecumenical Officer."

There I was, falling at my first hurdle, but I had a wily old friend called Ron Faires, who knew the ecumenical movement inside out. Ron told me, "I know what we will do. We will create a board of six people and set up our own company, which we will call the Peachcroft Church Trust. You know these days you can buy a company off the peg. They have done it in Northampton, so let's go and see."

The Northampton church was an imaginative project. They had bought an excellent site right in the centre of a new shopping complex, and it was open seven days a week, staffed by a rota of ecumenical officers. I knew this was what we wanted: a church right at the centre of the Peachcroft community.

Of course we ran into all kinds of problems. Radley College, who owned the land, reduced our promised acre to a quarter-acre and offered another quarter to a newly formed Community Centre. They approached us, and suggested we combine our resources and put up one building. "No way," I said. "We are not going to have our Sunday worship in a place reeking of beer."

Then our tight-fisted landlord offered us a ninety-nine year lease for a peppercorn rent. That suited us just fine, because our £20,000 had been well invested, and we could think seriously about plans for a brand-new ecumenical church.[3]

My tour of China, 1977

When still in Zambia, I had followed with great interest developments in China. By putting the production of food at the heart of 'the Revolution', millions of rural peasants were not only learning how to feed themselves, but were changing the entire economy of the country.

Perhaps they had something to say to us in Zambia. Kaunda had already taken a planeload of his ministers to China to see for themselves. They came back, made the right noises, and said to the president that in no way would the African peasantry ever set up 'communes'. I had asked Kaunda to send me on a trip to see for myself, but Mark Chona,

---

3 The church was built and thrives. See photographs opposite, and the present church and current minister's letter to Merfyn on p. 222.

the President's *eminence grise*, made it quite clear that the future of Zambia was capitalism, not communism. He had seen the ineffectiveness of Nyerere's vast 'villagisation' in Tanzania, and wanted nothing to do with it. He made it quite clear to his boss that Merfyn Temple the white man should not go to China, and that was that!

However on my return to the UK, I had joined the Society for Anglo-Chinese Understanding, and in 1977 I was given leave by the church in Abingdon to join a small group which once a year was invited to send a delegation to visit China, to see how the Communist Revolution was transforming their country. We each had to pay our own airfares, but once we crossed the border from Hong Kong, the Chinese took total charge, paying for everything from the best hotel accommodation, to first-class rail and air tickets.

Each member of the delegation declared their own particular interest. Mine was agriculture, with a special interest in maize cultivation. I knew that to declare an interest in the Church would have blotted my copybook, so like Brer Rabbit I 'laid low and said nothing', though I did keep my eyes open. Some of us wanted to see the schools, the prisons or the hospitals, but all I wanted to understand was how the Communes worked and how China had learned to feed its vast population. They knew I had been in Zambia, where maize is the staple diet, so they flew us up to the northern provinces, where I was to see great fields of ripening maize.

It is 7.30 am and we have just arrived off the train from the North – we left Harbin at 2.00 yesterday – trains are like Rhodesian railways – 4 to a cabin but much cleaner and more luxurious – 1st, 2nd and 3rd class. We as honoured guests of course travelled 1st – departure and arrival dead on time. Excellent dinner served on train. I did not write from the North because letters take 15 days. We are now going down to breakfast then out to spend the day in a P.L.A. camp (People's Liberation Army).

I am now just beginning to surface after the euphoric first experiences – getting quite a few glimpses behind the scenes – taking early morning walks in the back streets, and learning how to ask the questions which probe beneath the surface.

The visit to the North was tremendously exhilarating. Three days on the oil fields of Taching and three days visiting the countryside round Harbin. We are the first group of foreign visitors ever to have been

Wood carver, commune near Shanghai

allowed to visit rural communes N.E. of Harbin because it is a sensitive area – Heilungkiang Province borders on Russia. It shows the growing confidence of the Chinese in the success of their rural development programme that they are willing to let us see – these were not their showpiece communes, but better than average. Because we were the first foreign visitors, we were the subject of great curiosity. As we drove through one country town, the people lined the streets to wave and clap. In our two minibuses with Chinese Jeeps escorting us we had to behave like royal personages – our faces had to keep smiling and our hands waving. The streets were full because it was both the three-day celebration of the ending of the 11th Congress (confirmation of Hua Ku-Feng as Party Chairman) and the feast of the beginning of the rice harvest of the Korean Minority.

In Harbin the hotel in which we stayed on the 4th floor has a balcony looking out on the Central Square (hotel built by the Japanese in 1933 when they were in control of Manchuria). Every night there were processions in the streets with lanterns, drums, dances, fire crackers – the lot. One evening we went out and joined in.

> I must stop now. Am keeping very fit and surprisingly not putting on
> too much weight. Hernia no problem and I never have to stand too long.
> No tension in the party – we share rooms – different pairs in each place.
> Photography very frustrating – very difficult to 'snap' the things I want
> to record from train and bus windows. I'm just hoping I have enough
> good shots for a slide show – Very grateful to have Tom's camera which
> works beautifully.   *Letter to Audrey*

Of course the tour was a major exercise in Chinese propaganda to show
the world the wonders of Chairman Mao's great Cultural Revolution, and
indeed when I compared it with the general state of affairs in Zambia, I
was profoundly impressed. What an amazing change from the China my
father had found when he arrived there as a young missionary in 1910!
Then he had been allowed to preach the Gospel wherever he wanted,
and had built a big church in Canton. In 1977 no churches were allowed
to remain open. They had been taken over by the Government, who
strangely paid rent for them. All missionaries were strictly forbidden, but
unknown to me, Bibles were being printed and distributed in large numbers. The underground church was growing fast.

I was almost twice the age of the other members of the group, all
ardent Socialists who, when permitted to speak at the end of our many
sumptuous banquets, would clench their fists and call down curses on
our Government for their 'despicable' behaviour in Northern Ireland. For
them China seemed to be more Christian than Britain. "Surely," they said
to me, "can't you see it for yourself? When you missionaries were here,
millions died of famine or disease, and millions more were swept away in
the great floods of the first half of this century. Can you blame the Chinese who when they read the 'Little Red Book' call Chairman Mao their
God?"

They kept from us a great deal that they did not want us to see, and
we were always in the company of 'minders'. Once I had the inestimable
privilege of being lost for four hours in the streets of Shanghai and walking alone for 14 kilometres in the crowds. I pleaded guilty of having a bad
cold, and walked apparently unobserved along one of the main streets,
where I saw a blind beggar entertaining the crowd who threw money into
his hat as he sang Tibetan songs. There was clearly quite a large black
economy going on, for I saw many women who had made cloth slippers

in their homes, selling large bundles to local shopkeepers, and of course on every street corner were gangs of young men engaged in some kind of gambling.[4]

We were flown to the capital and given an official banquet. At an enormous round table we were given an endless meal of Chinese food. On either side of us sat our hosts, using their chopsticks to help us taste the other delicacies on the table. Unlike ourselves, the Chinese mix their food in a kind of glorious salad. One moment you are eating delicately fried fish, then a griddle cake dripping with honey, then a pork sausage and a sweet rice pudding.

Factory worker, Shanghai

I did keep a diary, but it is too long to quote. Some of my memories will stick for ever: the oil wells of Taching, the Great Wall, and early one morning in Mukden, seeing a man empty his potty in the street. Long meetings sitting at tables spread with white cloths, sipping endless glasses of green tea from multi-coloured thermos flasks. Everything had to be translated into English. To show my interest, I had to write down in my notebook complicated lists of annual food production figures.

But what so impressed me was to see how everyone was working, whether it was the peasants in the fields or the road sweepers on the city streets. Chairmen Mao had died the year before, and the country was in the hands of the Gang of Four. We were asked to 'criticise' anything we saw to be wrong. I spoke my mind when we were taken round a

---

4 At a time when any foreigner was the object of acute curiosity, we can hardly imagine the impression created by Merfyn's striking, tall figure.

generator factory making huge turbines for hydro-electric dams. The work force was clearly unskilled and ill-disciplined. Compared with the efficiency and skill I had seen on the Zambian copper mines, they made a poor showing. But the people to whom I voiced my criticism always had a pat answer, "It is the Gang of Four who are responsible."

From the fifth floor of the only multi-storey hotel in Beijing, I could see the twin towers of the city's Roman Catholic cathedral. On one, the wooden cross stood out clearly in the rays of the rising sun. On the other, the cross had fallen sideways and hung like a drunken man trying to commit suicide. China did not like 'missionaries' so when I put my occupation on my passport, I had simply written the word 'clerk', which was strictly true because after all, I was a clerk in Holy Orders. Early one morning before our minders had arrived, I slipped out to see whether anyone was there, but all the high barred gates were locked. Only a frightened janitor peered at me through the bars.

On our last day I came to the wide flight of steps which lead up to the front door of our hotel, and who should I see there but my old enemy Mark Chona. I greeted him in my best ChiBemba, then we went our separate ways. I wonder what he told Kaunda on his return. Perhaps he said, "Comrade President, I don't think there is any danger of our people becoming Communists. Those Chinese never seem to stop working." There were few cars on the road, but the main street of Beijing in the rush hour was one mass of bicycles.

Looking back on the China I experienced then, I realise how mistaken I was in my low opinion of its progress. What has transformed China from a Third World country to become one of the richest economies of our time? How is it that a country that in my lifetime expelled all its Western missionaries, has become one of the fastest-growing churches in the world? I wish I could live another ninety years to find out.

For All the Saints

WHEN THE WESLEYANS BUILT the grey-stone Trinity Church in Conduit Road a hundred years ago, Abingdon was a sleepy country town, just far enough from the City of Oxford to have a private life of its own.

In those days the Methodists were a fairly confident lot, and they made sure that their church spire soared into the quiet skies above the gently flowing Thames a good ten feet higher than the steeple of St Helen's Parish Church in the centre of the town.

Speaking to some of my friends who still worship in All Saints, they say, "We have great difficulty in remembering any of the many sermons you preached from the pulpit, but we do remember your prayers of intercession. We do so because you seemed often to pray for real people, describing in detail the context of their condition, whether it be spiritual or physical."

A few examples come to mind: one about Jimmy Barnes and Mrs McTaggart, and one involving the Fitzharry Secondary School, which was attended by a number of younger members of the congregation.

Jimmy Barnes and Mrs McTaggart

Saturday 23 October was the day of the church's Autumn Fayre. For this event, if for no other, all the congregation turned out. The Sunday School Hall was packed with people buying and selling their sponge cakes, their jams, chutneys, and white elephants to raise money for the Help the Aged Fund. As I was leaving the hall at 1.30 that afternoon with my purchases, I spotted two boys who seemed to be behaving in a most suspicious manner round the back of the church. Grabbing them by their collars, and

May Day 1979: Merfyn and some of the 'activists' of All Saints, on the steps of the church, about to set off on the annual cycle ride round the circuit.

towering over them in my ecclesiastical wrath, six feet of threatening clerical suit and collar, I shouted, "And what do think you are up to you scallywags, breaking down my boiler room door?!"

"Hey mister we ain't done nuffin," they said with wide-eyed innocence. "We was just walking across the playing field when we saw two big boys bashin' down the door with that there brick. When we come over to see what they was doing they ran off. Shall we go after them mister for you?"

"No," I said, suddenly relenting and feeling I had made a fool of myself, "come over with me to the office at the Lodge and I'll ring the police and you can tell them your story."

As we sat waiting for the police to arrive, our Church Steward came into the office and talked to the boys.

"It is very good of you two boys to help us catch these hooligans. I just can't understand why they should want to do a thing like that to us. We haven't done them any harm, so why can't they just leave us in peace?"

The next day was Sunday, and the police, who were keeping a special eye on the empty manse next door, caught the same two boys inside the house, breaking windows, smashing light bulbs and trying to set fire to the curtains. When we got an estimate for the repair of damage done, the bill came to £150. Since the police had caught them red-handed, they could prosecute and that let the Church off the hook. At least we would avoid the unpleasant publicity.

Everyone was prepared to forgive and forget the incident. That is everyone except me. I could not forget that sudden rush of shame as I laid hands on those two small boys. It was the younger of the two, aged twelve, fair-haired and blue-eyed who kept coming back into my mind, saying "I am not a vandal, I am an angel." Was he perhaps sent to us in Abingdon with some special kind of message?

I found out that his name was Jimmy Barnes and that he attended Lark-mead school, so I went to see the deputy head who said, "Yes, we all know Jimmy. He is not what you might call a bad boy, he just seems uncontrollable. I sometimes wonder if there is something wrong with his chemistry … "

So I got Jimmy's address, a small terraced house in Edward Street, only a few hundred yards from the church. The woman who opened the door smiled a welcome and invited me in, saying: "You must be the vicar of the Church Jimmy is in trouble with."

From the moment I stepped into the long low room which stretched from back to front of the house, it was obvious that either Mr Barnes had private means or he was a very skilful do-it-yourself man. The television set was hidden in a cavity in the stonework of the chimney piece, and tropical fish tanks had been cleverly designed to fit the panelled walls. Fred Barnes was the driver of one of those monstrous car transporters which delivered the products of the factories in Cowley to the distant corners of the British Isles. That was the root of the problem of Jimmy Barnes's vandalism. His father hardly spent a night during the week at home, and although she didn't go out to work, his mother had her hands full with two small children.

When I arrived, Jimmy was upstairs in his own room, which his father had never managed to finish off for him. He came down when his mother called him, bringing his pet hamster with him. We went back up to his room to see his very remarkable collection of birds' eggs. It was especially precious to him because he could never add to it, having been persuaded that it is a bad thing to rob birds' nests. It wasn't as though Jimmy didn't know who I was, because after all I was the man who had handed him over to the police, but he was obviously puzzled. Suddenly he said,

"Are you a psychologist or sumfin?"

"No" I said "I'm not a psychologist. I'm on my rounds."

"You ain't no milkman," said Jimmy.

"I used to be," I said, "but when I go on my rounds these days, I don't deliver bottles, I just go round seeing people."

"What sort of people?" he said.

"Any sort of people, that are in any kind of trouble, like Mrs. McTaggart down the road, who is in trouble because they have taken her husband off to hospital and she is eighty-four and she can't take it. And you, because you are in trouble with the police."

The last time I visited the house was on Thursday 23 December, and I spent most of the time letting Fred explain to me the difference between a Radar speed trap and a Vascar trap. All the time that Fred was talking to me, I could see that Jimmy was trying to get his word in. I knew the impending court case was hanging heavy over him. As I got up to go, he said he wanted to ask me a question but now he had forgotten what it was. He thought it might be about a bird he had seen which he couldn't identify, so I suggested he try to do a drawing of the bird and bring it around to Church Lodge.

At the stroke of ten the next day, there he was on our doorstep with his picture, but at that moment the telephone rang. It was a message from the lady at the Social Services.

"Please would the minister add his persuasive voice to all the other voices which were trying to persuade old Mrs. McTaggart, who was in danger of dying from hypothermia, to give authority to the gas men to move in to change her 5p in the slot to a quarterly account meter?"

When I put the phone down, there was Jimmy who seemed quite happy to spend the rest of the day with us, so I suggested he come with me on my rounds.

We found Mrs McTaggart in the cold kitchen of her Victorian red-bricked, bow-windowed semi, sitting upright on a bentwood chair as near as she could get to the single bar of a small electric fire. She said she had plenty of food in the house, and to prove it she lifted the lid of her bread bin to show us a few crusts at the bottom of their waxed paper packet. "I had no idea I was getting so low," she said, "I must go out and get some more bread from the baker."

Jimmy offered to go for her, but she refused and began to put on her threadbare coat. There was nothing she would let us do, least of all persuade her to sign the form to give the gas men authority to change her meter.

Jimmy went home for lunch as he had promised, but at 1:30 he was back on our doorstep clutching a plastic wrapped loaf of sliced, low-calorie bread.

"I told my mum all about Mrs. McTaggart," he said. "She said I could take her this bread if I liked, but the old lady might not take it because when people get old like that they don't like being given things."

So I said, "O.K., Jimmy, you come in and make her a Christmas card like the one you made for me and we'll take it round to her." So he sat at the desk with my coloured felt-tipped pens, and I showed him how to spell Mc-T-A-G-G-A-R-T. When he had finished we got a piece of sellotape and fastened the card firmly onto the wrapper of the loaf.

Just then I remembered that I had not arranged the chairs in the church for the midnight mass, so I asked Jimmy if he would come over to help me, as the church caretaker had gone home.

Before we started to move the chairs, Jimmy who was still carrying the loaf of bread, took it over to the Christmas tree and put it under the branches on the floor. I said, "What about taking one slice out of the packet and putting it on the high altar for God?"

"O.K." said Jimmy, "a slice for God, but how do you think he is going to come down and get it, unless we throw it up into the sky for Him?"

I didn't know how to answer. I just remember mumbling something theological and incomprehensible as we propped a slice against the stand of the big brass cross on the table.

We brought the dining-room table from the choir vestry and put it right in the middle of the church. I explained how all our people would come for a midnight feast and I said,

"I'll tell you what I will do, Jimmy, when they are all here tonight sitting round the table. I'll tell them about the bread you and your mum sent along for Mrs. McTaggart, and I'll take that slice of bread off the altar and put it with the other bread on the table there."

"Will you truly?" said Jimmy, with eyes shining so brightly it was as though he had already seen it happen. "Then when you tell them what I done, they won't think I'm as bad as what they thought I was."

We went out to take Mrs. McTaggart her loaf of bread. When we got to her house we found she had already gone up to the hospital to see her husband. In order that we would know just how far she had to walk each day on an empty stomach, we began to count the paces from her front door to the front door of the hospital: 1370, about three-quarters of a mile.

There she was, sitting bolt upright, silent and unsmiling by her husband's wheelchair. Jimmy gave her the present and she had quite a job undoing the sellotape.

I went along to have a word with the Sister in charge to see if we could find some way of persuading Mrs. McTaggart to have a meal at the hospital. When I came back, the old man, all twisted and slumping forward in his chair, was somehow feeding himself with a slice of bread. All the way home Jimmy kept asking me whether I had noticed the old man eating the bread, and the tame sparrow which had flown into the ward and was picking up the crumbs under his chair.

Prayer and action: The CUSA anniversary, 1980

I had been talking to the teenagers in Fitzharry School about Zambia's precarious economic situation. I had plenty of subject matter. By 1980 Zambia was in an economic mess caused by three things:

1. The price of copper had fallen dramatically on the world market.
2. Kaunda's refusal to buy oil through South Africa meant importing it by truck through Dar-es-Salaam in East Africa.
3. Mismanagement and corruption was rife throughout all Government institutions, including the copper mines.

As so often happens in a country like Zambia, it is the poor who suffer. I had heard from my friends that all imports of rubber tyres had been declared illegal, because of Kaunda's determination to stop trade with South Africa. This had brought to a stop all use of bicycles, which was a disaster facing villagers living in rural areas whose only form of transport for themselves and their goods was the bicycle.

I had told the Fitzharry students about the need for inner tubes. Then out of the blue came an invitation for me to attend the tenth anniversary of the founding of CUSA, the Credit Union Savings Association of

Zambia. I had been their first Chairman. The airfare would be paid for by the Government, so of course I accepted. What should I take as a gift? Why, a bicycle of course for Daniel, and as many inner tubes as I could raise money for. Fitzharry School gave generously.

I bought a small folding bicycle to put in the aircraft hold along with 120 inner tubes. On arrival I cycled up to State House on my mini-bike. Kaunda had been a patron of CUSA since its inception, so gave me a warm reception, asking Zambia Television to invite me to their studios to show off the bicycle and call the citizens of Lusaka to join in CUSA's celebrations. And what a celebration it was! The police band led the rejoicing people from the station all the way down Cairo Road, bringing the reluctant traffic to a halt.

I found that in the six years since I had left Zambia, the Secretary of the Association had done amazing things, not only training and employing a large staff but buying Pioneer House, a five-story building at the end of Lusaka's main street. The Secretary arranged for me to go to Chipapa so that I could present Daniel with his folding bicycle. Of course he never had occasion to fold it, and it was not long before it showed its total inadequacy for riding along Chipapa's tortuous paths.

For All The Saints

All Saints was the only English congregation to which I was appointed. I thank God for it, because the people became my dearest friends. This story is better told by members of the congregation to whom I ministered, than by myself. Fortunately, 50 years after All Saints was born, they published a little commemorative booklet, *For All the Saints,* from which I have taken the following extracts.

Merfyn Temple was an impressive preacher but he was a very emotional man. On one occasion he broke down in tears in the pulpit when he was preaching about something he felt very strongly about. There was an awkward silence as everyone wondered what was going to happen—he was clearly unable to continue with the sermon—and then Dorothy Beaumont stood up and said, "I think we should sing hymn number . . ." and we did. The organist began to play and we all sang, very quietly, seated, until he recovered.

A similar thing happened when a member of the congregation had a bad asthma attack in the service. It seems to be a standard Methodist reaction: if in doubt, sing something!   *Mary and Tony deVere*

We came to All Saints because it was the closest Methodist church to our house in Abingdon, but I have found that it matches my churchmanship as well as any Methodist church could. It's the best fit to what I believe about worship, which is that it should be liturgical, Eucharistic and honest. For me, the architecture says it all: the church was designed to be 'table-centred'. Many of our ministers—Tony Perry, Ron Berry, even Merfyn Temple, and supremely John Stanbury—have been men who believed that adopting your pet notions in the pulpit is not what worship is about. It's about celebrating the presence of God in this place. All Saints has maintained this stance through thick and thin, and I've done my best to support it.

Another impressive person was Audrey Temple, the wife of Merfyn. Audrey was a medical doctor who had practised in Zambia when they lived there. She was a beautiful person and clearly a saint: she spent her whole life supporting Merfyn. In their time we also got involved in a huge number of activities. Derek Pooley said Merfyn was wonderful at passing balls to people—by the time he left, the whole church membership was holding one or more!   *Paul Williams*

Back in the USA a group of friends and I had been writing and conducting feminist worship services, and when I came to England, All Saints felt very provincial—women's lib seemed to be viewed as a joke. I remember Merfyn Temple saying in a sermon that he had been on holiday with his wife and children, and he had realised for the first time how hard it was looking after babies; the congregation just laughed.

However, Merfyn was open to new ideas. When I asked him, "why do you always refer to 'sons of God' and not daughters?" he replied that it was Biblical. But he went away and researched it, and came back and said, "You're right, you can just as well say 'children of God'," and so he did. He allowed me to preach a sermon on the femininity of God. Some years later I instigated a service on an ecological theme, but by then I wasn't allowed to lead it because I was no longer a local preacher.   *Pauline Sykes*

The Entomologist

Our minister's ministry's shortly to cease
He's going to devote all his efforts to peace.
He surely won't think that this time of his life
Has been tainted by constant unint'rupted strife.
We've all grown to love his astonishing ways
And the outrageous sermons that sometimes he says.
His lifestyle has not been to everyone's like
Unless they wake, sleep and eat on a bike.
One day, on an outing to Oxford, I'm told,
He fell into the Cherwell and got very cold.
He didn't, it seems, standing firm in a punt,
Let go of the pole, a spectacular stunt,
Only matched by the swim and the subsequent trip
With the long-suffering ladies, and him in a strip
More in line with the athletes they first went to see
In Chariots of Fire at the town's ABC.

There's a story that's told and I'm sure it's not lies,
When a project of his caught the President's eyes.
Concerned that his household was wasteful to run,
He built a device that was not meant for fun;
A bio-efficient and composting loo
In a lean-to contained, to protect a fine view.
From the obvious input it made gas at nights
But you sat in the dark to avoid naked lights.
But last I must tell of a hobby that seems
To have featured for years, and is part of his dreams.
It's a passion for insects, not spiders or flies
But BEETLES with wheels; on his drive one now lies.
There's always one standing outside for the juncture
When 500 tyres all at once have a puncture.

I really don't know what we'll do when he goes
He's certainly kept all the saints on their toes.
Perhaps we'll relax. But I don't think we will,
For the spectre of Merfyn will be with us still,
Saying, 'Why not do this, or the other or that?
Let's build a coffee bar. Let's have a chat

About new kinds of service, the needs of the town
Or the world or the country. We've got to get down
To a challenging project that needs to be done
If a sense of achievement is going to be won.'

Audrey and Merfyn, you go with our love
Thank you for giving us all a big shove
And showing us all what we're able to do
When led by a vision and guided by you.

Read as a 'Farewell to Merfyn Temple' at a Church Concert on 18 June 1983

All Saints Church, Abingdon

Part Two
The Peacenik

PRAYER for PEACE

ACTIVE PRAYER
ONE YEAR OF PRAYER FOR PEACE

A meeting of reflection and celebration as we continue to proclaim the centrality of prayer in the struggle for peace.

ST. JAMES'S CHURCH, PICCADILLY, LONDON, W I.

TUESDAY 13th JULY 7.00pm

Introduced by Revd. Kenneth Greet (Moderator of the Free Church Federal Council)

MERFYN TEMPLE
recently returned from a personal peacemaking mission in Latin America.

"A lifted Cross is where the vertical and horizontal meet. Where prayer and action fuse, peace shines through."

SATISH   KUMAR
walked around the world taking a message of peace between people.

"to combat fear and free us from a feeling of helplessness we need to add the dimension of global prayer and positive meditation for world peace"

The meeting will include a period of silent prayer and meditation.

Music and singing from "PEACE CHILD" (courtesy the composer David Gordon) by the M.A.Y.C. Singers and Rock Band.

"Let us spread the good news that prayer is our strength"
Mother Teresa, announcing the Prayer for Peace at St.James's, 7th July 1981

Further details: The Caravan, 197 Piccadilly, London, W.1.
439 8498/771 4078

PLEGARIA por LA PAZ

Praying for Peace

In June 1984, I had arrived in Swaffham during the last days of my bicycle pilgrimage round Britain with the Prayer for Peace. I was preaching in the Methodist Church. The minister said, "We are so glad to have you here today, Merfyn; this pilgrimage of yours has captured the imagination of thousands of people as you have gone around the country. You have enfolded us all with prayer and I'm sure you have been making a very fine contribution to the peace on earth which we all so earnestly and prayerfully desire. Now we'd like you to talk to us."

"Let's begin by saying together the Prayer for Peace.

Lead me from Death to Life,
from Falsehood to Truth.

Lead me from Despair to Hope,
from Fear to Trust.

Lead me from Hate to Love,
from War to Peace.

Let Peace fill our Heart,
Our World, our Universe.

Peace · Peace · Peace

"It is intentional that the prayer begins with the individual: 'Lead *me* . . .' The seeds of peace must germinate in *my* heart, then they will flower naturally into the collective and the universal.

"A lifted cross is where the vertical and the horizontal meet. When prayer and action fuse, peace shines through.

"This ancient prayer has been marvellously brought to this country by a young Jainist monk called Satish Kumar. He has now become quite an important figure in Britain, as he is the President of the Schumacher Society. Schumacher wrote *Small is Beautiful*. Satish Kumar tries to live out his life in the light of Schumacher's beliefs, about not allowing things to get too big or organisations to become too impersonal, and that everything that can be reduced to the human level must be of God.

"Satish Kumar set out 20 years ago from his home in India. In his heart was this Prayer for Peace. He believed that the source of most of the trouble in the world was not in India, it was in the West. As he watched the great confrontation between Russia and America, he came to believe that he, an Indian-speaking monk of no reputation at all, should take this prayer to Moscow and to the President of the United States of Russia, he should go to the United States of America, and he should also go to London and to Paris. It took him two years to reach those capitals but he never took a lift, he just walked. Someone paid the fare for him to cross the Atlantic.

"When he came to England, he had begun to learn English and share his prayer with English-speaking people, and he didn't mind who he spoke to or who he prayed with, whether they were Jews or Muslims, Buddhists or Christians. And Christians began to recognise that this prayer contained so much of what they believed.

"So the Christian leaders of this country gave support to this prayer, phoned Mother Theresa and said to her, 'Will you come and launch this on behalf of all the churches?' This was at St. James', Piccadilly, in July 1981 on the eve of the World Disarmament Conference."

April 1982
To Tom Benyon, MP for Abingdon

Dear Mr Benyon,

I would like to make my personal protest to you about our Government's expenditure on arms.

I am deeply concerned at the accelerating arms race. I deplore the use of resources for military expenditure which are desperately needed to tackle the world-wide and domestic problems of poverty, hunger, ignorance and disease.

I urge you to do everything in your power to press Her Majesty's Government to be more active in seeking international disarmament, and to give full support to the forthcoming United Nations Special Session on Disarmament.

Yours, Rev. Merfyn M. Temple

22 April 1982
Editor, Abingdon Herald

Sir,

I am not always proud of being British, but I was very proud of our democratic way of life when Tom Benyon our MP arranged for a small delegation to go from one of Abingdon's largest public meetings ever held (on the Brandt Commission Report), to see Margaret Thatcher at 10 Downing Street.

Where else in the world is a little bunch of total non-entities given the opportunity, by someone whose political views they do not share, to express those views personally to a Prime Minister with whom they are often in total disagreement?

Many people who would wish to do so will not be able to attend the mass lobby for Survival being organised by the United Nations Association on Tuesday. But there is no reason why anybody should not write to Tom Benyon saying precisely what stance our Government should take at the UN Assembly.

With many others, I shall be urging Tom Benyon to say to Margaret Thatcher that we are tired of promises. We want to see evidence of determined action.

Yours, Rev. Merfyn M. Temple

2 May 1982
Minister's letter to All Saints

On Tuesday I went with five others from Abingdon to present to our Member of Parliament, Tom Benyon, a statement about our belief that military spending wastes resources, and the need for our Government to commit itself to:

- Substantial measures of nuclear disarmament and the creation of nuclear weapon-free zones;
- An immediate reduction in exports of conventional weapons, particularly to repressive governments;
- The steady conversion of armament industries to socially useful production both at home and overseas;
- The world's poorest to benefit most from the resources released by reductions in military spending;
- Government support for peace education.

Tom Benyon, good MP as he is, gave us a sympathetic hearing, but was totally unconvinced by the arguments we presented in support of our view.

I then went on to a meeting in Parliament's Grand Committee room arranged by the United Nations Association. One of the speakers was our own Dr. Kenneth Greet, who with great eloquence and passion spoke of the church as the one great supra-national organisation with authority to call for world disarmament. He finished his session by leading the 300 who packed the room in a 'Prayer for Peace'.

I came home on the bus knowing that we in Abingdon have been much too half-hearted in our prayers. I have decided therefore to be in the church for prayer three times a day, from 7.00 a.m. to 7.30 a.m., 12.30 p.m. to 1.00 p.m. and 5.30 p.m. to 6.00 p.m., and I invite you to join me when you can.

There seems to be some justification in Scripture for the connection between fasting and prayer, so I have decided to fast as well. By the time you read this the armed conflict between Britain and Argentina may have begun, which adds all the more urgency to our prayers.

29 April 1982
The Editor, Abingdon Herald

Sir,
I write further to my letter published in your issue of 22 April, urging the voters of this constituency to speak up about world disarmament.

Poor Torn Benyon! What chance do we give him to represent our views when only five of us went to Westminster on 27 April, and only one person that I know of wrote to him on this vital issue?

By this letter I issue a challenge to all Tom Benyon's constituents to take pen and paper and write to him suggesting what we, his constituents, believe to be realistic and potentially effective proposals for the Prime Minister to take to the United Nations World Disarmament Conference which opens in New York on 7 June.

My challenge is this: *That ten thousand people from this constituency write individually to Tom Benyon expressing their view on world disarmament before 7 June.*

To give a little edge to this challenge which is designed to rouse us from our political inertia, I am committed from 7.00 a.m. on Saturday 1 May:

- To fast on nothing but orange juice until such time as Tom Benyon can tell me he has received ten thousand letters on this subject.
- To spend my meal times praying for peace in my church. (It is my hope that people of all faiths will, as occasion suits, join me there or in their own churches at these times.)
- To give what I save on food to the implementation of the recommendations of the Brandt Commission relating to world development and world disarmament.

Yours faithfully, Rev. Merfyn M. Temple

9 May 1982
Minister's letter to All Saints

Thanks to all who have been giving me such magnificent support in our praying for peace. Although I was alone at the beginning, there is now always somebody praying in church at 0700 and 1230 and 1730. We sit sometimes silent and quite still waiting for The Inner Light, sometimes we offer extempore the prayer of our hearts.

Many of you will be asking yourselves why it should be your minister of all people who has been singled out to take up an exposed position at this time. If I am truly your servant, why did I not consult you before taking a risk to my health which could affect my service?

I understand your concern, and it makes me love you all the more that you should care so much. However, it is my hope that this is not some quixotic gesture, but rather a carefully considered plan of the Holy Spirit for one of His soldiers in the battle for peace. He knows that:

Arms race protest — by fasting

By PETER ALHADEFF

A CHURCH minister is going on a strict fast to stir up protest against the nuclear arms race.

Nothing but orange juice will pass the lips of the Rev. Merfyn Temple from breakfast-time tomorrow.

Mr Temple, Minister of All Saints Methodist Church, Abingdon, plans to keep up his fast until 10,000 letters of protest against the arms race have been sent to the MP for Abingdon, Mr Tom Benyon.

He said: "I spent 30 years in Africa and am very anxious that we recognise the damage we do to the Third World by our expenditure on armaments."

Mr Temple, 62, decided to go on a fast after only

© *Oxford Journal, 29 April 1982*

- I am able to go without solid food for forty days because He has twice tested me before.
- That what the world's poor need is not guns but food, and that anyone who speaks for them must be a hungry man himself.
- That there are many to whom He speaks who need a nudge from me before they will speak out themselves in his name.

But is not the figure I have set of 10,000 ridiculously high? It may be, but let's wait a bit and see what the Holy Spirit is going to do. If each one of you would write to Tom, and share your letter with another, then the miracle could happen. Daily I say Francis Drake's prayer:

"O Lord God, when Thou givest to Thy servants to endeavour any great matter, grant us also to know that it is not the beginning, but the continuing of the same unto the end, until it be thoroughly finished, which yieldeth the true glory; through Him who for the finishing of Thy work laid down His life."

April 1982
To Tom Benyon, MP for Abingdon

Dear Mr Benyon,
More and more ordinary people are saying that the existing stocks of nuclear weapons, and the continuing manufacture of all kinds of weapons, seem greatly to threaten rather than defend the world's citizens and their children.

Let us ask the Government to act with a sense of urgency when they consult at the United Nations Session on Disarmament on 7 June.

- Let them consider as a matter of dire necessity working hard to limit a further proliferation of arms and to reduce existing stocks.
- Let them be seen to be discussing such topics as nuclear-free zones, even if this would imply a re-appraisal of NATO defence policies.
- Let them consider the danger of allowing arms sales to continue as at present.
- Let them work decisively to develop the UN Security Council as a more effective peacemaker, realising that the more powerful nations must be prepared to sacrifice some privileges to assure smaller nations that there is justice to be found in the Council.
- Finally, let the Government suggest forcefully how monies diverted from arms-making could be used to make war more fully on the human evils of hunger and disease. Let, for example, the Brandt report be debated as a basis for giving from our privileged wealth to the poorer citizens of the world. Seen against their needs, Europe even in recession, and Great Britain even with 3 million unemployed are prosperous.

Yours etc., Merfyn Temple

16 May 1982
Minister's letter to All Saints

Last Sunday was a day to remember in the history of All Saints. There we were, in deep confusion of mind and heart and spirit over the Falklands crisis, and a young man named Joseph, from the Lebanon, stood up to quote those now unforgettable words of Martin Luther King: *"either we learn to live together like brothers or we die together like fools."*

Joseph has come to Britain to study accountancy. He told us how the Christians in his own Maronite church had through the centuries been in conflict with the Muslims, but in defeat and disillusion with war as a means of settling disputes, they had come to see that the only way of overcoming hatred is with love.

We in Britain today may be on the brink of an experience which is new in our recent island history—the experience of defeat in war. Of course there are never any winners in war, for the dead are always losers, but we in Britain do believe we won the first and the second world wars. I hope and pray that whether we 'win' or 'lose', the experience will help us forever to renounce war as a means of settling international disputes, because nowhere in the teaching of our Lord Jesus Christ can we find anything to legitimise the use of modern weapons with their awful capacity to inflict suffering and death.

Each one of us has his or her own strongly held opinion about the responsible use of force. We must try to look at each occasion when the use of force is required, on its merits, and try to see each situation in its world wide and historical context. We shall come to different conclusions, because there is no universal slogan or catchphrase that we can apply to every situation, that will produce a single simple answer.

The answer for me and the answer for you is not going to drop down from heaven, nor will it leap out to us from a single verse of Scripture. Each one of us in our armchairs before our television screens, or listening to the radio, or reading the newspaper in one hand and the Bible in the other, must sweat it out before the Lord, for whatever we do or say must be 'in His name'.

House of Commons SW1A 1AA

Dear Mr Temple

Thank you very much for your letter of 19 May. Yes, we are keenly in favour of a much higher priority for disarmament, and have pressed the Government for a debate in the House on the UN Conference, so far without success.

Yours sincerely, Shirley Williams[1]

---

1 The support of Shirley Williams must have been heartening to Merfyn. At that time MP for Crosby, and a founder of the Social Democratic Party in 1981, Baroness Williams of Crosby has maintained her pacifist principles. She is currently a member of the Parliamentary Group for Multilateral Nuclear Disarmament and Non-Proliferation.

Lambeth Palace, SE1 7 JU

Dear Mr Temple

Many thanks for the copies of your correspondence with Mr Benyon.

I am very glad that you are encouraging people to use the 'Prayer for Peace' and I enclose for your interest a message being read on my behalf at a service on the evening of 6 June at Westminster Abbey.

With all good wishes

Yours sincerely, Robert Cantuar[2]

Letters from members of All Saints and other local churches

Dear Mr Temple

I am writing to let you know that both my husband and I have written letters to Tom Benyon, calling for a positive contribution by Britain at the UN Special Session on Disarmament in June. We both feel that something must be done and there is no reason why Britain should not set an example to the rest of the world in these talks. We believe that the arms trade should also be halted and that money spent on nuclear weapons should be used for Third World development.

We sincerely hope that the fast we have heard you are making will be concluded after messages of support like ours have reached you. Our thoughts are with you and also with the millions of people in the world who have no control over their lives.

Dear Mr Temple

I read about your fast for disarmament in the local paper, and just want to write some words of encouragement and solidarity! I have been connected with the Women's Peace Camp at Greenham Common since September, and as I expect you know, the camp is about to be evicted by Newbury council for infringement of a bye-law. One of our supporters, arrested on our blockade in March, is doing a five-day fast to bring the eviction to public attention. She is doing this in Bournemouth. With the Falklands so prominent in the headlines, our publicity is minimal (and local) but we must persevere and keep our struggle in the public eye. People like you are the backbone of the movement, because you have the courage of your convictions.

---

2 Robert Runcie, Archbishop of Canterbury from 1980 to 1991. At this time, Runcie was about to welcome Pope John Paul II to Britain, and despite much criticism, was making serious proposals for union with the Roman Catholic church.

Dear Mr Temple

I have seen your letter on the subject of world disarmament and your personal response and feel impelled to write to tell you that, however sincere your motives, which I do not doubt for a moment, in my opinion your letter—with its underlying threat—amounts to no less than moral blackmail. I am sure you cannot see it in this way, or you would never have presumed to put this kind of pressure on your fellow-citizens and fellow-Christians.

As I said earlier, I respect the sincerity of your intentions and also have the greatest admiration for your self-discipline and willingness to risk your own health in the cause of world peace. This certainly gives one cause to examine one's own conscience.

Dear Rev. Temple

I write as a member of Trinity Church expressing my own point of view. I do not know whether or not you have called off your fast until our MP receives the 10,000 letters you demand. You will never get that number or even a tenth of it.

In an ideal world, there would be no poverty or famine. But this is not an ideal world and we have to accept that. Opting out of it will do no one any good and leave a very bad taste in the mouths of your fellow-Methodists.

My husband and I have covenanted for years to Oxfam and give generously to other charities. I am sure thousands of others do so also. There is not much else ordinary people can do to help the Third World. What price the British people in the Falklands if this country had opted for disarmament? Some common sense needs to percolate through to some of these rather hysterical publicity-seeking 'doves of peace'.

I hope you will think again and remember your wife, family and church.

May 1982
Open letter to Tom Benyon

Dear Tom,

A great deal of confusion has arisen over my challenge to the people of your constituency to write to you on the subject of World Disarmament. I think this can be avoided in future if you and I would carry on a public correspondence by open letter in the Press. May I start by asking you three questions:

1. Believing that you and I as democrats should be seen to be together in the fight against ignorance, apathy and people's feelings of political impotence, will you encourage your constituents to write to you expressing their views about World Disarmament before the meeting of the United Nations Conference on Disarmament on June 7th this year?

2. Do you agree with that recommendation of the Brandt Commission Report which states that: "The public must be made aware of the terrible danger to world stability caused by the arms race, of the burden it imposes on national economies, and of the resources it diverts from peaceful development."

3. Will you join me in the Market Place Abingdon at noon on Sunday 6 June to pray Mother Theresa's Prayer for Peace?

Yours sincerely, Rev. Merfyn M. Temple

(Letter sent to four local newspapers—none published it)

25 May 1982

Dear Merfyn,

Thank you very much for your letters.

I am contacting the Prime Minister's office to find out what her intentions are relating to the World Disarmament Conference. I am confident that we will play an important role in this conference as our Government is anxious to support multilateral disarmament and will play its part.

I know you are not a pacifist and in this respect we have views in common. I believe, for example, that the Government's actions over the Falklands issue to be correct. There has been so much press comment over our position in this matter any further comment from me is possibly unnecessary. Several constituents who have written to me are highly critical over the Government's position and with them I disagree. I believe that if we withdraw our troops at this time it would lead to further escalation of violence in other areas; Gibraltar, Hong Kong, West Berlin, for example. Also, of course, the fate of the Islanders is of paramount importance and it would be quite wrong for us to leave them to the fate of government by a regime with which neither of us can have any sympathy.

In answer to your third point I do support the Prayer for Peace. I hope that this movement grows and is not regarded as the preserve of those who believe that peace can be secured by our laying down our arms in the vain hope that this gesture will be copied by others. Disarmament can only be achieved by tough diplomacy and negotiation. The Falklands issue demonstrates how brittle world peace is.

I am glad you are well. I should be most distressed if you damaged your health. I have the highest regard for your sincerity of beliefs and your Christian concern for peace and those in the Third World. I wish that all Christian leaders regarded their responsibilities with the same dedication as you do. The world would be a better place.

Kind regards,
Yours sincerely, Tom

25 May 1982

Dear Merfyn,
Thank you so much for your letter and details of the action being taken by yourself and the Abingdon and District Council of Churches, in the cause of peace and disarmament.

I strongly support your stand on international disarmament, and am deeply impressed by your combination of prayer and action—'the strongest combination in the world'. I hope and pray that both the Vigil for Peace on 6 June, and the response to your prophetic fast, will help significantly to alert both our government and people to the urgent need to put our full weight behind the United Nations Special Session on Disarmament, when it opens on 7 June.

The present tragic hostilities in the South Atlantic serve to underline the standing menace to world peace which the present arsenal of world armaments constitute.

Please give my best wishes and heartiest support to the Working Party for Social Responsibilities of the Abingdon and District Council of Churches, and to the Council itself, for the initiatives it is taking. All power to your elbow, and greetings in Christ's name.

Yours sincerely,
John Newton, President of the Methodist Conference.

From Merfyn's diary

24 May   Woke up feeling offended by Church's attitude to war. Wrote to Vicar of Abingdon expressing deep concern.

Delivered letter by hand.

Cycling home, knew I must say the Universal Prayer for Peace in Market Place, Port Stanley, at noon, 6th June not Market Place, Abingdon. Use money from house sale to charter small boat to Falklands.

Found a wounded sparrow on steps of Church.

From atlas saw that nearest neutral port to Falklands is Punta Arenas in Chile. Put up notice on front wall of house.

Enlist here for:
THE INTERNATIONAL TASK FORCE FOR
PEACE IN THE FALKLANDS
NO PAY – IRON RATIONS
Vessel 'SPARROW'
Flag   UNIVERSAL PRAYER FOR PEACE
Destination PORT STANLEY
E. T.A. 6 JUNE 1982
E. T.D. WHEN FUNDS AVAILABLE
Donations to date £19,000

25 May   Bridging loan arranged. Air tickets purchased to Punta Arenas, also sheepskin jacket. Press conference Westminster Central Hall, B.B.C. interview. Wept for anguish of those bereaved by war. Offered rent-free accommodation on retirement.

26 May   Left home to catch flight no. PA 97 from Heathrow, 1100.

Mission Falklands, 1982

27 May 1982, inflight Miami – Santiago, Chile
Telex to Colin Morris

TELL JOHN NEWTON I WOULD LIKE HIM CONSIDER INVITING PRESIDENT OF METHODIST CONF OF ARGENTINA TO BREAK THE BREAD AND DRINK THE WINE WITH HIM IN THE CENTRAL HALL WESTMINSTER AT NOON ON JUNE SIX STOP

ASK DAVID WILCOX BAPTIST MINISTER ABINGDON WHAT SPECIFIC ARRANGEMENTS HE IS MAKING TO ENSURE THAT THERE ARE TEN THOUSAND LIVING EPISTLES ON THE MARKET SQUARE ABINGDON ON JUNE SIX STOP REMEMBER IMPORTANCE OF WILLIAM BLAKES MINUTE PARTICULARS STOP LOVE

From Merfyn's diary[1]: Thursday 27 May

We are circling over Santiago Airport, unable to land because of low cloud. My first sight of South American soil is a line of jagged hills tipped with the orange flame of the rising sun.

Now that we are expecting a 72-hour truce before 6 June, the most difficult part of the mission is made easier. I wonder what kind of ship I can charter for the £20,000? Perhaps an ocean-going tug? I don't know.

God the joker

We are still circling, and I am laughing a bit about my last fifteen minutes at home. I had done everything except write to Jane, Robin, Ruth and Tricia, when the door bell rang, and there was a man, who in spite of my

---

1 Diary entries and letters are taken from *Angelus for Peace in the South Atlantic*. Reproduced with permission.

Man with a mission

VICAR'S WAR ON TASK FORCE

❝ The peace movement

THE DO-OR-DIE Abingdon vicar who intends to liberate the Falkland Islands in the name of peace revealed his incredible plans in full to the Journal this week.

Rev Merfyn Temple of All Saints Methodist Church, Abingdon, told us how he was going to:

■ Try and enlist the support of his long

■ Raise the United Nations flag of peace in Port Stanley on June 6, whether it is occupied by British or Argentine troops.

Mr Temple, 62, said the idea of launching the mission came in a moment of inspiration on Monday morning.

Only hours later an anonymous Christian promised £19,000 to help finance the in-

Rev Kenneth Kaunda for his support because he had supported him in his struggle for Zambian independence in the 1960's.

"We're old friends and we stay in regular contact," he said. "I'm sure he will help my mission.

"I also hope to get the Archbishop of Argentina to come

with us so we will be truly representative of peace."

The fearsome British naval blockade around the islands holds no fears for Mr Temple.

"There are great dangers but I don't believe we will be fired on — God will be with us."

He flew out to Chile on Wednesday.

© *Oxford Journal, 27 May 1982*

saying I had one foot on the bus, proceeded to tell me that I was totally irresponsible in the way I was spending the £20,000 anonymous gift. It should have gone directly to feed the hungry, or to build the new youth centre we desperately need for the young people of the Peachcroft Estate. All that would happen to the £20,000 would be that it would end up in the pocket of Lloyds, the shipping insurers of 'Sparrow'. It upset me for a bit, because I am relying on 100 per cent backing in prayer by our church, but then I realised that if he thought I was going to get as far as having 'Sparrow' insured, he must have a great deal more faith than many others I know, who cannot begin to believe that it is anything more than a colossal practical joke—well it is, of course, but it is God who is the joker.

An Orthodox priest

The fog over Santiago proved too thick to land, so we have turned back to travel north 1000km to Antofagasta, where we shall have to refuel, then return to Santiago, as this plane must go back to Miami tonight. There is only one plane a day from Santiago to Punta Arenas, so I shall have to spend the night in Santiago.

When I went to get a drink of water from the galley, there was a very large bearded priest, who smiled and asked if I spoke Spanish. He is an Orthodox priest from Santiago, Fr Galindo. I gave him a Prayer for Peace

Clergyman flies to Falklands

A Methodist minister flew off yesterday on a "way out and crazy" mission to end the fighting in the Falklands.

The Rev. Merfyn Temple plans to pray for peace in Port Stanley's main street, and believes this could succeed where diplomacy and bloodshed have failed.

"This may be a Quixotic gesture, but at least it is trying to bring it to the attention of the world," he said, as he prepared to leave his wife, four children and church in Abingdon.

Mr Temple began a liquids-only peace fast on May 1, and hopes to continue it until his prayer meeting on the Falklands at noon on June 6 — the day before a UN disarmament session in New York.

He hopes the Pope will ask Argentina and Britain to declare a truce for the day, and that the Red Cross will allow him to fly its flag on a vessel he hopes to charter from Chile and rename The Sparrow.

"I don't know whether it will be the British, or the Argentines who will be in Port Stanley then — but whoever it is, there will be a lot of bloodshed," he said.

"My family is totally supporting me, and so are most of my church here.

"It does seem so way out and crazy, but the whole war is crazy. You have to go in from the outside with something as illogical as prayer."

Mr Temple is taking only ten dollars towards the cost of chartering a vessel strong enough to withstand the South Atlantic weather. But an anonymous donor has promised £19,000 "to use for God."

© *Oxford Journal, 29 April 1982*

pamphlet which was interpreted for him at length. I told him of my mission, and he said his spirit was with me and that he would call all his people to pray every day at noon.

The Carrera

By the time we landed, my 'plane to Punta Arenas had long since departed. I knew no one in Santiago. I felt very lost, unable to speak a single word of Spanish, but I had one dollar left and that was the price of the bus fare to the centre of town. I was dropped outside this fourteen-storey hotel, the Carrera.

A helpful person at the desk looked up Iglesia Metodista de Chile, so with the $12 given me by Carlos, I took a cab to the Episcopal Office in Sargento Aldea St. where I was greeted by Thomas Stevens, a Chilean theologian. Thomas took me in, listened courteously to my story, and gently suggested that although Punta Arenas is geographically the nearest land to the Falklands/Malvinas, the political problems between Chile and Argentina make it an unlikely perch for a sparrow. He suggested Montevideo in Uruguay because Red Cross Hospital ships are using it already in this war.

Then Thomas rang his friend Raimundo Valenzuela, who was about to depart for a service in a Roman Catholic church. It is the week of prayer for Christian unity, which the Southern Hemisphere holds the week before Pentecost, whereas we hold ours in January.

Warmheart

We were greeted at the church by a warm-hearted, friendly, dumpy little priest in a baggy black suit, face all wreathed in smiles and his warm soft hands in a permanent handshake. We met in a kind of church hall, seated antiphonally with quite the biggest candle I have ever seen in the centre between us. Five chairs had been set out on a low platform with a reading desk in the centre.

We took it in turns: the previous priest from whom Warmheart had taken over only a month ago, then a middle-aged lady, an American of the Mary Knoll Sisters who had worked in Chile for many years, then me, then Raimundo, then Warmheart. It all started in low key with a song and a guitar—what a lovely, lovely voice the guitarist had—then there was free prayer, just thirty-second petitions with a great number joining in. Chileans seem to pray on their feet instead of on their knees.

Then we passed the peace; what an outpouring of love it was! How we hugged one another! One middle-aged sweetie, who said she was Argentinian, kissed me and gave me a white rose which I am pressing in my Methodist Hymn Book at St. Patrick's hymn, "I bind unto myself today the strong name of the Trinity". I think it is the purest, loveliest, most powerful hymn I know.

Saturday, 29 May

Spread Shalom by radio

Woke up a few moments ago wondering how many languages there are in the world. We need to broadcast the Prayer for Peace in as many possible languages at noon on 6 June. If it is given to me to be one of those through whom God shall teach the Nations the things that belong to their peace, I must spread Shalom. Shalom is what the Jews were always on about. Peace for their promised land which flowed with milk and honey.

There is still much to be done to release from people's hearts the power of prayer that is hiding there, if everyone in the world is going to be praying the prayer in their own tongue. Before 6 June, every radio broadcasting station in the world must have the Prayer. It must be early next week so that they can start teaching the people how to pray. We don't need to bother about the press and the TV as their coverage is so limited.

Talking in other tongues

I am thinking that when the BBC rings me at 14.00 hours and asks me to say the Prayer for Peace I ought to be able to say it in Spanish, but I wonder who is going to teach me? Pentecost is all about being filled with the power of the Holy Spirit and beginning to talk in other tongues. We must learn to speak especially in the tongue of our enemy. At this moment, Spanish-speaking Argentina is supposed to be my enemy. The fact is that this whole war is due to a colossal misunderstanding, which could have been avoided had we been able to talk about being led 'from fear to trust'.

My spirit is low

My spirit has been a bit low this afternoon. I had been building up some kind of expectation for the BBC telephone interview at 14.00. Patricia Guarachi my delightful bilingual secretary has taught me to pray the Prayer in some kind of tolerable Spanish, but the BBC producer said there would not be time for it on the Sunday programme.

Indeed the whole interview was unsatisfactory from my point of view. I had fooled myself into believing that my interviewer had understood what I am really on about, which is the death of ten million children every year, but he does not seem to understand. He wanted to hear either that I was beginning to get significant support from a few well-known people, or that I had decided to pack up and go home. He wanted to hear about a little ship with steam up waiting to sail from Punta Arenas with half-a-dozen big names lined up in the crew, and here am I, stuck on the wrong side of the South American continent, talking about a dream-boat in some yet undecided Atlantic port in Uruguay or Patagonia.

Hope for a truce has almost died

Then I went down to buy a copy of *Time* magazine in the hotel foyer, and read of the mounting carnage of the Falklands war, and America's growing involvement with the British. I read of one high-ranking Argentine official who said, in a voice nearly choked with tears, "Each death of a British soldier pains me as much as the death of an Argentine one. This is all madness. I hope tomorrow someone steps in and stops this lunacy."

Sunday, 30 May. Pentecost

I tried to catch David Wilcox before he left to take his 10.30 a.m. service at the Ock Street Baptist Church, but he had gone. However, Ann his wife came through on the line, and I was able to tell her that I shall be saying the Prayer in Spanish this morning while they are praying in English. "Well done, Merfyn," she said. Those two words have lifted my spirit, because I am able to see a little more of God's secret plan.

Templo San Francisco de Asis

After I had finished lunch of asparagus soup, yoghurt, honey and unripe banana, I put through a call to Raimondo Valenzuela. He invited me to go along at 4.00 pm to the final service in the Week of Prayer for Christian Unity to be held in the oldest church in Santiago, Templo San Francisco de Asís.

We were 24 dignitaries up front. Everyone from the head of Chile's Franciscan Order in his brown habit, to Monsignor Bernardino Pinera Obispo, Secretario of the Episcopal Conference of all Chile, he in scarlet cloak and biretta, I in my black Methodist clericals. You can tell how long the aisle is, because I had time to tell Monsignor Obispo of my mission to the Falklands and he to say that my best bet is to get on a Red Cross ship in Montevideo, which confirms the advice given me by Tom Stevens.

What a long service! and what a lot of standing! but fantastic singing led by an accordion, guitars and tambourines. Somehow Raimondo had arranged to slip me into the programme right at the end. He said I could say the prayer. I asked if I could bear witness to my mission. He said OK, but two minutes only.

I unrolled the linen banner and hung it round my neck. Everyone could see the prayer as we processed down the aisle back to the church door, where we stood in a line greeting the people. They did not just shake hands as we do after a service in All Saints; they hugged me, pressing their warm bodies against the banner on my chest.

This is the mission

I know now quite clearly what this mission is. It is to mobilise the prayers of the whole world to pray the Universal Prayer for Peace in a continuous orison around the world for twenty-four hours before the opening of the

World Disarmament Conference on 7 June. We have just a week to do it, and I have yet had no reply to my telex to Pauline Webb on whom I must rely so heavily.

It does not really matter any more who is in command of Port Stanley at noon on 6 June, nor do I need to be there with my banner, because the prayer can be said in the market place whatever happens. The mission now is as sensible and as rational as can be, but the joke is that I had to go crazy and to come half across the world to make the dream come true. Mind you, it is still totally irrational to think that we can stop war by praying about it, but that must be another of God's jokes, the biggest joke of all.

I have just had an idea. I am going to blow some of the money which I transferred to the bank here on a fantastic party in the Carrera Hotel. Warmheart will be mine host, and we will invite the poorest families of Santiago to come to the feast. What an ecumenical picnic that would be!

The following telegram was sent from Edinburgh to Pope John Paul II on 31 May:
> YOUR HOLINESS WE RESPECTFULLY ASK FOR YOUR PRAYERS AND SUPPORT FOR MERFYN TEMPLE THE BRITISH METHODIST MINISTER WHO HAS BEEN FASTING SINCE THE FIRST OF MAY AND WILL CONTINUE UNTIL THE SIXTH JUNE WHEN THE UN DISARMAMENT CONFERENCE OPENS. TEMPLE IS NOW IN SANTIAGO ATTEMPTING TO TRAVEL TO PORT STANLEY TO PRAY FOR PEACE THERE ON THE SIXTH OF JUNE. TEMPLE'S DISTRESS AT THE WAR AND DETERMINATION TO ACT FOR PEACE HAS GONE LARGELY UNRECORDED IN THE BRITISH MEDIA WHICH HAS CONCENTRATED ITS ATTENTION ON THE WAR AND ON YOUR HOLINESS'S VISIT. CONSEQUENTLY WE HAVE TAKEN THIS ACTION TO PLEAD FOR WITNESS TO TEMPLE'S PRAYERS WHICH REFLECT THOSE OF OURSELVES AND MANY OTHERS WHO ARE SIMILARLY ANGUISHED AT THIS UNNECESSARY WAR IN THE SOUTH ATLANTIC.

> The signatories to the telegram are:
> Rev. Ron Ferguson, Leader, Iona Community, Glasgow.
> Ms Kathy Galloway, Worker in the Peace & Justice Resource Centre, Edinburgh. Rev. Donald Macdonald, Minister of St. Columba Church, Glasgow. Mr Iain Macdonald, Director of the Church of Scotland SRT Project, Edinburgh. Rev. Donald Ross, Organiser, Church and Industry, Church of Scotland, Edinburgh. Ms Helen Steven, Peace and Development Worker, Iona Community, Glasgow. Rev. Kenyon Wright, Warden, Scottish Churches' House, Dunblane.

Monday, 31 May
Solidarity and prayer

I have just had a conversation with my son-in-law Colin Quine. Colin gave me a quotation from somewhere which he feels may be helpful. It goes like this: "We need both solidarity and prayer, for prayer without solidarity is playing games with God. Solidarity without prayer indicates that we have not realised how serious the situation is." Still mankind makes war not love. What is this act of solidarity we have to make? I was wakened at 3:45 this morning by the sound of laughter from down the corridor. They sounded so happy I can only think they were making love.

Perhaps that is what Colin is talking about when he says that solidarity has got something to do with incarnation. There was a great deal of body language being spoken at the service on the night I arrived here. Perhaps what we all have to do about peace, in addition to praying for it, is to seek out our enemy and make love. I know from experience that the best love-making comes after confession and reconciliation. Indeed, the love that flows is the act of reconciliation.

Tuesday, 1 June

I was saying to myself just now, "What are you doing, Temple, lying on your bed praying when you might be organizing a boat from Punta Arenas or Montevideo? Five days have gone since you arrived in South America and there are only five days to go before you are due in Port Stanley." But then I remembered St. Patrick's prayer, "Christ behind me, Christ before me" and then the thought came to me: "When God works he works like lightning." If He does as much of a miracle in the next five days as He has done in the last five, everything is going to be OK. It is only man who delays God's plans by not taking the trouble to find out what His secret plan is.

I have just had a call from Radio Oxford. They really have a problem. Either they are talking to a lunatic, a chap on a super ego trip playing some crazy game of dice with forty grand, or they are talking to one of the sanest men on earth, who is saying that the world has gone off the rails and only God is strong enough to lift it back on again. Anyone, but anyone, who prays sincerely in faith for peace is giving God a helping hand. It is as simple as that.

My fast is ending

When I started my fast, I said it would be orange juice only until Tom Benyon, MP, had received ten thousand letters about disarmament. Since then I have been modifying the fast. First on the advice of my brother and sister ministers, I set the date of conclusion at noon on 6 June however many letters had been received by then, because some people felt I was subjecting them to moral blackmail, as Bobby Sands had done.[2]

Then on the thirteenth day of fasting, my body began to shout for relief and the shouting drowned out the whisper of my prayer, so I bought a yoghurt maker from Timothy Whites, some longlife milk from the Co-op, and some wild Mexican honey from Frugal Foods, and that was my diet with a little soup, until I came here and added oatmeal and fruit.

I first said I would end my fast in Abingdon market, or on the banks of the River Thames. Then I asked Edward Carpenter, Dean of Westminster Abbey, to end it in the Abbey on 6 June. Then I thought it would be in the Market Place of Puerto Argentina, Port Stanley. After I wept this morning I knew I could end it today, 1 June, at the celebration of peace let loose in the Ball Room of the Carrera Hotel. How God keeps messing up my plans!

The farewell party at the Carrera

The great party I had arranged did not turn out at all as I had expected. The first hitch came when the hotel Catering Manager said he could not possibly allow the hotel menial staff to come to the party. I had arranged with the management to stick up about twenty large posters of the prayer all round the ballroom and the hotel staff knew something different was happening.

They were surprised also that there was no wine. I had told the Catering Manager we should not need any because the Good Lord is quite capable of turning fruit juice into whatever is required to make us exceedingly happy.

When the hour of 7 p.m. came only three guests had arrived, two young men and a girl who are students at the Protestant Theological College here in Santiago.

An hour later, we were only twenty, including Patricia Guarachi my interpreter and secretary. However it was a super charismatic meal. Towards the end, one of the theological students said we did not know

---

2 An IRA 'freedom fighter' who died of a hunger strike at the Maze prison, Northern Ireland

each other's names so we went round the circle saying who we were. I started and when it came back to me I fortunately noticed a lonely waiter standing behind the long buffet table. I asked him his name and he said he and his family were good Catholics and he believed in the Prayer of Peace. The waiter later on came from behind the table and joined hands for the saying of the Prayer and the Grace. Then we all embraced each other and gave the kiss of peace.

We had tried to invite some people in off the street, but had failed, so in the end we got large sheets of paper and made great bundles of *bocados canapes surtidos, empanaditas cocktail de pino, empanaditas cocktail de queso fritas*, etc., and took them home to feed the poor. I went up to my room with a bit of a stomach ache. I should have known better than to break my fast with caviar.

Wednesday 2 June
I visit Santiago's prison

One of our number had told us that her husband is in prison in the Santiago Gaol, and that she will be going with her friend, a charismatic prison visitor, to see him at noon today. I confess I hesitated when she suggested I went along too, because the international calls are coming in thick and fast, but I pulled myself together just time to realise that the intercessions of prisoners for our mission to the Falklands/Malvinas are even more important than the prayers of the Holy Father himself.

I spent an hour and a half in Santiago's central prison. I found it, apart from the grim-faced guards, a very human place. No prisoners wear uniform and it is quite impossible to know who is inmate and who visitor. Fifteen or twenty of us met in a small chapel. Someone had a guitar and we sang 'Glory, glory Hallelujah' to the tune of 'John Brown's Body'. We then prayed and I talked about how I came to be here.

Here were the 'small fry' of Santiago's sinned-against: the petty thieves, embezzlers and debtors. They all promised to pray the Prayer of Peace, "Lead me from falsehood to truth, from despair to hope". I pray that they will put their hands into the hand of God and allow him to lead them now. We all embraced one another and I dashed off for another confusing session in the Bank of South America.

I travelled on the airport bus with an American, who introduced himself to me, having seen me on the Chilean television last night. "And which part of the Islands do you come from?" Since the only islands that have been in my mind for days are the Falklands, I was at first confused, and then realised he meant the British Isles. He is a very high-powered gent who speaks Spanish, has lectured in Oxford in Third World economics and, when he was in the American State Department, rubbed shoulders with all the Latin American military people.

> *1 June 1982*
> *To:- Mons. Herbe Seijas*
> *Secretario General de la Conferencia Episcopal, Montevideo*

Dear Herbe,
The bearer of this letter is an English Methodist Pastor who feels he has been called by God to give a Testimony of peace between Great Britain and Argentina, as he will tell you soon.

He sold his house in England and afterwards he travelled to Latin America with that money. His intention is to reach Malvinas Islands and then to pray for peace between Argentinian and English people. He is carrying a beautiful prayer whose origin is Hindu and he has christianised it invoking the Lord at the end of it.

He has been in Chile, has shared in an ecumenical act on the day of Pentecost, and it seems to me he is a man of God who really wants to serve the cause of peace.

I will be very thankful if you could pay him attention for a short while, so you could see the way of helping him with his mission. It is possible he may be able to take advantage of one of the hospital ships which are carrying wounded to Montevideo, so he could reach some English Navy ship and then he could see what to do.

> Kind regards,
> (Signed) Bernardino Pinera C. Obispo
> Secretario General de la Conferencia Episcopàl de Chile

We arrive in Montevideo

I noticed a nun get on the plane. She took a seat alongside us. As we came in to land I asked Patricia to speak to her about our mission and show her the letter from Bishop Bernardino Pinera Obispo to Bishop Herbe Seijas. She said she is Mother Mary of the order of the Good Shepherd in Montevideo, and a car was coming to meet her and perhaps we would like a lift.

'Wayout, crazy'— but not just another crank

Herald reporter Peter Aldaheff meets the Methodist minister who, at the age of 62, sold his retirement home to finance a one-man prayer mission to Port Stanley.

Merfyn Temple in characteristic pose: his aim is to reverse the upward spiral of the arms race and channel the money saved into helping the poor.

The Rev. Merfyn Temple himself described his solo peace mission to the Falklands as "way out and crazy," and the opinion was no doubt echoed by many who read of his journey.

But those who know him best recognised the decision to sell his house and head for the South Atlantic armed with a bible as typical of a man who has spent his life bucking the system.

Mr Temple's record of getting results through protest and direct action make it impossible to dismiss him as just another crank.

As the task force was steaming into the South Atlantic Mr Temple, Minister of All Saints Methodist Church in Abingdon, was already in the headlines with his fast to stir up protest against the arms race.

As he entered the fourth week of his hunger strike he surprised everyone by abruptly departing on a solo peace mission to the war zone.

He admitted at the time that his plan to pray for peace in Port Stanley's main street on June 6 the

of going to Port Stanley came to him in the early hours of the morning as he was cycling back from delivering a letter expressing deep concern about the churches' attitude to war to the Vicar of Abingdon, the Rev. David Manship.

It was 5.25 am on Monday, May 24, when it happened: "Cycling home knew must say the Universal Prayer for Peace in Market Place, Port Stanley, 6th June, not Market Place, Abingdon," says the terse telex message.

Just a week earlier, he had proposed a vigil for peace in Abingdon Market Place which would include saying the World Peace Prayer first said publicly by Mother Teresa, the Yugoslav-born Indian missionary.

Mr Temple's abrupt change of plan starts to look a little less surprising in the context of his *curriculum vitae* at the back of the report.

Merfyn Morley Temple was born of Methodist missionary parents in London 62 years ago and spent his early childhood in Chi-

© *Abingdon Herald, 24 June 1982*

Mother Mary's car turned out to be the convent minibus, and three elderly sisters had come to meet Mary. They told us that our plane had been delayed because two British planes had come to take the wounded to hospital. They said two are in the hospital here. I must go and see them as soon as possible. A new dimension is being added to our mission.

On the way into the hotel, I sat with the driver on the front seat praying the prayer while Patricia sat in the back fraternising with the nuns. She had been to a convent school and they made her feel very welcome. She said "They are so warm and simple. They make me feel at home in a strange country I have never visited before." Is this what it means to have a Christian name and be a member of Christ's family in all the world?

Before we got out of the bus I led them through the Prayer in Spanish, then gave Mother Mary a big kiss, and we walked through the great marble pillars of the Victoria Plaza. It makes the Carrera seem like a village inn.

I have just heard a ship hooting in the harbour. I hope it is not the hospital ship leaving.

I have asked Audrey to contact Kenneth Greet to see if he can suggest some way to give me status as Honorary Methodist Naval Chaplain. I still hope for a declaration of truce on 6 June.

Thursday 3 June

After finishing my diary this morning, I took a taxi to the British Embassy. I thought they might like to know I was around, but they were not interested. You can hardly blame them, as their officials are working flat out night and day on the arrival and departure of hospital ships. That hooter in the night was the departure of HMS Hecla.

As I wrote John Simpson's name in my diary, he rang to apologise and say he had just heard that a Vulcan bomber had landed in Brazil, and he is off there pronto. However, I have had a long interview in my bedroom with another—Gibson of BBC radio, and a rather funny one with a Canadian broadcaster from Toronto, over the telephone. She must think I am bonkers, because she said, "How do you think that when the Pope and other world leaders have failed to get a truce, you can? What kind of real support have you got?" I replied, "I cannot stop the war; only God can, but I can pray. Anyway I already have fantastic support." She said "But what is it?" "The prisoners in Santiago Gaol," I said. I could feel her freeze on the line. She quickly brought the interview to an end.

Satish Kumar, the author of the Prayer for Peace, rang me from his home in Devon. He sounded a bit disappointed that I had failed to hire a small boat in Punta Arenas, enlist a crew of British and Argentinians and one or two important people, and sail into Port Stanley harbour. He wants to see a 'Greenpeace' operation which would confront the opposing forces with a demonstration of the power of non-violence to quell the storm. He feels that our mission for peace will have simply petered out if all that happens is me sailing on a slow hospital ship to minister to the sick and dying.

He could be right. The Greenpeace way is one very significant way of witnessing for peace, and at the beginning I did think of Sparrow as a greenfinch, but I think we must get our long perspectives into focus. My little witness is only part of a far, far bigger thing. To raise the flag of the Prayer for Peace in the Falklands and see it shot to pieces would be a gallant thing to do, and half the world would cheer, but how much more significant it would be, if when the cease-fire sounds there is no song of victory from either side but only the troops at prayer, thanking God that their lives have been spared and that they can meet each other to join hands and say the Prayer of Peace.

Incommunicado

A couple of hours ago the BBC rang from London to book a telephone interview with me for 14.50 and I had a good conversation with Julie Lloyd the interviewer. I hope nothing goes wrong this time as it did with John Simpson's BBC television interview.

The call from the BBC came through on the dot of 14.50 but then something went wrong in London: at first all I could hear was a faint, faint voice, then Donald Duck, then the echo of my own voice. I began to feel someone was trying to stop me talking to the media, and that is a sure sign of paranoia. To be incommunicado, to feel cut off and isolated, is a chilling experience. I must try and get some sleep if only those elusive mosquitoes would allow me.

17.00: the silence is broken

The silence has been broken by a call giving me the names of two international air charter firms. I have put through calls to both, and will ask for estimates for chartering a plane capable of taking me to Goose Green or another airstrip on the Falklands/Malvinas as soon as we hear of a truce, which I hope will be dawn to dusk on Sunday, 6 June. How I get from Goose Green to the Market Place in Port Stanley only God knows. If there is no truce in the South Atlantic, I shall say the prayer in the Plaza, Montevideo at noon and thereafter every day until truce is declared. I intend, if necessary, to move my residence from this expensive hotel to Mother Mary's convent if she will have me.

Friday 4 June
The nerve of failure

Last night before I went to bed I rang Audrey to see what joy she had got from Kenneth Greet in the matter of getting me appointed as an emergency Naval Chaplain to join a hospital ship to go to Port Stanley.

There is no joy. The process of appointing a British naval chaplain takes months and there is apparently no way of speeding it up so in the end it is red tape that will bind me here in Montevideo. At least I am released from the feeling of doubt that had I arrived at Montevideo earlier, I might have been able to get on HMS Hecla.

I got into bed knowing I had finally to face the possibility of failure of our mission. Then there came to me the words of Phillip Potter, general secretary of the World Council of Churches, which were spoken to me at a conference I had addressed in Mindolo on the Copperbelt in Zambia in 1958. I had spoken of the church's failure of nerve in the face of the need to act on the issue of political independence for the country. He replied that what was needed was 'the nerve of failure'.

With lack of sleep I become desperate

I woke up with the words of Jesus to the rich young ruler in my mind "Go and sell everything and give to the poor". "I have done that small thing, Lord," I replied. "So what does it mean?" The rest of the night I was kept awake by a mosquito, so I had time to work it out. These words call us all to total commitment to our Lord, so that in the words of the Collect, we shall "have grace to love what you command and desire what you promise".

I have decided, as soon as the world wakes up, to seek out another charter company and see if I can hire a plane. I know there will be problems of getting insurance and a pilot willing to fly.

You will all say this is sheer madness and an empty gesture, but before you dismiss the idea, think about it. Are the British and Argentinians really so besotted with war, that if given due warnings by the United Nations and the Red Cross, they would shoot down a defenceless civilian plane? Of course they would not and you know it. Think again: if it were to be Ted Heath or Kenneth Kaunda on that plane, would not the guns of Port Stanley fall silent? If you called the troops to listen and to pray the Prayer of Peace, they would be with you.

Saturday 5 June
No truce and no joy

It was about 16.00 hours yesterday that I finally recognised that there is going to be no truce on the 6th and I had better go home. The next plane leaves this afternoon.

I told Patricia and we went out together for a meal. We ordered a meal of tasty Uruguayan sea fish and ice-cream meringue. A poor boy off the street came in selling packets of chocolate-coated peanuts. So in The Eagle's talons ends the flight of our sweet sparrow.

Don Quixote and Sancho Panza

I bought in the hotel tourist shop a beautiful piece of Uruguayan sculpture. It is Don Quixote in his rusty armour on Rocinante, with Sancho Panza trailing after him on his long-suffering donkey. I think of my beloved people in All Saints as being like faithful Sancho. He shared his master's ludicrous adventures, which arose from his insane ambition to redress the wrongs of the world. He was well aware of his master's shortcomings, but was quite incapable of avoiding their consequences.

I say the prayer on the plane at noon

Once again I missed the bus, but was able to get a fast taxi and reached the airport on time. We were delayed in Rio de Janeiro, so I could not say the prayer at noon in Miami as I had hoped. Over the Caribbean, I wrote the following note to the captain:

"*I am a passenger in seat no. 31K. I am a Methodist minister of the British Methodist Conference from Abingdon, Oxfordshire. I am on a peace mission to say the Universal Prayer of Peace in Port Stanley. I had hoped to say the prayer at noon today 7th June in Miami but owing to delay cannot do so. Any chance I could say prayer in English and Spanish over your tannoy when present film ends?*"

He replied that he did not have authority to grant my request, so at noon I said the Prayer and kept the vigil while all the other passengers stood in the aisles of the Jumbo Jet waiting to disembark.

Monday 7 June

I arrived home in Abingdon on the local bus at 11.30. My wife did not recognise me in my garish South American rig. Pinned all along the radiator in the hall were messages of love from our Junior Church: WELCOME HOME – IT'S A SHAME YOU MISSED THE BOAT – WHAT A PITY! And Caroline Shaw had drawn a picture of a sparrow on her nest.

Thursday 10 June

I recorded a talk about the Universal Prayer for Peace for the Falklands Service on the BBC World Service, and said the Prayer in English.

Better late than never. I wonder why I had to travel 26,000 kilometres and spend £6,000 when all it needed was a 50p telephone call to Pauline Webb of the BBC. It must be another of God's jokes.

Monday 14 June

Today white flags flutter over Port Stanley, and British troops are flushed with victory.

Now begins the long search for peace in the South Atlantic, and I feel the hand of Cardinal Raul Silva H. on my head.

> ". . .The Lord has imposed on us this mission of peace. It may be hard at times, yet we are to continue on going until we are all one, as is the will of the Lord."

Make me a channel of thy peace Lord. 'Llevame' - Lead me.

From local supporters after Merfyn's return

Dearest Merfyn

I was very moved by your telex messages. They enabled to us to live through those days with you. In spite of all the 'stops' your experiences came across direct, fresh and vivid.

I think your action was a sublime one—a response of obedience to a call of God, for which He must have had His reasons, the results of which though perhaps apparently disappointing in that you didn't personally reach Port Stanley, to fly the banner of peace, have been and will be important and far-reaching in ways not always obvious or measurable. I know its effect in **my** heart—an inspiration and challenge that will last all my life. . . It has challenged people to consider the insularity of our safe and comfortable ways of living and thinking and shaken our complacency.

Thank you for showing the courage to go to the South Atlantic, for taking the risks, for demonstrating your love and care. It has changed us; and God will nurture the seeds you have sown. It's **very** good to have you back in our midst. Our need for you is very deep. Carry on being 'an instrument of God's peace'!

Pauline Sykes

Dear Rev. Temple,

This evening I was babysitting for my good friends Gill and Tony Rose, and they showed me a copy of your 'Angelus for Peace in the South Atlantic'. I feel privileged to have had the chance to read it and, having read it, I feel so uplifted by your account of your experiences that I must write and congratulate you on your successful mission.

Yes, that's right! Having read your experiences, in no way can I call your mission a 'failure': the only 'failure' was on the part of the media to give you adequate coverage! Clearly, you didn't achieve your original objective of saying the Prayer for Peace at Port Stanley on 6 June, but as it turned out, the war had still one more horrific week to go through at that time, and the consequences of trying to fly in there at that time of high tension would almost certainly have proved fatal to you.

Your success, instead, lay in your whole positive action of travelling so far, as an individual, with your mission clear before you, and in the massive impact you clearly made on all those with whom you came into contact. The inner strength you took with you must have passed on out to so many people, whether they were leaders of various Churches, or ordinary people, such as the Argentinian woman who read your diary, some of it has passed into me, for your example will, I know, inspire all of us in the Peace Movement to continue to speak out and stand up for the peace which we all believe is the only way that will help our civilisation go forward.

Dear Rev'd Merfyn Temple,

I thank you for your kindness in sending me the report of how you tried to say the Universal Prayer for Peace in Port Stanley; I cannot think that you have failed, for all things that are good and done for peace in the name of the Lord will reap their reward, if not now, then in God's good time. I think all your efforts were wonderful as you went forward in the strength of the Lord. I feel so inadequate to comment on how to pursue this mission, but would ask you to read Isaiah 37:14, which I did when I read your report, the Lord may impart some words of comfort from this text, and that your message of peace was spread before the Lord and in his way answered, also your safe return to your loved ones, from so great a distance. God bless you, your family, your members in Christ, as you continue to seek peace and pursue it in His name.

3 June 1982
House of Commons SW1A 1AA

Dear Reverend Temple

Thank you very much for your letter and I was interested to read of your correspondence with Mr Tom Benyon. Governments and Members of Parliament do respond to popular feeling and they can be influenced particularly if the pressure is coming from a broadly based public opinion. I believe the organisation of churches can play a very important role.

You will be interested to know that I have been involved for the last eighteen months in the work of the Independent Commission on Disarmament and Security Issues. Our Report entitled, 'Common Security: A Programme for Disarmament' has been published this week by Pan Books and I held a press conference yesterday to launch the British edition with Mr Ramphal who was also a member.

A copy of the Report has been presented to the UN Secretary-General by the Chairman of the Commission, Mr Olof Palme, and further press conferences will be held as additional national editions are produced. The Commission was formed along very similar lines to the Brandt Commission, and indeed arose out of it following a recommendation that further work should be done in the area of disarmament and its link with development. It would certainly be useful if you could stimulate interest and lobby your local MP and the British Government and try to persuade them to support this Programme of Action, which I hope will be referred to during the UN Second Special Session on Disarmament.

Yours sincerely, David Owen[3]

11 January 1983

Dear Miss McMullen,

Vacancy for a Minister in the Tabernacle. Port Stanley. Falkland Islands

I write in response to the call from the Falkland Islands for a free church minister (published in the Methodist Recorder of 3rd December 1982) and in reply to your letter which sets out the expectations of the Tabernacle Council and the 'Penguin Project' for such a person.

---

3 Like Shirley Williams, David Owen was one of the 'Gang of Four' who broke away from the Labour Party to found the Social Democratic Party. Then at the height of its popularity, the SDP might well have won the 1983 election had it not been for the huge boost that the Falklands war gave to Margaret Thatcher and her Conservatives.

Having served the Methodist Church since 1942 I am applying to the Methodist Conference this year to become a 'Supernumerary'. This means I shall be free from 1 September to take up an appointment in another church.

I spent 30 years of my ministry in Zambia where I had a wide experience of pastoral care, evangelistic outreach, teaching and administration. Since returning to Britain in 1974 I have been a Circuit Minister of the Wantage and Abingdon Circuit with pastoral charge of one town church and two village congregations. During the past 8 years I have been involved with a great deal of pastoral counselling and spent much of my time in ministry outside the structures of the church, eg. alcoholics, young offenders, and those who are mentally, emotionally and physically handicapped.

Should I be appointed as Minister of the Tabernacle I would respond with enthusiasm to the opportunity of paying regular visits to outlying farm settlements, for by choice I have spent most of my ministry amongst rural people. For me their social, economic and political development has been a continuing concern.

I am aged 63 and in good health. I am married with four children, all independent, and three grandchildren.

Rev'd Merfyn M. Temple,
Methodist Minister, Wantage and Abingdon Circuit.

24 February 1983
Rev. Paul Charman, East Ham.[4]

Dear Paul

Thank you for taking so much trouble to answer my letter of 17 Feb so fully, so frankly and so constructively. It was just the kind of letter I needed to make me sit down and try to clarify my own thinking.

First I must try to clear out of the way a very personal problem which is bugging both me and my family. Why do I persist in my desire to visit the Falklands? Am I going there to satisfy some profound need in myself? To prove something to myself? To try and show the world that my abortive attempt to reach Port Stanley last May was not the failure it felt like and that all that money I spent was not wasted after all? Am I not persisting in a kind of very personal arrogance in saying that I am

---

4 Paul Charman was directing the move to recruit a Free Church minister for the Falklands.

going to do what I am going to do because only I can do it and no other? Was my offer to be the minister of the 'Tabernacle' an excuse to use that opportunity to bolster my ego? Is the idea of a house of prayer to pray the Prayer for Peace another escapade? a giving way to the temptation to "tempt God" to establish the Kingdom by another spectacular? Why the Falklands anyway? Why not Belfast or Beirut or Greenham Common or the Church in Abingdon? Are you not, Temple, trying to prolong your active life instead of trying to lose it? . . . I think I have said enough for you to get the gist of my personal problem.

The only way I know of dealing with this personal problem is to recognise that there is an element of truth in every one of these self-accusations. When I become a supernumerary and cease to come under the authority of the Methodist Conference, I am given the awful responsibility of having to understand God's will for me as a free agent of the Spirit. How much more simple it is to be a Methodist minister than a Methodist layman!

I now turn to you, Paul, as I do to others, to help me to test my vocation to go to the Falklands. Now as best as I can I will try to spell out that vocation.

The Universal Prayer for Peace, particularly in the last line: "Let peace fill our heart, our world, our universe" is for me another way of saying "God has allowed us to know the secret of his plan . . . everything shall find its perfection and fulfilment in him" (Eph 1:10). I believe that each one of us has to discover for himself what tiny part he is called to play in the working out of the secret plan.

I have a vision of the day when there is a ceremony in Port Stanley when the flag of the United Nations is raised and the Falklands/Malvinas are renamed "The Peace Islands" or Isles of Peace. When both Britain and Argentina will renounce all claims of sovereignty and give the Islanders themselves the right to live on the islands without the need of a military garrison but under the protection of the United Nations.

The practical means to make that dream come true are:

1. To establish a centre in Britain which will be the focus of all who work and pray for Britain to give up its claim of sovereignty over the Falklands.

2. To establish a centre in Argentina which will be the focus of all who work and pray for Argentina to renounce its claim to sovereignty over the Malvinas.[5]

---

5 The remainder of the letter was lost; hence the abrupt ending.

Protest and Arrest, 1983

Dear Doc, Monika, Mikael and Martin,[1]

It is very remiss of me not having replied to your last letter, nor have I any excuse—just put it down to the old sin of procrastination. I cannot possibly fill you in with *all* that has happened in the last six months, but a ticker-tape version of events might read something like this:-

- Rev reads in Guardian that K.K.[2] is to make a state visit to U.K. Arranges for K.K. to preach on peace in St. James', Piccadilly

- Rev and Audrey invited to 10 Downing Street for luncheon party with K.K. and Betty—Maggie [Thatcher] asks Rev to 'say grace' which he does, but using the 'prayer for peace'. Geoffrey Howe[3] comments 'what a beautiful prayer!'.

- Rev is invited to royal banquet, meets Maggie again and takes her to task for not letting Argentinians visit graves of their dead on Las Malvinas.

- Rev applies for post as free church minister to 'The Tabernacle' in Port Stanley; he is not even short-listed, but told politely that the Tabernacle selection committee regard him as 'too old and too radical'.

- Rev is instrumental in raising £35,000 for new premises at his All Saints church for community needs—youth, elderly, sick and poor.

- July: leaves All Saints in blaze of glory—many tears shed—end of eight years of very happy ministry.

---

1 Dr Gustav Krapf was a theologian in Zambia and adviser to President Kaunda on social policy. He and his family became close and life-long friends with Merfyn.
2 Kaunda was President until 1991.
3 Then Chancellor of the Exchequer. Appointed Foreign Secretary later that year.

- Rev and Audrey put up pre-fabricated garage in garden of son-in-law near Reading to store some furniture, obtain second-hand caravan to park in son-in-law's drive.

- Robin and Patricia have small terraced home under the shadow of Brixton prison—offer 3 rooms to parents. Rev fixes up cellar as workshop for lathe.

- Audrey takes over Beetle and moves each week round family—Sats to Monday at Clapham—Tuesday/Wednesday in Luton (daughter Ruth and granddaughter Abigail)—Thursday/Friday in Upper Basildon, near Reading, Jane's home.

- Rev begins to work on plans for a pilgrimage in 1984, hopes Mikael and Martin will join him on their bicycles for some part of the journey.

- Rev begins to limber up for protest—confronts the police at U.S. Bomber base, asks to be allowed to say the Prayer with USAF chaplain, meets with blank refusal.

- Rev cannot take part in Greenham Common protest because of his sex, so distributes copies of the Prayer to police as they drag off women.

- Marches with 200,000 protestors on 22nd Oct.

- Stops all traffic in Central London for 3 hours when 2,000 protesters sit down in Whitehall.

Can the chaplain come out to pray?

Abingdon's go-it-alone Methodist minister, the Rev. Merfyn Temple — who embarked on a one-man peace mission to the Falklands last year — joined members of Christian CND at a three-day peace vigil at RAF Upper Heyford at the weekend.

He was one of a group of campaigners who asked to see the base chaplain, Capt. Thomas Gallenbach. "We just want to meet him and pray with him. That's all we ask," said Mr Temple, pictured here talking to police officers at the base.

A Ministry of Defence policeman made inquiries, and told the protesters that the chaplain was not there. "Please write him a letter," said the officer.

Mr Temple tried to walk on to the base, but was stopped. He said he would sit outside the base and wait for the chaplain.

One campaigner said: "The House of God is always open."

"This isn't any house of God. It's an air base," replied the officer, patiently.

Over at Abingdon, there was a different kind of protest this week — a peace picnic for the mothers of Abingdon Peace Group.

© *Abingdon Herald, 26 May 1983*

- Gets dragged off from entrance to 10 Downing Street by two hefty policemen—congratulates commanding officer for his gentle handling—officer replies with a smile 'It's a pleasure, sir.'

In half an hour I leave to hold a candle with other Christian CND protesters in Parliament Square. We have to make light of it all—marches and protests are full of joyful celebration of the Prince of Peace, but when I stop to think about it my heart grows very heavy—not because I care what is going to happen to us, we madmen of the West, some day in the future when they explode this monstrous thing; but because now, now, now a million children die because we will not feed them nor quench their agony of thirst. It is not enough to pray for them from the safety of our comfortable pews, nor hope that some day, somehow, all will be well. The Peace Movement all over the world must grow and grow until our demand for an end to the arms race becomes so insistent that even the Principalities and Powers must pause in their madness to listen to the truth.

With all our love, Merfyn.

PS: After writing this letter, I went to protest about Cruise to Parliament, was arrested at 19:30 hrs and spent 8 hours in prison cells of the Metropolitan Police. I have been released on bail with 300 other protesters. My case will be heard at the Highbury Magistrates Court on 29/11. Over a hundred Greenham women were also arrested—pray for us that our protest may 'go on, and on . . .' Thirty Quakers were arrested last week—when asked by the police who their leader was, they replied 'The Holy Spirit'. The police have quite a problem on their hands when they take the Holy Spirit to court!

16 November 83
The Editor, The Guardian

Worm's Eye View of the Police in Parliament Square on the Night of
15 November 1983

I was arrested last night at 19.30 and charged seven hours later with obstructing the thoroughfare at Carriage Gate, Parliament Square. Most of the time was spent in a cell at a police station with ten others, though I did have two hours locked in a cage in a Black Maria waiting to be 'processed'.

The way I was handled, perhaps because I had my dog-collar on, increases my respect for the Metropolitan Police. I received nothing but courtesy and good humour, indeed the two hours in the cage were enlivened for all twenty of us in the Black Maria by the police driver, who surely had missed his vocation as a stand-up comic.

However, one youngster in our cell told me how he had been standing on the steps of St. Martins-in-the-Fields, wondering whether he ought to make his public protest, when he was swept into a 'police net' and handcuffed on the floor of a police vehicle. I have no way of corroborating his story.

I do not know how many other ministers of religion were arrested last night. I had hoped I might be in custody with the Archbishop of Canterbury, who I believe is not altogether happy about Cruise; however I understand he was making a speech in the House of Lords at the time, about the obscenity of video nasties.

Yours faithfully, Merfyn Temple

5 January 1984

Dear Anna-Lena

Your card arrived this morning as I was preparing my defence for the hearing of the case brought against me by the Metropolitan Police for demonstrating against the coming of the Cruise missiles. I was arrested at the gate of the Houses of Parliament.

I had clearly decided to tell the court that my only fault was to stand quietly holding a candle of peace to bring light into a world living under the dark shadow of Cruise missiles. But I had no witnesses to support me in my plea that it is always and everywhere the duty of Christians to shine with the light of God.

I was praying when I was interrupted by the knock of the postman at the door. He had only one letter—it was the letter from you. As I read your comforting words to me, "I wish you a joyful new year of 1984 fulfilling the task laid upon you by our Lord", my heart leapt for joy, because I knew that holding my candle was the task the Lord had laid upon me when I went to pray on that cold November night beneath Big Ben.

So I got on my bicycle and cycled to Highbury Court, determined that the love of my Swedish friend would shine on the police officer who arrested me, the lawyer who prosecuted me, the clerk of the court, and the three magistrates who sat on the bench.

When I was allowed to speak in my defence, I spoke about the candle in my hand when I was arrested, and then I produced from my pocket your letter and showed the magistrates the picture of the candle on the envelope. Then I read them your letter and they became quite silent, the whole court became quiet. The magistrates conferred together, then announced that I was guilty on both counts, for had I not broken the law in refusing to move when asked to do so by the police? But in spite of being guilty, I was given an unconditional discharge, which means I paid no fine, nor was I "bound over to keep the peace". I think the magistrates were saying, "This man is guilty under the law, but he is not guilty in the eyes of the God whom he worships and obeys, therefore he is not to be punished."

I have little doubt, Lena, that it was your letter which moved the hearts of the magistrates and all others in the court. None of the other 100 protesters who were arrested with me have been dealt with in this way. "It is the Lord's doing and wonderful in our eyes."

May our dear Lord bless you and keep you in His holy peace which passes all understanding.

Yours faithfully, Merfyn Temple

Pilgrimage round Britain, 1984

From Merfyn's sermon at Swaffham, June 1984

"I was on my way to Punta Arenas; we were circling over Santiago, where I was to catch my connection. I had been introduced to Cardinal Raul Silva, Archbishop of Santiago. I felt he was a very saintly man, so I asked him to bless me which he did. Then he said, 'We have to pray to the Lord that he enable us to convince our fellow men that war is a monstrosity. The Lord has imposed on us the mission of peace. It may be hard at times yet we have to continue on, until we are all one as it is the will of the Lord.'

"It was this commission from the Archbishop of Santiago which filled me with the desire to keep on going. I failed to get to the Falklands, but I came back to this country as determined as ever to fulfil my commission. I said to myself: if Satish Kumar, an Indian monk, can because of his beliefs walk on his flat feet from India to Moscow and then on to Paris and London, why cannot I, a Methodist minister, get on my bicycle and take this prayer to the people of England? This as a stage towards the final destination of this journey—although of course there is no destination to a pilgrim, but at least the time must come when there is reconciliation between Argentina and Britain over the Falkland Islands.

"I divided my journey into about 28 'laps', each of about 30 miles, roughly following the English and Welsh coastline. Much support came from my own church, though I spoke about the prayer in Westminster Abbey and in the cathedrals of Canterbury and Bristol. When in Scotland, I was welcomed both in the Anglican and Roman Catholic cathedrals.

"The preparation for the journey took about five months and the journey itself took two, my greatest support coming from the Bahà'is."

Proposal for a Pilgrimage With the Prayer for Peace[1]

Purpose

1. To assist in placing the prayer at the centre of our concern for justice and peace.
2. To encourage local groups:-
a. to learn more about how to pray for peace
b. to pray with one another across boundaries of race, colour and creed
c. to engage in the studies of the issues of justice and peace
d. to emphasise the threefold nature of peace: individual, communal and environmental.

The point of departure for the pilgrimage is the belief that peace and justice are God's gift, given in response to making ourselves available to receive it.

Encouragement for this pilgrimage is being given by the sponsoring body of 'Prayer for Peace' whose chairman is Bishop George Appleton, former Archbishop of Jerusalem and author of numerous books on prayer.

7 November 1983: To Satish Kumar

Dear Satish,

I write to you on my 64th birthday and ask you to celebrate 64 years of life on earth for me and another sunrise for all creation.

Probably the thing to emphasise for *Resurgence* readers is that the pilgrimage will provide the opportunity for *all* people of faith to pray together for peace to 'fill our heart, our world, our universe'.

In addition—or perhaps in the first place—I have decided to travel on a bicycle, so that I can invite anyone to join me for all or any part of the pilgrimage. For the mobile bookshop, a caravan will simply be a support vehicle, and I shall ask for volunteers who own a car with a towing hitch to pull it from place to place; farmers with Land-Rovers might give a hand. The bicycle is important because it is symbolic of the importance of challenging macrodeath with micro-life, and any technology at the human scale which is totally within human control is good.

---

1 Merfyn would 'publish' broadsheets such as this, and send them round to his huge circle of friends and contacts. See also *Millions of Small Holdings*, p. below

LEAD ME FROM DEATH
to LIFE from FALSEHOOD to TRUTH

LEAD ME FROM DESPAIR
to HOPE, from FEAR to TRUST

LEAD ME FROM HATE
to LOVE, from WAR to PEACE

LET PEACE FILL OUR HEART,
OUR WORLD, OUR UNIVERSE...

PEACE • PEACE • PEACE

Prayer for Peace
Pilgrimage
April - July 1984

I intend to spread the news about the pilgrimage far and wide, especially in Europe and over the Atlantic, because I see the possibility of individuals and groups from overseas including in their summer holidays a week or two travelling joyfully with us in this pilgrimage of prayer.

Peace be with you

Merfyn

A PILGRIMAGE ROUND BRITAIN WITH THE PRAYER FOR PEACE

The purpose of the Pilgrimage is to put prayer at the centre of our concern for justice and peace, believing that peace is a gift from God given as we become open to receive it.

The map shows the places and dates when the Prayer for Peace will be said at noon each day. Prayer will be encouraged to cross boundaries of race, culture, creed and politics. When given opportunities pilgrims will offer to speak about prayer to individuals and groups and to lead the study of the great issues of justice and peace of our day. They will be glad to receive invitations to preach on Sundays and will bear witness to the three-fold nature of peace—individual, communal and environmental.

The pilgrims will travel most of the way on bicycles. There will be a support caravan equipped as a mobile bookshop and a "PEACE—PRAYER—JUSTICE" information bureau.

Rev. Merfyn Temple (supernumerary Methodist minister) will lead the Pilgrimage and invites anyone to accompany him on the whole or part of the journey. Pilgrims will expect to be self-sufficient for their own transport, food and accommodation.

Wherever possible local groups are being encouraged to welcome the pilgrims, to arrange a local programme and to help tow the support caravan from place to place.

The Prayer for Peace pilgrimage: itinerary (opposite) and an introduction (above) published as a leaflet

23 November 1983

Dear Fiona and Dewi,

We need to find a little local group in each place to make local arrangements, e.g. where to park the caravan to best advantage as a mobile bookshop, and ask for volunteers to tow the van from place to place. Would the local Christian Aid committee be the right group, or would they be too busy in May? Are there likely to be Christian-centred peace groups in most of the towns?

Good speech by Sonny Ramphal on Monday, and a good one yesterday by Kenneth Greet at the British Council of Churches, but I begin to think we must move beyond words to determined action. If indeed "the manufacture and possession of nuclear weapons is an offence against God", then all who support them—Thatcher, Habgood et al.—are *ipso facto* offenders, but who dare ask for their excommunication? I spent last weekend in York, doing some preparatory work for the pilgrimage. I worshipped on Sunday with the Friends—marvellous experience for a Methodist minister to be able to keep quiet and know that it is not expected of him to say anything! Almost I am persuaded to be a Quaker.

Living in London is a great experience—so much is happening and my trusty old bicycle gets me anywhere I want to be and costs nothing. I am being much influenced by the leaders of Christian CND as we move from dignified protest to rather undignified civil disobedience. My case comes up at the Highbury Magistrates Court, and I am trying to decide whether, like Janet King, I have a conscientious objection to paying a fine.

ps: I shall be joining "Cyclists against Cruise" in Parliament Square this evening. Presumably if you keep moving, however slowly, on a bike you can't be nicked for obstruction.

Dear Mary,

I enclose a copy of our "Proposal" and would greatly appreciate your comments. At the local level in your area I would appreciate your help in arranging:

1. A central location to park a mobile bookshop and to announce the arrival of the prayer for peace pilgrimage

2. A nearby hall to display books and literature for sale

3. Local initiative in organising half-day or evening seminars/meetings on every aspect of how to pray for peace—with especial emphasis on outreach to local peace, devotional, development and environmental groups

4. Invitation to preach and take services

5. Hospitality.

We are still at an early stage in planning—the fluid stage! when we are very open to suggestions from others.

Yours sincerely, Merfyn M Temple

From Merfyn's diary

Sunday 1 April

Heart-warming send-off from St. James [Piccadilly] in the morning, where I preached on a text from 1 Corinthians, and Westminster Abbey in the afternoon. High point: Nicholas as he helped me pack my panniers and offered me a couple of small chocolate Easter eggs, enquiring "Grandpa? What's all this for?" Unable to find succinct answer. Mumbled something about God's secret plan of peace for the world—not satisfactory.

In the Abbey I asked the congregation how they would answer Nicholas' question. There were a number of distinguished people in the Abbey: there was Satish Kumar, once a Jainist monk who brought this ancient prayer from the Hindu scriptures to the West when on his own pilgrimage he had walked round the world with it. There were leaders of the Bahá'i faith, ministers of the Christian religion, at least one poet. But it was the saintly Dean who had preached with such humble authority over this simple ceremony, who stood up and gave the answer. "Nicholas," he said, seeking him out in the chair he occupied alongside David Lewis, "What's all this for? It's all for you."

The east wind blew more strongly as we stood outside the Abbey gate, waiting for the Dean to put on his anorak to accompany me on his bicycle over the Thames. I had lost my gloves, but a gentleman offered me his—he was a visitor from Italy and I was glad of his immediate response to my need. I think without those gloves my fingers would have been frozen that night.

As I followed the dean round Parliament Square, I was amazed at his confidence on the road. Buses slowed down for him and the taxi drivers hooted and shouted as he established his right of way amongst them. He cut a swath for me through the traffic, and I began to wish he would come all the way to Dartford. But before he left me, I found that I was being escorted on my left by a young cyclist and on my right by the hooded form of the vicar of Dartford who had come to guide me the twenty miles to his house. The warm welcome his family gave me, and the encouragement I received from the hard-working Catholic, evangelical, and truly radical priest was more than adequate reward for that first cold journey of this pilgrimage.

Monday 2 April

I arrived at the Coach and Horses, which was my rendezvous on the out-skirts of Rochester, to be met by a man about my own age, who had come out to escort me with a small group into town. He explained that he was not a regular peace worker, but a member of the fraternity of the Pilgrims of Santiago, and he presented me with a palmer's scallop shell. As he told me how he had cycled last year to the Cathedral in Santiago I felt a glow of admiration for him, recalling my own experience in Santiago in 1982 when I had been asked to say the Prayer for Peace in Spanish at a great service during the week of prayer for Christian Unity in the Cathedral of St Francis of Assisi. It was much later in our connection that I discovered he was talking about Santiago in Spain, while I was talking about Santiago in Chile.

By this time we had reached the Cathedral, where I was greeted by the dean who, seeing the scallop shell which I had pinned to the pocket of my tunic, exclaimed, "How appropriate! the pilgrim's shell is our Cathedral emblem," and he took me to see the motif of the scallop shell in glass and wood, and then to many memorials of this ancient Church. At noon we said the prayer together, the Dean himself leading it movingly in German and in fluent Russian. He told me that for the last forty years he has been building bridges with fellow-Christians in Russia, believing that to dispel ignorance and build greater understanding with those whom we so glibly call 'our enemies' is a vital element of all peace-making.

During the prayers, a Cathedral official handed me a note from one of my colleagues to say that the car towing our support vehicle had broken down and was stranded at a service station on the outskirts of the town. Perhaps it was a necessary reminder to me that the spiritual and the material are deeply interwoven in our daily lives. I was given another reminder by a schoolboy that day, who saw me in my clerical collar riding down a hill with my cycling cape flapping in the wind, and shouted: 'Keep it up Batman!'

In the evening there was a small gathering in a local church and we talked together about peace, pilgrims and prayer. People are surprised to find a Church minister travelling with a Hindu prayer. They seem to think that by now everyone in the world should have heard of the Lord's Prayer, which must be the final word on prayer. It needs a prayer like the Peace Prayer to help them to believe again that getting forgiven depends on us forgiving the 'Argies' and the Russians and the punks next door. For the coming of Christ's kingdom on earth means giving up dependence on bombs to bring it.

Tuesday 3 April

I was met on the outskirts of Canterbury by seven cyclists and a television team. The cameraman, who squatted on the floor of his station wagon with the back flap open, asked me to follow him down the dual carriageway keeping two cycle lengths away from him. As his car gathered speed, I changed into top gear, struggling to keep up, and began to breathe hard.

"What did you say?" he shouted.

"I'm saying the prayer for peace," I said.

"Then say it louder," he said, and ordered his sound effect man to push out the mike on a kind of fishing rod extension to dangle over my head as I pedalled desperately along behind.

So I arrived in Canterbury panting the prayer for peace:

"Lead . . . me . . . from . . . . death . . . to . . . life. . ."

Outside the Cathedral I was met by an impressive line of dignitaries: the Mayor, the Vice Chancellor of the University, a Bishop, the dean and many other church dignitaries. The television camera took it all in, and I was interviewed by their reporter.

"Why a bicycle?" she asked.

"Because the bicycle is God's greatest technical gift to this generation. For three-quarters of the world's people the bicycle is the life-line to get the sick to the nearest rural clinic, to get the children to the nearest central school for their high school entry, to get the produce of the land to the market. I ride a bicycle because the poor need bikes not bombs."

"Why a Prayer?" she asked.

"Because the peace the world needs is the peace of God, which is beyond their understanding and seems the more elusive, the richer and the greedier we become . . ."

The reporter looked just as puzzled when I finished as when I began. How can it be otherwise for someone who does not know about the other dimension?

In the Cathedral, we prayed in the Chapel of Thomas à Becket. We made a full circle round the central candle. Each person as he/she said the prayer in his/her language, lit their candle from the centre. Fourteen languages used. Final prayer said by a blind lady in Esperanto.

9 April – Winchester

Greeted by a small band of peace people on the outskirts of the town. Walked with the Prayer for Peace banner to the Cathedral.

At noon prayed the prayer in seventeen different languages as a sign of international yearning for peace.

During lunch hour, spoke about the prayer in Sixth Form College.

In the evening, good gathering in the Methodist Church Alresford. A visitor chanced to come in and spoke of how she and her family had used the prayer every day for the past two years and how it bound them together even when they separated.

Spent some time with Bishop John Taylor who shared his concern for those members of his flock whose consciences are deeply troubled as they earn their living working in industries connected with the arms trade and the production of nuclear missiles. We prayed together for them in the Bishop's private chapel beneath the great painting of the head of a cosmic Christ.

14 April – Exeter
Prayer at noon in the Mint Methodist Church. Well supported by members of the Bahá'i community. Six people came to the evening meeting.

On Sunday morning, Palm Sunday, the minister of the Mint arranged that pilgrimage should be the theme of the service. In place of a sermon I rode into the church on my bicycle with the banner and spoke about the Prayer for Peace to a congregation of 250.

15 April – Torquay
The Bahá'is arranged a meeting in the Town Hall. Greeted by the Mayor and his wife. There is an active inter-faith group here and we had the leader of the Hebrew congregation singing a prayer and a Bahá'i, a Sikh, a Muslim and a Christian all spoke about the unity we find in prayer.

I was given hospitality in the home of a retired officer from the Shah's army in Iran. He old me how twenty years ago he would play 'war games' with tactical nuclear weapons when on exercise—how whole divisions would be wiped out in seconds and the entire battle utterly devastated. "We were playing with toys twenty years ago," he said. Now the weapons we have are unimaginably destructive. No man who is obedient to the laws of a merciful God could ever, ever contemplate firing a missile with a nuclear warhead.

Merfyn continues the story in his Swaffham sermon
"On Good Friday, I cycled up to Camelford in the West Country. It was one of those unbelievably beautiful spring days, just before the leaves had come fully out on the trees. The sunlight filtered through them onto the

PEDAL POWER OF A PEACE PILGRIM

City is first stop on minister's marathon

A 64-YEAR-OLD pilgrim arrived in Rochester yesterday — on a bicycle.

Methodist minister Merfyn Temple plans to

bike — and I was a minister in Zambia for more than 30 years!"

Mr. Temple will be calling at more than 55 towns in England, Scot-

© *Chatham Standard,*
3 April 1984

Vicar cycles for peace

A CYCLING vicar visited Rochester on the second day of his Round Britain Pilgrimage for Peace.

Methodist Minister the Rev Merfyn Temple prayed in Rochester Cathedral

retirement to lead a four-month pilgrimage round the country, stopping each day at noon to say the Peace Prayer.

Mr Temple, 64, has chosen to travel by bike because he thinks it is the most ecologically an

© *Kent Evening Post, 4 April 1984*

Pedalling for peace

RETIRED Methodist Minister Merfyn Temple stopped off in Brighton yesterday as part of an 1,800-mile pilgrimage to spread the word.

He aims to cycle round Britain in three months, visiting 60 towns and cities during his

the Prayer for Peace — a 2,500-year-old prayer translated from the original Hindu Scriptures.

He said: "Since being brought to this country 20 years ago, the prayer has been translated into 40 languages. I chose this time to make the

© *Evening Argus, 7 April 1984*

woodland floor. As you travel on that road there is a stone wall on the left, so you look across straight into the faces of the violets, the primroses and wood anemones, and it was magical. And I was thinking, now this is the absolute embodiment of Spring.

"I cycled on, and came to a tiny farmhouse called Barton's Farm, where a family, Pam and Nick and their two children, had set up a little organic farm, to teach people simple organic farming. And they had just a few goats and a cow and they'd got some field where they grow vegetables. Two ex-students have felt so much the need to try and live as much as they can close to their environment that they've come with their wives to settle nearby—a little community there. When I arrived at their house, they said, 'We are just busy planting the new potatoes. It is Good Friday, the day for planting potatoes.' As evening came we went out to the *poustinia*.

"I said, 'What is a poustinia?'

"They said, 'Poustinia is the word for desert in Russia. It is either a place of quiet, or peace in the heart. You have come to us today and you are a poustinik, that is one who goes into the poustinia.' They took me into what had once been a pigsty. You had to bend almost double to get inside and it was whitewashed. They had repaired all the windows and there was a candle burning in the centre, a few emblems on the wall and there was just one book on the table in the centre of the room. It was John Taylor's 'The Go-between God'. Pam explained to me, that earlier that day they had come to the poustinia to read the story of the crucifixion with their children and now as dusk fell they wanted to be quiet together. We gathered there, totally quiet, even the small children were silent, and in that very simple place, we experienced the 'peace which passes all understanding'.

"The next day, nobody had made arrangements to meet me to say the Prayer for Peace, so I went up to the top of the cliffs above Wellcombe on the coast. As I climbed the cliffs which were carpeted with primroses and tiny celandines, I was saying to myself, *be careful, Merfyn, don't put your foot on a primrose because tomorrow you are going to meet Satish Kumar and he believes that no living thing should be destroyed.* There I was, scrambling up the cliff trying to get there by twelve o'clock to say the Prayer. I thought, *this is the nearest point I shall ever get to America.* So I shouted the Prayer across the waves of the Atlantic Ocean to President Reagan, but the wind blew it back in my face. No one was listening.

"But then I saw the gulls riding the wind. They were coming right up beside me so I said to them, 'Take the Prayer on angels' wings to the President of America.' Then I climbed down the cliff. May the Coast-guards forgive me, because getting down to the beach was a very hairy experience. Then I climbed over those great granite slabs of rock they call Gull Rock which go right out into the sea, and I said the Prayer to the fishes and told them to take it to Japan, and all round the world.

"When I told Satish Kumar about this he said, 'Let me tell you about my spirituality. I have a cow whose name is Hazel. Every morning when I wake up Hazel is waiting to be milked, so I can't lie in bed. I walk through the dew in the garden with a bucket over my arm, then taking the three-legged stool I put my head against her flank. I love to hear the rhythmic splashing of the milk; it is music in my ears. I say the Prayer for Peace and I am at one with the whole of God's creation.'

"As I left Hartland on my way north through Wales to Glasgow and Edinburgh, Satish, who had borrowed a tricycle to accompany me, was walking up the hill to Clovelly. We stopped for a moment to watch a gold-crest feeding in the branches of a larch tree, and then he said, 'Mahatma Gandhi used to say that the bicycle and the sewing machine are the only truly environmentally sensitive machines ever made by man.'

"Neither of these inventions can get out of control. Unless you go down Porlock hill without any brakes! There's a sense in which the whole ramification of the arms business has actually taken the control out of our hands. How important the bicycle is to the poor in Africa! How would the sick ever get to hospital without being carried on a bicycle? How would children get to school? I once knew a boy who was in the seventh year of his education who had had to travel a long distance to school every day—I worked out he'd travelled 8000 miles to and from school to get his education.

"I knew that when mothers or babies needed injections, the clinics were so far, spread so wide, you needed to get on a bicycle to get your child to get that life-giving injection. And as for supporting the economics of the Third World, the bicycle is essential. In 1977 I went to China on a brief visit. I remember being taken at night from the airport to the only big multi-story hotel on the boulevard in Peking, and being wakened in the morning by what I came to call 'China's dawn chorus', the ringing of thousands of bicycle bells. Looking out of the window and seeing them coming ten abreast, wave upon wave through the mist, the Chinese going to work. Then going down into the street and seeing them coming from the countryside, thousands of people on bicycles and tricycles heaped with cabbages, tomatoes, all the produce of the countryside, and suddenly realising that a quarter of the world's population depends upon the bicycle."

"Perhaps the high point of the number of religions which were saying the prayer was in Bristol Cathedral. We had a whole hour, from noon on the day I arrived, and for the first time in its history, that ancient Christian shrine resounded to the chanting of the leader of the Hindu community with their marvellous prayers, finishing up with Aum, which is their word for God—it is just the expiration of your breath. Then a young Muslim stood up. He spoke with tremendous conviction about his belief in prayer, "My Lord Allah God has bidden us to pray five times a day." All we Christians hung our heads in shame, for it is sometimes a problem for us to remember to say the prayer for peace even once a day.

"Then we had a message from the local gathering of the Buddhists, then the leader of the Jewish synagogue stood up to fill the church with that marvellous chanting of the Scriptures. First the Prophets then the Shema. There was a lady who stood up with trembling knees. She was a Quaker. She told me later that she had never spoken in public before, but there she stood in that great Cathedral to read the marvellous words of the 'testimony of peace' of the Quakers, written 300 years ago. Then there was the West Indian woman who was the leader of the St Paul's multi-faith, multi-racial team in the difficult minority area in Bristol. And finally, a slip of a woman stood up and said in rather broken English, 'I'm from Chile. Two years ago my brother was arrested and has been held in prison without trial. This week I have had information that he's been brought to trial and been condemned to death.' In Spanish she led us in this Prayer for Peace for her brother."

Letter to supporters, May 1984

I have now completed the first stage of my pilgrimage with the Prayer for Peace. Seven hundred miles came up on the cyclometer as I rode into Gloucester on Saturday 28 April.

First may I say to all who have opened their homes to me and made me feel so wonderfully welcome, a general word of deep gratitude. At

The pedalling pilgrim . . .

THE WHEELS of peace rolled into Salisbury on Tuesday morning as Methodist Minister Merfyn Temple's bicycle pilgrimage around the country reached the cathedral city.

Mr Temple set out from Westminster Abbey on April 1 — but this was no April Fools' joke.

He's visiting 57 cities all over Britain to carry the message symbolised in the Prayer for Peace.

The bicycle was donated by Raleigh, reflecting the help and co-operation Mr Temple has received since he started out on his epic journey.

"It was hard going at first, but I've staggered along and I'm sure I'll be

© Wilts and Hants Times, 16 April 1984

Prayer from cycling minister

THE Methodist minister who is cycling round Britain to deliver a Prayer for Peace in every major town passed through Totnes this week.

The Rev Merfyn Temple's pilgrimage is intended to reach people of any religion, race or belief in a multi-denominational sup-

Pictured above, he walks along the Plains and up Fore Street, flanked by

His pilgrimage was launched at a special ceremony in Westminster Abbey on April 1 attended by

Mr Temple is no ordinary minister. At the height of the Falklands War, he attempted to

Twenty years ago, he fasted for 14 days at the tomb of David Livingstone at Westminster Abbey.

© Torquay Herald Express, 14 April 1984

first I tried to write to you individually, but the days have been so full of pedalling and praying and preaching and listening, that there has hardly been time for anything else.

How have I fared and how has the prayer fared on this journey?

Every day without fail, we have said the prayer at noon at the appointed place. Sometimes I have been met by television cameras, the mayor, the Bishop and representatives of a dozen different faiths. Sometimes I have been met by the Curate and his wife. Sometimes we have had a police escort as we marched behind the banner into town, and sometimes I have arrived un-noticed and slipped away alone.

The following is a factual account of the pilgrimage thus far:-

The prayer has been said in six cathedrals and outside two, in ten churches, six public places, at two military bases and on one clifftop and on one quay. The prayer has been said in twenty different languages and by Sikhs, Jews, Muslims, Bahá'is, Catholics, and Quakers. Thirty meetings to relate prayer, peace and justice have been held in various places such as Civic Council chambers, nonconformist chapels, Friends Meeting Houses, farm kitchens and in a pig sty converted to a quiet room for prayer and meditation.

I have spoken on five occasions in schools. Local commercial and BBC radio stations have recorded interviews six times. In Bristol I had a live audience of 150,000 on a Thursday morning and in Gloucester a live audience of 6,000 on Sunday.

The Merlin bicycle given to me by Raleigh of Nottingham has performed magnificently. The attempt to support the pilgrimage with a travelling book van has not been entirely successful and so has been abandoned. From 8 May the pilgrimage will consist of one man on his bike—Merfyn and his Merlin.

For those of you who still await my coming, may I say that there are plenty of copies of the Prayer for Peace pamphlets still available, and they can be despatched from this address in response to a telephone call or a postcard. More important than the number who can be persuaded to gather for prayer, is the vast local audience waiting to be addressed by the prayer through local press and radio.

From the diary: 11 May – Bridgend

We met in the Tabernacle, a Welsh Congregational Chapel. Roger, a young Catholic from Cardiff, said the prayer in Japanese and a young woman from Hong Kong in Chinese.

Speaking of the phrase "Lead me from Hate to Love" I confessed my hatred for Margaret Thatcher. "With all my guts I hate her," I said. "I try not to hate her as a person, but I hate all that she stands for. When she appears on the TV I switch it off. I cannot stand being lectured."

A voice came from the back of the chapel: "Peace, Peace, Peace," then a woman stood up and with the hint of a Dutch accent behind the Welsh lilt of her English she said: "At the beginning of the war the Germans bombed my village in Holland and we escaped to Arnhem. Then one day from my back garden I saw the sky full of planes and young men coming down on parachutes out of the sky. As they floated down they were shot to pieces and I watched their bodies dangle on their strings bump down to earth. I began to hate the Germans who murdered them and I hated Churchill who ordered those young men to jump to their death. I cried and I cried and my heart was black with hatred.

"Then I got married and I was given six sons, and I knew that if I ever let them know the anger in me they would grow up to hate the Germans and then I would sow in them the seeds of a third world war. Every day I prayed to be led from hate to love, and my prayer has been answered and all my sons are free to love our old enemies.

"Please don't hate Margaret Thatcher. Help her by loving her to understand that the only way to Peace is to stop fearing the Russians and the Argentinians and start trusting them."

Merfyn continues his sermon at Swaffham

"Another very moving occasion was in a tiny chapel in a valley above Swansea. This chapel was built three hundred years ago by one of Cromwell's soldiers coming back from the Civil War. I had been invited by the people in the chapel to say the Prayer with them one Sunday morning. With me was Ezekiel Landau, an Orthodox Jew who had come all the way from Jerusalem just to say the Prayer with me, on this mountain. We had been in dialogue for many months and he had become my friend.

"I went to see him there, and we understand each other perfectly in the sense that he is one of the leaders of the Jewish peace movement in Israel, totally in conflict with the policy of the Israeli Government. Especially about the settlement of the Israelis on the West Bank of the Jordan. And I said to Ezekiel, 'I suppose I as a missionary of nearly four generations, I should be saying to you, I've got ten minutes and I can convert you from being a Jew to becoming a Christian, and I suppose you should be saying to me, Merfyn, you've got it all wrong, Jesus wasn't the Messiah; but we really haven't got time for that today because we are both concerned, I as Christian, you as Jew, to find God's purpose for peace in the world.' And then he went on to explain to us, as no Christian could, the meaning of *shalom*. This idea of wideness, openness and

'Premier in danger of hell fire'

PRIME Minister Mrs. Margaret Thatcher is in danger of hell-fire, a Methodist minister claimed in Gloucester yesterday.

The Rev. Merfyn Temple was criticising her announcement last year that she was willing journey so far by public apathy about the dangers of war.

He was also highly critical of the Thatcher Government's continuing defence of the

© The Citizen, Gloucester, 30 April 1984

inclusiveness, he said, tells us the Holy Land is not just Holy for us Jews, there must be a place for Palestinian Christians, Palestinian Muslims, Palestinian Jews.

"When we had prayed the Prayer together, I in English and he in Hebrew, we were joined by a young African student from Northern Nigeria, who said, 'I'm going to pray this Prayer in Hausa, the language of 100 million people in Northern Nigeria.' When he finished, a woman stood up and said, 'I am from South Africa; I'm a refugee from apartheid because I cannot believe that the white people should oppress the black people in the way they do.' She said, 'I am going to say the Prayer in Afrikaans, the language of the white oppressors of the blacks in South Africa, because there must be reconciliation, I as a white person with my black friend from Northern Nigeria.'

"Back in Winchester, I had put the big banner of peace up outside the Cathedral, to be met by a tall distinguished-looking gentleman who said, 'What are you doing, coming here talking about peace? There's no war on. You tell me where the war is, then I'll talk to you about peace. We've had peace for thirty years. You tell me where the war is.'

"Well, I didn't have my wits about me, otherwise I would have said: 'Well what about the millions of children who die who don't need to die? They die because we are so preoccupied with our scientists inventing new weapons and spending our money on these dreadful things that we can't really supply water and medical aid to millions of children.' But he just turned on me and said, 'How old are you, young man?' Well I was slightly flattered that he said young man, so I said 'I'm 64.'

"'Well,' he said, 'I'm 76 and I'm a rear-admiral, and I'm telling you we've got no war on, so don't you come here talking about peace.' And it is this false sense of security which makes us say 'Well perhaps it's going to be all right, perhaps if we can just keep a bit ahead of the Russians, perhaps it will keep them quiet.' The consequences are that the rest of the world is not at peace, and we do not have the authority to enable it to have the peace it needs because we ourselves are so involved in this mad arms race. And so in the end we have to come down to the question, what can we do about it? Can we do anything about it?

"Bishop John Taylor asked me to come round to his house for a cup of tea. One of the things we talked together about was the rising arms spiral. He said, 'This unilateralist-multilateralist debate is a red herring. The real issue is just a straight issue between rearmament and disarmament. It has to be one or the other. We either believe we should re-arm to keep pace, or believe we must now start to disarm. There must come a cut-off point, a moment when everyone says, "Stop! Freeze!" Then we can start cutting down.'

"And John Taylor was saying: we know this, but we know that neither Chernenko, nor Reagan, nor Thatcher, nor Miterrand, nor any world leader is going to say stop, because every one of them has a vested interest in actually maintaining the situation. For all their words, they know that politically their position depends on them not embarking on disarmament, but continuing with rearmament.

"So don't let us put our trust in princes. The only thing is for ordinary people to be so convinced that it is totally immoral that we go on with the arms race, that one by one they will stand up and simply say 'No!' There's absolutely no reason why ordinary people like ourselves can't just say, 'There's nothing worse than that I should ever give my consent to the destruction of my enemy in this way.' It cannot be justified by anything we read in Scripture. Jesus said, 'Love your enemies.' You cannot love them if you threaten them. You cannot threaten them with retaliation if you love them; therefore it is ordinary people just quietly saying 'no' and joining with others who also say 'no'."

Letter to supporters after the end of the pilgrimage

It has not been possible to write individually to all of you who so marvellously sustained me in body, mind and spirit during my recent pilgrimage round Britain. This circular letter is a poor substitute, but it carries my deep appreciation for all the loving kindness and tender care you showed me wherever I went.

You may recall that I carried two saddlebags on my trusty bicycle (over 2054 miles, 'Merlin' suffered no other damage than one broken spoke). In the right-hand bag I stowed away all the good things that happened, all the funny and moving things. On the left I packed the sad things which happened when the Prayer for Peace was diminished and ignored. These were immediately emptied down the kitchen sink on my return. By the time I got home, the bag on the right side was full to the flap. Now it overflows as more and more stories come in, of how the Prayer goes on and on, giving life, truth, hope, trust, love and peace to all who now weave it into the fabric of their lives.

A few like myself, have had the direction of our life's pilgrimage changed by the Prayer, but for most simply to be reminded again of the deep significance of prayer has given a new lightness to their step along the way, and kindled afresh in them the vision of *shalom*. Each time the Prayer was said in so many different languages by people of so many faiths, a tiny charge of energy was fed into the world's international power grid for peace.

The purpose of praying the Prayer for Peace was encapsulated for me in the answer Edward Carpenter gave to my grandson Nicholas' question: "What is all this for?" "Nick, it's all for you," said the good Dean. This became an all-consuming desire for me as I journeyed on— that Nicholas, his brother Jonathan, their cousins Abigail and Rachel, and all the world's children should be given the opportunity to know peace and possess it.

As I met with saintly Bishops, gentle Bahá'ís, valiant Jews, serious Quakers, determined Methodists, thoughtful Buddhists, disciplined Muslims, joyful humanists, beautiful Hindus, dedicated Anglicans, gallant Wesh monks and funny old agnostics, I was given a glimpse of what John Taylor, Bishop of Winchester, calls ". . . the universal inner place of the human spirit where attitudes are re-shaped and directions changed." So just saying the Prayer is in itself a creative act.

Many of you are asking what next for me as one who carries the message of the Prayer. Even before I arrived home, I was invited to join a group of pilgrims who are walking to Assisi to visit the shrine of St Francis and I have been asked to go to France to talk about the Prayer, but I have discovered the truth of T.S. [Eliot] who declares that in the end we find ourselves back at home where we started and know the place for the first time. I no longer want to talk about prayer; I just want to pray it.

I have been offered a disused Methodist Chapel in the village of Quick's Green, only four Merlin minutes from Nicholas' home. My wife and I will make a garden there and turn it into our home. I have also been offered partnership in an organic farm, eight Merlin minutes from the Chapel. We start in September to prepare an acre for the bio-dynamic production of vegetables following closely the methods of Masanobu Fukuoka. Thus I hope not only to say the Prayer, but to live it in meekness, sharing it daily with my grandchildren.

I am being encouraged to write up the diary of my pilgrimage, and perhaps when the days draw in, I shall make the time to do just that, because I would like to share with you all the good things that happened on that journey, and the even better things that are coming out of it.

"What I want to say to you today, is never give up. It may sometimes feel that we are making no impression on the situation, but those of us who believe that there is only one way to create the political will to create a world consciousness for peace, must believe that we are much nearer the top than we may have ever thought. And one of the ways is simply to get on quietly with this task of creating the conditions for peace, the atmosphere of peace, in people's hearts, Bring them to understand it's God's purpose simply by praying this Prayer for Peace."

Part Three
The Organic Prophet

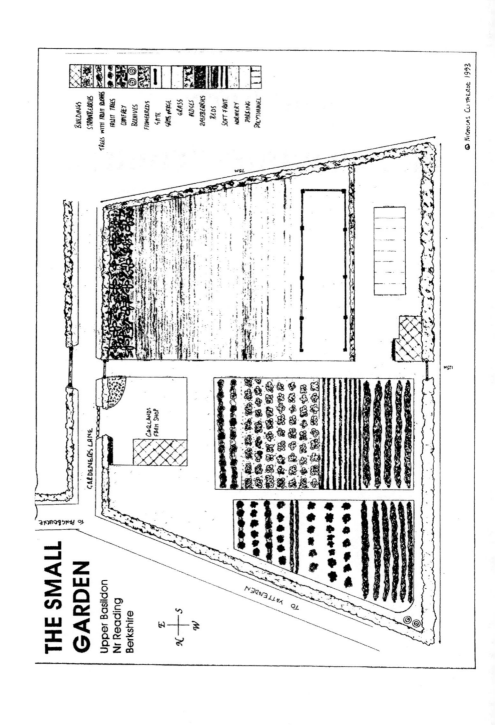

THE SMALL GARDEN

Upper Basildon
Nr Reading
Berkshire

Legend:
- BUILDINGS
- STRAWBERRIES
- TREES WITH FRUIT BUSHES
- FRUIT TREES
- COMFREY
- BEEHIVES
- FLOWERBEDS
- GATE
- GRASS VERGE
- GRASS
- MOLES
- RASPBERRIES
- BEDS
- SOFT FRUIT
- NURSERY
- PARKING
- POLYTUNNEL

GARDENERS LANE

GARLANDS FARM SHOP

TO PANGBOURNE

TO YATTENDEN

© NICHOLAS CLITHEROE 1993

The Small Garden

IT IS CALLED 'THE SMALL GARDEN', not because it is a little garden but because it is beautiful.[1] When I first saw it that summer day many years ago, it was a green field encompassed by trees and an unclipped hedge of hawthorn and wild privet.

This is the story of how we watched an acre and a half of grassland become a little farm where fruit and vegetables and flowers grow.

It all began in 1984, when my daughter Jane offered to help a local farmer make butter from his surplus milk. We'll call him Gerard, and he farms organically. That year his cows were giving more milk than he could conveniently sell. Perhaps it was that the grass and the herbs in his meadows were sweeter, and the hay they had fed on through the winter had been richer than ever before. Anyway, the gentle Jerseys had never been more contented. In the early morning and in the evening, he had no need to call them in, they stood waiting for him at the milking parlour door. Added to the problem of disposing of the milk, was what to do with all the extra eggs from the flock of hens which ranged freely across his fields. Like most small farmers, Gerard had been slipping steadily into debt. His friendly bank manager had been very patient, but the overdraft kept growing every month.

One day as he rinsed his buckets and sluiced the dairy floor, he had one of his brilliant ideas. He would make butter and ice-cream from the surplus milk and open his own little shop at the farm gate. That evening

---

1 Merfyn was by then a keen follower of E.F. Schumacher's ideas as set out in *Small is Beautiful*. He would also have been thinking of the Small School, that Satish Kumar and others had founded in Hartland, Devon.

he got out his calculator. All night he worked on his sums, until it was time to go down and meet his cows in the morning. But he could not make the figures add up to make any kind of profit that would even begin to reduce his overdraft. It became clear that for the shop to succeed, there must be more on the shelves than organic milk, organic butter, organic ice-cream and fresh brown eggs from organically fed chickens.

A few weeks later my daughter went to help out in the farm kitchen. As Gerard turned the handle of the churn, Jane formed the butter into golden pats. They talked about the need for another enterprise on the farm to make the shop a paying proposition. Gerard began to have another of his brilliant ideas.

"I know what I'll do," he said. "I'll set aside an acre or two on the farm for an organic market garden. I'll fill the shelves of my little farm shop with organic fruit and vegetables. I can see those shelves already, weighed down with creamy organic cauliflowers, white winter cabbages as big as little footballs, bunches and bunches of cherry-red radishes all arranged in a nest of lettuces—bronze-leaved Lollo Rossa, Webbs Wonderful, Iceberg and Little Gem. In the winter we'll have Alaskan leeks, and Brussels sprouts, curly kale, Jerusalem artichokes and everlasting spinach. In summer, there will be as much fruit as we can possibly pick—rows of little baskets brimful of strawberries, and trays of punnets filled with succulent raspberries. We'll have blackcurrants, redcurrants, white currants and fat hairless gooseberries. When our customers walk into the shop, they will find themselves in a place filled with the fragrance of fresh-picked coriander, mint, thyme, and flowering camomile."

He paused for a moment, his head soaring above the clouds. Jane went on patting the butter. There was silence between them, the only sound the slap and clatter of the Scotch hands she used to shape the butter into half-pound packs. She said, "I think it is a great idea, but how do you imagine you are going to grow all that wonderful stuff and run a shop on top of everything else you do? Cows don't milk themselves, and free-range chickens can't be trained to collect their own eggs. What is going to happen to all those experiments you are carrying out, like growing Stone Age wheat for thatching straw?"

Gerard never liked his brilliant ideas to be examined too closely, but had had to admit that he already had far too much work to do on the farm as it was. There was another silence, then he said defensively: "I'll just

have to get someone to help me. We can get a good premium on the sale of organic vegetables so we can employ an experienced organic gardener for production and put a manager into the shop. We should be making a good profit within a year, and it will not be long before I start paying off the overdraft. I've got a stable on the farm that I can turn into a shop. I'll use the old Ferguson to plough up one of the fields, there's loads of muck in the cowshed, the hen-houses are deep in droppings and I've got a beautiful muck-spreader in the barn. We can use the little old Howard rotavator to prepare the beds and there are plenty of tools with no handles in our garden shed."

Blueprint for organic food

I was sixty-six at the time, ready to settle down with my wife and draw my pension from what in my father's day they called 'the Worn-out Ministers' Fund'. However I felt far from worn-out. I had come to live in a caravan, parked in the drive of my daughter's Berkshire village home. Jane came home from her butter-making, and told me about Gerard's brilliant idea for an organic market garden and a farm-gate shop.

The weeks went by, planning permission was granted for the conversion of the stable, and a person appeared who had experience of the retail trade, to help run the shop. But no one appeared, even on the distant horizon, offering to grow fresh fruit and vegetables. Gerard was desperate, because the brilliant idea could not work without the organic food supplied fresh from the field. He began to clutch at any straw. I was the straw he clutched.

What I had to offer was just a spark, a desire to dig, and the hope of supplementing my pension. My experience of growing things in an English climate was minimal. True, I had made compost heaps in Zambia, but that is not difficult in a place where the sun shines most of the year, and the temperature was above 20° most of the time. For eighteen months, I worked an allotment in Oxford, but the only thing I grew successfully was Russian comfrey. Yes, I loved digging, and one of my most precious possessions is a stainless steel spade with an unbreakable haft. Another  is the Zambian hoe sent me by Kenneth Kaunda when he heard I had taken on the allotment. Gerard suggested I go and see him on his farm.

It was a beautiful day in late summer. He took me first down Adder Lane, the bridle path which runs right through the farm, to see his herd of Jerseys. We found them gathered in the shade of a line of old hawthorn trees. He knew each one by name and they knew him. Then we saw his flock of laying hens ranging wide across the field by the road that runs between the Red Lion and the Beehive. Finally we came to the home farm field, which the chickens had left not long before, an acre and a half of grassland gently sloping from north, south-facing and ideal for irrigation. It was entirely surrounded by a thick hawthorn hedge, which had been secured by wire netting to keep the chickens in, and the foxes and the muntjac deer out.

There and then we agreed on the broad outline of the plan. Gerard would supply the land and the tools, while I supplied the labour. I would sell the produce to the shop at wholesale prices and we would share the proceeds of the crop. It seemed a sensible sort of arrangement; after all, half the Indian subcontinent grows its food on this basis, the landless peasant share-cropping with his master. We divided the field into four plots for a four-course rotation. Gerard ploughed it up while I cleaned out the chicken houses for their rich manure. It was a hard job scraping the perches and the slatted floor with a paint scraper, their droppings set as hard as varnish.

Neither of us had any experience of gardening on this scale, but Gerard lent me a book called 'The One-Straw Revolution' by a Japanese called Masanobu Fukuoka. He is a world authority on what is sometimes called the 'no dig, raised bed, deep mulch' system. This was to be our bible, though I felt some disappointment that I would not see my silver spade flashing in the autumn sun. Gerard said it would take too long to mark the raised beds all by hand, so we would have to borrow a potato ridger.

"We made such a go of it—it took time to learn the lessons. There was one occasion when we planted out our first lettuces; I had 1,000 lettuces to plant, and Audrey and I went to see the garden on a Saturday and there were all these little lettuce plants flopping on the ground. We dug down and found that there were leatherjackets in the ground, because leatherjackets live on grassland, and when we ploughed up the grassland we hadn't ploughed up the leatherjackets, so they destroyed the lot. So I said we've got to replant, and this time Audrey said I'll come and help you, so we planted out another 1000 lettuces, and Audrey planted them out with the same care. It was a marvellous experience, and the point came when we were growing carrots and selling them through the farm shop that we had set up, and these carrots were going to a hotel a few miles from the village.

"Now attending that hotel was Egon Ronay, and he had this dish that they had prepared for him. And he said 'These carrots! I've never had anything like them. Where do you get these carrots from?' 'Oh,' they said, 'there's an old clergyman, he has a garden, we get them from him.' So a few weeks later, he was at another village, on the Thames, and the same thing happened, they had two gourmets from France who said, 'Where are these carrots from?' He said, 'There's a man up on the farm.' He wanted to know about the carrots, and we set up a special blind tasting operation to find whether our carrots were different from others. Anyway it was a very great success. I knew organic gardening had a future."[2]

---

2 Interview with Rev Merfyn Temple by John Pritchard, 2006, Methodist Church Oral Archive project, British Library reference C640/146 tape 5 side A © Trustees for Methodist Church

Some Thoughts on the Future of Garlands Organic Farm[3]

Because of its history, Garlands has a head start in the scramble for land on which to practise organic farming. There are now few farms left in England which have been preserved for so long from chemical sprays and fertilisers. At all costs Garlands needs to be conserved for the future development of organic farming throughout the world.

Economic viability

For Garlands to become economically viable, it must not only generate enough income to support a family, and enough to sustain the annual costs of farm maintenance, but it must also generate confidence for long-term investment.

The importance of livestock

The development of part of the farm for intensive pick-your-own fruit and vegetable production points the way forward, but to sustain the fertility of the land, it will be necessary to include livestock. The provision of an adequate supply of high quality farmyard manure is essential. The labour required for the management of the livestock would have to be paid for from the proceeds of sales. The livestock operation would need to be kept separate from the production of fruit and vegetables as a self-financing department of the farm.

A centre for agro-ecology

As Garlands develops as an economically viable proposition, it can become a centre for the demonstration of the principles and practice of ecological agriculture, and a place where people can come for periods of instruction in the techniques of bio-dynamic farming.

Radiating the message

Already the Department of Agriculture of the University of Reading has shown an interest in bringing groups of overseas students to visit Garlands, to see how organic vegetable production is carried out. One woman from Zambia was placed on the farm to receive a week's training this year.

There is a real possibility that Garlands might be used by local schools as a place to visit to learn about agro-ecology.

Purposes on behalf of the Methodist Church Oral Archive project.

3 Another of Merfyn's 'broadsheets' circulated among his many contacts, for discussion and fund-raising. See also pp 69 and 146.

A five-year plan

Starting from 1989, I believe a realistic five-year development plan could be drawn up with a view to Garlands Farm becoming a viable economic proposition by 1995.

2 May 1993

Dear Ian,

Audrey and I are working flat out in the garden now that Spring has sprung. We have taken in four mentally handicapped young men to work with us to teach them the basics of organic agriculture and set up a demonstration of what we magically mucky rascals can do with his land when the Good Lord shows us how to use it properly.

Yours ever, Merfyn

11 August 1993

My dear Barnaby,

You would hardly recognise the small garden now. There is now a spanking new shop where our muck heap used to be. The polytunnel was blown away in the gale and I have moved my 'HQ' to the western hedge of the field. Since April I have been working five hours a day, five days a week with a small group of handicapped people in a project of training, therapy and rehabilitation. We are constructing another poly-tunnel 65 x 21 feet for growing winter crops, and I have started a worm farm to provide locally produced compost.

Yours ever, Merfyn

Organic Odyssey, 1989: Nairobi to Lusaka

DURING THE LAST FIFTEEN YEARS Zambia had become no more than a happy memory. Suddenly my peace was disturbed by the call of an old African friend, Job Mayanda. He told me what was happening to the land in the Southern Province of Zambia, and asked for my help. Deforestation, overgrazing, neglect of conservation and the misuse of chemical fertilizers had resulted in serious erosion and degradation of the soil.

There was no way I could give Job Mayanda 'no' for an answer. Five years cultivating the Small Garden had convinced me, not only that God is green, but that His way for the future of farming was the organic way. I was sure it was right for England, but not so sure it was right for Africa. I had heard recently of the highly successful Organic Farm Training Centre near Kitale in Kenya. It was necessary for me to go and see for myself: I would travel from Kenya to Zambia.

I could not leave our garden until after the autumn harvest, but would need to be in Zambia before the onset of the heavy rains in January. There was no money for the journey, so I asked my family and friends to sponsor me with a penny a mile, and a prayer a day. My grandchildren and great-nephews and nieces gave me enthusiastic support, especially for the part I planned to tackle on a mountain bike. I decided to travel light and, within the limit of seventy days, to do as much as possible of the journey on the ground. This would mean travelling by any means of transport available and living off the land.

I received a letter from President Kaunda, warmly welcoming my intention to visit Zambia again. This set the seal on the expedition. The following are extracts from my diary.[1]

---

1 This is an edited extract from *New Hope for Africa*. Reproduced with permission.

Kenya: organic farming, Kitale

It has been a strange and wonderful experience to come here to Manor House. I would change the name to The Garden of Eden, because only God could have planted it here. Everything is being done far, far better than ever we do it in our small garden in Upper Basildon. The cabbages are twice the size, the carrots fatter and longer, the climbing beans climb higher and the spinach grows thicker and a deeper green. I know we grow the best organic vegetables in Berkshire, but they would not stand a chance of any certificates at the Kitale Show. The compost here is richer, yet the weeds are fewer. Everywhere there are beds of comfrey, which is used not only to give soft, green content in building the compost heaps, but also to feed the rabbits and the pigs.

There is a flock of sheep and a herd of goats for meat, and three cows for milk; their dung will be used for the bio-gas plant that is being constructed. Eight grey donkeys frisk and bray in a field by the gardens, ready at any time to be inspanned in harness made in the leather workshop here. They pull the locally constructed donkey-carts and the ploughs on the ten-acre farm, where the maize and finger-millet crops are grown to feed the whole community.

During lunch, a proper African meal consisting of domed plates of ugali, maize meal porridge, with boiled cabbage and wild rabbit stew, I was told how it all began. In 1981, at an international conference in Nairobi called to discuss renewable sources of energy, a little group of Kenyans determined that something must be done to establish systems of sustainable agriculture. At this time a man named Patrick Peacey, who had been a teacher at the Manor House Prep School, was still mourning the death of the school ten years before. He told the Kenyans that the buildings at Manor House might be available, but that roofs were falling in, doors and windows had been stolen, and it would need a lot of money to make it habitable. They went to the Government and got a kindly but dusty answer.

Then a little miracle happened. Peacey met a young American woman in Nairobi whose parents had a deep commitment to environmentally friendly farming. The upshot was well over a million East African shillings, given for the restoration of Manor House buildings for agricultural training.

After lunch a young woman arrived, to take me to see her father's farm. She is the sister of Festus, and I had asked to meet their father because he is a small farmer, who for the past three years has been carrying out, on his own land, all the practices recommended by the Manor House.

The old man's farm had no shape or form. The two acres of ripening maize drifted down amongst the cabbages, the onions, and the cultivated amaranthus. The goat-pens and the chicken-run straggled through the banana grove. The pawpaws mingled with the guava trees. Here and there were lines of French marigolds to keep the aphids under control. Beds of black nightshade spinach reduced the nematode population in the soil and the scent of fresh goat manure rose from the compost heaps. He has set such an example as an organic farmer that when people visit Manor House and say, "All this stuff may be OK for the younger generation, but you will never persuade the old farmers to take it up", they are taken out to the old man's place. There all the arguments stop.

UGANDA: 31st October to 2nd November 1989

Travelling by car, bus, truck and taxi, I crossed the border into Uganda on my way to Kampala, from where I hoped to sail across Lake Victoria to Mwanza in Tanzania. I spent the first night at the Catholic Mission house in Bungoma and was treated to wonderful African hospitality. The next day I set off for Jinja.

I got to Jinja late in the morning but found no taxi that would take me on to Kampala, so I clambered aboard a seventy-seater bus, and had the bike tied on the roof. I was hungry and thirsty, but did not want to get off the bus lest I lose my seat. A small middle-aged woman saw my predicament, and speaking good English offered to negotiate through the window for a 'soda', the generic term for all Cokes, Fantas, Sprites.

When we came to the bus station in Kampala, I could hardly believe my eyes. This central parking space lies in a hollow, and you look down on the shining roofs of thousands of taxis and hundreds of buses. As the bus draws in, it is surrounded by packs of boys stretching their hands through the bus windows, shouting for the privilege of carrying the passengers' bags to taxi or bus for the next stage of the journey. My new-found friend said, "Follow me; these boys have not all come here to help you, many have come to steal things too."

She found her own barrow-boy, and told him to take the bike as it was lowered from the roof and fight off any others who wanted to handle it.

From out of Africa

■ Ready for adventure — the Reverend Merfyn Temple and his bike ©   Pictures: ROZIE STOTT

I asked the woman if she knew anywhere I could leave the bike in safe hands. She lived out of town, but she was sure her daughter Fiona, who is a lawyer, would look after it. She said, "Go to her office over there in Spear House and give her this note." It read: *I found this man on the bus, please help him.*

I showed Fiona the map of my journey, the paper about it, and the letter from Kenneth Kaunda. She read everything quickly, asked me a few questions, and took me to an empty seminar room, where she said we could talk undisturbed. Then she told me about herself.

"I took my law degree here at Makerere University, where amongst other things I was leader in the debating society and very much interested in the women's rights movement. At first I could not find a job, but I am now a legal officer of ACFODE (Action for Development), a non-governmental organisation that was formed by women in 1985, to stimulate the awareness of the nation to their potential and rights, as well as to expand the involvement and visibility of women in Uganda's development."

Vicar gets on his bike to teach villages

By DAVID WILLIAMS

CRUSADING vicar Merfyn Temple is off to spread the word about organic farming by trekking through Africa on a mountain bike.

And the Reverend Temple's trip has the blessing of his old friend, President Kuanda of Zambia.

The vicar, from Thames Avenue, Pangbourne, spent 30 years in central Africa helping to resettle the country as land commissioner.

Since returning to Britain and retiring from his post as minister of All Saints Church, Abingdon, he has grown organic vegetables on a 1.5-acre plot in Upper Basildon.

Now his gardening experience is in demand among his former friends in Africa, where intensive chemical farming has destroyed the soil.

Mr Temple decided to set off on his mission when an old farming friend from Zambia, Job Mayanda, wrote: "Come and tell us what to do. May God in his kindness bring resurrection to the dead lands of our Tonga people."

And as the churchman prepared to depart, he received a remarkable message from the president saying: "Just a few days before I learned of your proposal I had a premonition of your coming and it was an answer to my prayers."

On October 25 Mr Temple will travel to southern Zambia then get on his all-terrain bike to spread the green message to the most inaccessible villages.

After cycling around Britain only two years ago, he is confident age will be no handicap.

"I know people think I'm eccentric," he admitted. "They are right, I am, but I know this is very important.

"When I was last in Zambia I helped create the problem by encouraging people to use fertilizers, so I will now be helping to create the solution.

"For the first two years we will start up organic farming in one place as a demonstration with people coming in to take short courses.

"I am really going because of my experience in running the small garden in Upper Basildon with my wife.

"It is only about 1.5 acres but we manage to grow enough fruit and vegetables for our family and several others in the area.

"Zambia will be a real homecoming."

© *Reading Evening Post, 19 October 1989*

She was of medium height, slender, and immaculately dressed in black skirt and white blouse. She said she had some work to do, but would like to take me home for lunch to meet her mother again. Meanwhile she arranged for me to be interviewed by the editor of the women's page of Vision, Uganda's daily newspaper.

By midday Fiona was ready to go for lunch. We squeezed into a mini-bus taxi and alighted at a large, rather dilapidated building, with a sign saying Tile Factory; in the yard were a few piles of cement-cast roof tiles. Fiona, apologising that her house was not all she would want, led me round the back to meet her mother. I was not expecting an impecunious lawyer to be living in a palace, but I was quite unprepared for the sight that met my eyes.

At some time in the past, a watchman's shack had been built against the factory wall. It consisted of mud walls and smoke-blackened corrugated-iron sheets. There were two rooms. The inner one contained two mattresses slung on rickety wooden frames, where Fiona, her mother and her daughter Phyllis slept. The outer room contained a bunk-bed which stretched the full six feet from wall to wall. Here four young boys slept. The remaining space, six feet by five feet, contained everything else that these seven people owned.

Fiona's mother, dressed in the same blue Ugandan cotton print dress she had been wearing on the bus, was sweeping the trodden earth around the cooking fire. I was invited in to sit on the only little chair they owned and had space for. After a meal of stewed smoked meat and groundnut gravy, sweet potatoes and spinach, Fiona took Phyllis outside, and her mother came and sat on the floor in the doorway and told me her story.

"My husband was a teacher who had done some of his training at Birmingham University. I am a primary school teacher and we used to live in the eastern part of Uganda. In the last week before he fled, Amin ordered all educated people in our area to be killed. Then the soldiers came and murdered my husband. Most of my friends fled, but I needed to stay in my house for the sake of my children, and I had nowhere to go.

"On 24 February 1988, I was in the house alone, when a gang of men with guns and pangas smashed down the door and broke in. They said they wanted money. I said I had no money, but they said I was lying because all teachers had money and I must show them where it was hidden. I said I had no money, because I had not been paid. One soldier pushed me to the ground, holding a *panga* at my throat, and others began to ransack the house. The man made me take off all my clothes and I lay on the floor naked. He lifted up his panga to kill me but at that moment there was a loud crash from the room next door. The man with the panga went to see what had made the noise, afraid the others might have found money. I ran and hid in the bushes. After a long time I peered out and all the soldiers had gone. When my children returned from school, we just ran. We had nothing. So in the end we came to Kampala to Fiona, but she was living in just one room with a friend. Last year we managed to find this place, but there are no jobs for teachers. All the jobs are taken by the first ones who ran away from the east."

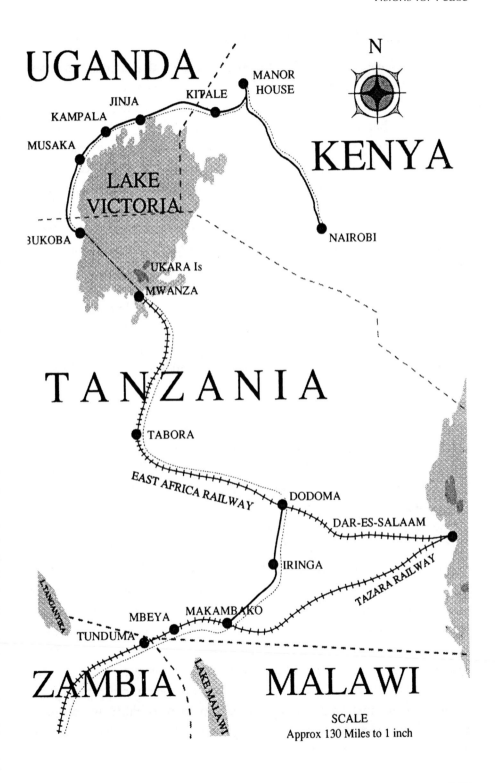

On to Tanzania: 3 to 6 November

Tanzania was like another world. No buses bulging with passengers, no men clamouring to get their taxis full. All I could see were a few men and women sitting around under the trees, looking as if they were waiting for something to turn up. What in Uganda had been a well-graded road had deteriorated into little better than a cart-track. A ramshackle Land-Rover arrived, and I clambered aboard, being assured that I would be taken to a place where I could get a bus to Bukoba. An hour later the Land Rover driver announced that he was not going any further, but that I should get on my bike, and a kilometre further down the road, I would find a bus to take me to Bukoba.

I bumped along on the bike for a good four kilometres, till at a fork in the road I saw a bus. Fortunately, before I boarded it, I found it was going in the opposite direction. A passer-by suggested I should sit under a tree, where a small boy was roasting kebabs, and the bus would come.

No bus came, and I was getting thirsty. I found a mud hut where cups of tea and roast bananas were for sale, but I could only eat half the banana before it stuck in my throat. I was exchanging addresses with a Muslim I had met, when they said a lorry had arrived.

I went out onto the road, and there was a five-ton lorry piled high with bulging sacks. About twenty-five people were perched on top. The driver said he would take me to Bukoba, ninety kilometres on, if I was prepared to ride outside. Sitting on the roof of the cab was a very portly man with heavy, dark horn-rimmed glasses, wearing a well-cut jacket.

'Are you a priest?' he asked.

'Yes, a Protestant priest,' I replied.

He gave me a hand and pulled me up. They threw the bike on top of a mound of green bananas by the tailboard, and we set off in a cloud of dust. The only way I could keep myself from falling off was to cling to the arms of a young man in front and wedge my feet against the legs of another.

I began to chat to the man with the horn-rimmed glasses. He was a retired inspector of schools, who had taken a diploma in education in Britain at Exeter University. I asked him what was in the sacks we were riding on. He said they were full of dry cow-dung being transported from a government ranch to the secondary school in Bukoba. How appropriate, I thought, the organiser of the organic revolution in Africa riding to victory on a load of muck!

In Tanzania: 6 to 11 November

I discovered that the next ship to Mwanza was leaving that evening. Having managed to buy a ticket from a couple of honest fellow passengers, I spent an uncomfortable night on board ship and arrived in port at dawn.

From Mwanza to Dodoma was an equally crowded twenty-four-hour train journey. I spent the night at a Christian Conference Centre in Dodoma and set my goal to reach Iringa the next day[2].

The railway bus to Iringa was full and I quickly discovered that there was no chance of getting a private bus, taxi, or anything else, so I set off on my bike hoping to get a lift for the 200km journey. Unlike other towns I have been in on this trip, Dodoma does not seem to have any outskirts. It just suddenly stops and the barren bush-country of the Wagogo people begins. The dirt road is badly corrugated and quite sandy in parts, so I was thankful for the balloon tyres of my bike and its low gears. It was a beautiful day, my seventieth birthday; I had the wind at my back and was quite sure that the good Lord would get me to Iringa to light my birthday candles.

Fortunately, at intervals of four or five miles, I found a little 'hotel' selling warm Pepsi Cola, or warm sweet tea, or just a cup of water. At one of these a beast had just been slaughtered. Its skin was pegged out on the hard baked ground, its bones and flesh hung on a rack over a smoking fire. A boy was toasting the offal. For twenty pence he sold me a tasty morsel of liver. That was my breakfast. For lunch I had a Pepsi and a fresh fried doughnut.

By 2.00pm I had been in the saddle for five hours and I was reduced to pushing the bike. It seemed a long time ago that I had had anything to drink. My lips were cracking, and my mouth furred up. Ahead of me I saw three figures, women, judging by the cloths wrapped around them. They had carrying-poles across their shoulders, with large calabashes on either end. I pressed on to catch them up, but they were swinging along at a good pace.

Under the shade of a Baobab, they stopped for a rest. I caught up with them and they gave me a drink as I sat by my bike in the shade. I heard

---

2 The next day was Merfyn's 70th birthday, and he was looking forward to spending it with friends in Iringa: Roland (the editor) and his family.

the sound of a vehicle approaching and struggled to my feet. It was an empty white UNDP pick-up, with a white man driving. He did not see me. Whether, if he had done so, he would have stopped, I shall never know. With his passing went my last vestige of hope that I would reach Iringa to light the candles on my cake.

From behind me came the sound of music. I turned to see another Land Rover with a full-length roof rack, five red jerrycans strapped to the rear and a blaring loudspeaker at the front. As they stopped to pick me up, I found myself perched on a bundle of religious tracts with three other African men in the back of a travelling bookshop, belonging to the Tanganyika Press. It was too noisy to carry on much of a conversation, but it was not long before we stopped at a village. The music attracted a little crowd of men and women who came out to greet us. There was much hugging and clasping of hands and a call for 'soda'. I treated everyone to a bottle apiece and two for myself. The tall man, who was obviously leader of the team, explained that although we were on the way to Iringa, he would not get there for a couple of days. The next day he would find someone to give me a lift into Iringa.

So we travelled on through the afternoon, stopping now and again to play the music, deliver a number of letters and greet the people. By six o'clock we had come to a large cluster of houses where we were to stay the night. We were parked in the shade of a tree right in the centre of the village and soon a crowd began to gather. There must have been a hundred children of all ages as the microphone was fixed up and the people collected to hear the preaching. A Muscovy duck and five tiny ducklings quacked and squawked at my feet.

I sat on a chair feeling a bit sorry for myself. I was hungry and desperately disappointed: Iringa was still sixty miles away. Far away down the road I saw lights again and as they drew nearer, I could see by their position that they were Land-Rover lights. I said, Please God, let him turn off and rescue me. The Land Rover slowed down and bumped over to where the dried-fish sellers had spread out their smoke-blackened fish on racks in the moonlight. A man got out dressed in khaki uniform and began bargaining with the traders. After a while he noticed me and in perfect English said, "What am I going to do? I must have some fish to take home to my wife and they want seventy shillings for a fish [20p]. I cannot pay that."

"You can," I said, "I will buy you all the fish on the rack if you can get me to Iringa tonight."

He laughed and went on bargaining. Then I saw another man get out of the cab, dressed in a safari-suit; he seemed to be the boss. I told him my story and could see that he did not believe a word of it.

I pleaded with him, saying that I had travelled in a much smaller space on the train from Mwanza. I could leave the bike on top of the Tanganyika Press van and it could follow tomorrow. The man shook his head again, but his friend weighed into the argument on my side. He said, "This man says he is a priest and I believe him. That is how priests travel. They suffer. He has suffered all day on his bicycle and he is prepared to suffer again."

I did not wait, but squeezed myself into the vacant corner. We roared off at tremendous speed, and I was thankful for the child, as he acted as a kind of counterweight, preventing my head from hitting the roof as we went over the deep gullies of the wickedly eroded road through the mountains. But nothing mattered now. Somehow I would hold on until we got there.

Iringa pit-stop

I did get to Iringa that night, but could not get in touch with Roland on the phone. He found me the next morning at the hotel in town, and drove me in triumph in a white Land Rover to his house. Behind the wrought-iron gates Fiona his eldest daughter was jumping up and down with excitement; soon she was joined by Tania and Naomi shouting "He has come! He has come!" The security-guard came to unlock the gate and there was Tandy, Roland's Papua New Guinean wife, to give me one of her warm Pacific Island hugs.

The room I entered was decorated with balloons, and on the table was a big chocolate birthday cake, made as the figure of seventy, with coffee-butter icing and seven candles, each representing ten years. They have a beautiful spacious house, simply and sparsely furnished; in one corner is a large playhouse with door and curtained windows, which Tandy had made out of a big corrugated cardboard box. In the afternoon I slept a little, and at four o'clock the guests arrived. The candles were lit, I was crowned with a paper crown that Fiona had made for me and they sang Happy Birthday, first in English, then in Tandy's language. How good it was to be among friends again.

I slept all through the night and awoke wonderfully refreshed. Roland refers to my coming here as a 'pit-stop'. He has found a local cobbler to mend my shoe, and spent some time in adjusting the brakes of my bike and sorting out the stiff derailleur gears.

Next afternoon we went out a few miles from Iringa to see a dairy farm, run by the son of a retired agricultural officer who bought the farm many years ago. Over the years a unique system of cattle management has been developed, which is entirely organic and indigenous. In the pasture-lands the native acacia trees have been preserved, while the others have been cleared. Not only do the acacias provide shade, but they are leguminous, their root-system providing nitrogen for the grass. The farm looks like spacious parkland surrounding an English stately home.

There is arable land too, for growing maize for food and making silage. Perhaps the most amazing thing for me is that this young man is steadily replacing tractor-cultivation with cultivation by oxen. He has found that by crossing his Ayrshire milk-cows with Sussex bulls, he gets a good draught animal. This visible evidence of practical organic pasture-management reinforces my belief that indigenous organic farming provides the best way forward for most of Africa.

I spent long hours with Roland in discussions about his concept of grass-roots development. The Ismani area, in which he hopes to encourage the emergence of base communities, bears a great resemblance to the conditions in Zambia's southern province. The constant use of artificial fertilizers has increased soil acidity, reducing maize yields. In the days before chemicals were used, ten bags of maize per acre were normal, but today three bags is the average.

The only way in which this desert will ever be made to blossom as the rose, is to initiate a process by which the local people undertake the task themselves. There are no quick and dramatic answers to their problem, but Roland has made the first tentative steps along the way which stretches a hundred years on.

Roland was taking a week's leave and had planned to take us all in the Land-Rover to spend time with some friends in Southern Tanzania, dropping me off somewhere along the line in order to get the TAZARA Railway into Zambia.

As planned we found the railway at Makambako. To our dismay, there are only two trains a week, one going through at 2 o'clock tomorrow morn-

Saying goodbye, Makambako railway station, Tanzania:
Roland and his daughters perched on Merfyn's bike

ing and the next not until next Wednesday. I had promised Kaunda that I would be in Lusaka next Wednesday; so we said a sad goodbye. Roland and the family left me booking my ticket on the station platform and booking my bike into the parcels office, to be sent on its own way to Zambia.

A gent in a grey suit sidled up and asked me what I was waiting for. When I explained that my train did not leave until 2.00am, he said with a sympathetic air, "This hotel closes at 10.00pm and I shall have to turn you out. Your train does not leave until 4.00am. You will get very cold waiting for six hours. It will be too crowded in the waiting room, as hundreds of people travel. Why do you not take a room and sleep here? I will tell the security-guard to wake you in good time before the train arrives at 4.00 in the morning."

"How much will a room cost?" I asked.

"A room upstairs costs 1,000 shillings. A room downstairs costs 750 shillings."

I found I had exactly 750 shillings in my money belt, so I gave it to him and he gave me the key. I slept, but woke at 2.15am to hear the hoot of a train. I threw on my clothes, woke the security-guard, who was fast asleep in his blanket on the office floor, and rushed out. I had to climb over the security-fence and I began to run down the road towards the headlight on the engine, which I could see shining through the darkness. I began to pant and I heard my wife's little voice in me saying: *Merfyn, is it worth it? I would much rather you missed the train than die of a heart attack.*

I slowed to a trot, but broke into a run again with a long blast from the train's whistle. I still had a hundred yards to go to the station when the train began to move. I cut off diagonally through the waste ground, leaping over the bushes to intercept the train. I ran alongside the moving train, grabbed a handrail with my left hand and swung my foot onto the step. I had my bag in my right hand and I tried to hook the handle over my thumb, leaving my fingers free to hold the other rail. I held on for a few yards, but as the train gathered speed my fingers slipped and I fell off.

I picked myself up, none the worse for my fall, and I went back and stood by the roadside. I prayed, *Good Lord, when you gave me my bit part in this drama, you never told me it was a comedy. It's all very well, but how are you going to get me to catch up with my bike in the guard's van on your blessed train?*

It was not long before I saw lights approaching. It was an enormous twelve-ton Mercedes truck, towing a twenty-ton trailer. The driver, a bearded Tanzanian, fortunately spoke a little English and I explained my predicament. He told me to get in, which I did, squeezing myself on the front seat. How quickly my luck had changed! Instead of being cooped up for hours with hundreds of people in a third-class carriage, here I was tooling along the open road at sixty kph in a Merc.

I knew that the next place where the road and railway-line converged was Mbeya, two hundred kilometres to the south. If we kept going at that speed, we would be able to catch up with the train, but soon we slowed to walking pace to negotiate the gaping potholes where the road surface had crumbled.

At 3.30am we stopped, so that the lorry boys could get a plate of egg and chips at a drivers' road-side cafe. I hoped we were travelling at least as fast as the train, but there was no way of knowing, because the road and the railway track do not run side by side. We reached the Mbeya hills at dawn and finally the driver put me down at the railway station.

The spacious waiting-room, which would do credit to any provincial airport, was empty. That must surely mean that the train had come and gone. I found a man pacing the polished pink and green terrazzo floor. "Has the train to Tunduma left?" I asked.

"No," he replied, "It is not due in until 7 o'clock." I sat down on one of the newly varnished hard-wood seats and watched the well-dressed passengers arrive to join the orderly queues that were beginning to form.

On through Zambia: 12 to 15 November

I rejoined the train, and my bicycle, at Mbeya, and we crossed into Zambia later in the day. I was glad of a hotel at Kapiri Mposhi, the end of the TAZARA line.

The next morning, a heavily laden bus from the north drew in. Enough passengers got off for me to get on, so I decided to travel on to Kabwe, forty miles to the south on the road to Lusaka. It was as crowded as any bus I have been on. I managed to get a seat on the aisle, but I had to crouch, because the woman standing on my side of the aisle had a baby on her back whose bottom protruded over my head. I hoped it had a clean nappy on.

Two seats back were two women in white dresses with black head-scarves. They said they were members of the African Reformed Church and I said I was a member of the United Church of Zambia. "Then we are brothers and sisters," they said. About half way, when I was wondering if I might have to ask the driver to stop to let me out for a breather, the women began to sing and everything changed as others joined in.

When I got to Kabwe I was desperate for a shower and some clean clothes. I found the best hotel in town, and slept well, keeping the whining mosquitoes at bay with applications of Jungle Formula. A copy of the *Times of Zambia* was pushed through my door the next morning; the banner headline on the business page of the paper read: *AGRO-CHEMICAL FIRM TO OPEN RURAL OUTLETS*. It was the story of how a new chemical-fertilizer company was opening with the intention of getting fertilizers out to the most remote rural areas. I closed my eyes and said a prayer: *Strengthen the hand of thy servant, O Lord, and help him deliver Zambia from the hands of her enemies.*

It was noon. I could not face another journey on bus or train. Lusaka is only ninety miles to the south on a reasonable tarmac road, so I set off on the bike, past the smoking chimneys of the lead and zinc mine. Twelve miles further on, I was just wondering where I could find a drink, when I saw a thatched shelter with a woman selling Fantas. I parked the bike and drank a bottle. An elderly man in a tattered coat and a cloth cap brought me a cup of *munkoyo* beer[3]. I greeted him in Chitonga, and he asked me where I was going and where I had come from. I told him, and after we had talked awhile, he said, "You are the Reverend Merfyn Temple. I have got the book which you wrote about our President called 'Zambia Shall Be Free'."

We shook hands delightedly, and a small crowd began to gather, most of them young men and school children. I showed them Kaunda's letter. My friend called everyone to gather round and said, "Take a look at this man. You are too young to know him but he is the great friend of our President, and he helped us in the struggle to get our Independence."

With this heart-warming reminder that I am still remembered in Zambia, I cycled on, wondering where I might find myself at sunset. A yellow Toyota pick-up passed me, drew in to the side of the road and stopped as if waiting for me to catch up. A bronzed white man got out and flagged me down. I stopped. He held out his hand and said, "Merfyn Temple. Do you remember me?" I had to confess that I did not.

"I am Boria Pilblad," he said. "I was one of those Swedish volunteers who came out to help you when you started the first youth camp at Broken Hill in 1964. I now have a little chicken-farm a mile down the road, there on the right."

I spent that night with Boria and his Zambian wife, and the next night with a Bahá'í scientist with a passion for trees. The journey was long and hot, and as I neared Lusaka I was weary and saddle-sore. However there were to be no more lifts, and no one came to greet me on my arrival in Lusaka.

Lusaka: 16 to 23 November

I went in search of my old friend Justin Zulu, with whom I used to work in the National Institute of Public Administration. I finally found him in one of the large office buildings near the Milk Marketing Board. Justin is

---

3 A weak beer made from kibbled maize and the root of the *munkoyo* tree.

now the deputy Permanent Secretary in the Ministry of Commerce and Industry, and occupies one of the two hottest and most powerful seats in government. There are four telephones on his desk: the red one is the direct line to the president in State House. When he finally got through to Kaunda's private secretary, he was told that the president was expecting me, but would have to delay a meeting with me, as all the heads of the Front Line States were arriving for a one day summit-meeting.

After imposing on Justin and his wife Elizabeth for four delightful but increasingly embarrassing days, I was getting impatient. I wrote an urgent letter to Gloria Sleep, his private secretary, pointing out that although the President was obviously a busy man I was anxious to be on my way to the Gwembe Valley. However Justin returned that evening with a message from State House saying that I was to see the President at 11:00 the next morning.

By 8.30am, Elizabeth and I were watching the television, because we had heard that His Excellency the President had called a press conference to which he had invited all the ambassadors, and all the press. Kaunda came on the air and started by saying he had called this conference before the end of this 'momentous year' to review the state of the nation. He then went on to say, "I have invited my old friend Merfyn Temple to meet me at 11 o'clock this morning for discussions about organic farming. I very much believe in organic farming and after my discussions with him we shall have lunch with members of our National Agricultural Society."

I put on my suit with clerical collar and arrived at State House at 10.45am, wheeled my bike up the steps and contemplated the large stuffed lioness, which reclines on a circular mat in the marble-pillared entrance hall. A slightly surprised aide-de-camp ushered me into the great waiting room with clusters of white leather armchairs and settees grouped around glass topped tables. I sat in lonely state, sipping a glass of iced Fanta and thinking about the first time I was here in 1957 when I had come to see the Governor, Sir Arthur Benson. I was wondering what to say to a friend I had hardly seen for more than a few moments in all of thirty years. We had been very close during the years of struggle for independence, but since Kaunda became President, we had never spent more than five minutes together.

The private secretary led me into the long room where the Cabinet meet. It must have been a great dining hall in colonial times, the oval mahogany table surrounded by forty red leather-backed chairs. I waited nervously shifting from foot to foot, then an aide appeared and said, "His Excellency would like to see you in his private study."

Kaunda was sitting in a big leather-backed chair at his small private desk. He stood up and there was a moment of embarrassment until he stretched out his arms and we hugged each other. I think we both cried a little. I said that when we were young we had seen our visions together and now that we were old we should not be afraid to dream our dreams together. He told me about how he had dreamt of my coming and then the letter had arrived saying that I was on my way.

I told him my story and when I came to the bit about the different religions praying for me on different days of the week, his eyes lit up and he said, "I have been thinking a lot about that Bible text 'They shall turn their swords into ploughshares'. I want to find out if a similar idea is in the Upanishads and the Bhagavad-Gita and other ancient books. I have been under unbearable pressure these last few months, not only with affairs of State, but also on the international scene; but when I go for my annual holiday to my private lodge at Mfuwe in the Luangwa game reserve, I shall take all my books with me and see if I can find the same thought in them all."

Chipapa and Kafue: 24 and 25 November

The next day I went to Chipapa. Nothing seemed to have changed, though the bougainvillea bushes on the right of the veranda had grown into trees whose branches provided cool shade over half the house.[4] The one on the left had climbed thirty feet to the top of a *musekese* tree, making a cascade of purple blossom to hide the rusting body of the yellow Toyota pick-up, which we had used to take vegetables from the irrigated garden to the market in Lusaka.

I walked down to the dam, and the sight of its blue waters took my breath away. Chipapa is still for me one of the most beautiful places in the world. A few women were fishing, the older children sat chatting and laughing in the shade of the *makoka* trees, and the younger ones had made long thick ropes of twisted grass, which they used to sweep the

---

4 Merfyn lived in Chipapa from 1967 to 1974, in a modest house built for him by the local people. See Volume One of his memoirs, *Zambia Stole my Heart*.

shallow water on the lake's margin up the sloping sand, leaving tiny fish flipping their silver tails on the shore. A big herd of cattle came down to drink. Numbering at least two hundred, they all seemed to be in prime condition.

The irrigated garden, where sixty families once cultivated their own small plots of land, had long ago been abandoned to the thorn trees and tall elephant grass. The big four-inch outflow pipe had become silted up and no one knew how to clear it. By the time I returned to the house Sarah and Daniel had arrived from a funeral. Sarah's sweet smile was the same as the one she gave me when I first arrived twenty years ago. I hardly knew Daniel, now almost blind, very deaf and moving uncertainly. We sat and talked about all the people who had died.

"Zunda is dead," they said.

"But he must still be only in the middle of his life," I answered.

"He died from eating poisoned grain, the same food which made me very sick," said Daniel. "It happened only four months ago and ten of us were taken to hospital for three weeks. Zunda and another died there and all the rest of us are still sick but we have been sent home."

Daniel's neighbour Moses Zumbwa was dead too, but we found his son John, desperately trying to get a few corrugated-iron sheets put temporarily over part of a new house he is building from sun-dried brick, before the rains came. He offered me a seat on his buckskin-covered deck chair, drew up his stool, and we began to talk. John told me that in 1989 he was working at the Mount Makulu agricultural research station. He had had to take early retirement in order to come home to look after his mother who had become very ill.

I began to tell John and his young friends what this area was like when I first found it twenty years ago. I told them that it hardly looked any different, though the trees were taller now, and the fields even more arid and desolate than they were back then, and the cattle were looking bigger and fatter.

I told them how I had brought the 'Green Revolution' to Chipapa by bribing Daniel, with the promise of a new two-furrow plough and bags of fertilizer and bags of hybrid seeds, to demonstrate in his own fields how land which had produced four bags of maize could be made to yield twenty bags. It was such a successful demonstration that I brought a load of Chiefs in my truck from Kasempa three hundred miles away to see it. A hundred farmers in Chipapa formed a co-operative, borrowed money, seed and fertilizer and, in the following year, planted one hundred acres of maize. The rains failed that year. Instead of reaping twenty bags each, they got nothing and landed themselves deep in debt. The so-called Green Revolution was a disaster for Chipapa.

It was after this failure that we had managed to get the outflow pipe in the dam wall mended, and Chipapa's years of prosperity began. The people paid off their debts from the sale of tomatoes, peas, beans and irrigated maize. The rainy seasons got better and they were able to purchase fertilizer again. The yields of grain went up but the soil began to get poorer. The drought returned and the pipe in the dam wall got blocked again. "We are back where we started twenty years ago, though the soil is poorer now and no amount of fertilizer will ever take us back to a yield of twenty bags again."

John Zumbwa and his friends had nodded and grunted with agreement all through my story. Then they told me something I did not know. They said, "You remember you once asked Godfrey Kalambalala the young herd-boy how he could be up in the hills all day without water, and he told you there was a stream of 'white water' there."

Now I was nodding and grunting my agreement.

"You remember how we made plans for a cattle-camp in those Mpande hills and an expert came to advise us about an insemination scheme to improve the quality of our beasts? The story we are going to tell you now is a different story. The charcoal-burners came, first in twos and threes and then they brought their families. Every day now we see the trucks passing here carrying big loads of charcoal up to Lusaka. Without the clothing of the trees the hillsides will be left naked."

I knew what they told me was true, because as we crossed the railway line at Chipongwe, a Land Rover piled high with charcoal had passed by. On the hillsides there were no longer any trees, only the secondary growth of green from the hacked-away stumps. There was a long silence. Then John Zumbwa spoke.

"As long ago as last May we heard you speaking on the radio from the BBC in London. We knew you would come and we have already started making plans. We have cleared all the ground round the broken outflow pipe of the dam. A local European farmer has promised to help us and now we are just waiting for him to come. I am the new chairman of the irrigated garden group. As soon as the water begins to flow, within a week everyone will be ready to begin work on their plots. I have ploughing oxen and donkeys on the way.

"You will remember that when you were here you could never persuade any young man to stay in the village to work the land; they all rushed off to find work in the towns. The only ones remaining were those with no education. All that has changed. These five young men are only a few but they are all well-educated. There are many more like them in the villages. They have understood that living a life of unemployment in the towns is hard and difficult. They have now returned, and are waiting to be guided into ways of making a good living from the land."

Sarah came to call me for a bath; it was the same tin bath that she had filled with water, twenty years ago on the day of my arrival. I was tired, so went early to bed, as the only light I had was a piece of string stuck through the lid of an ink-bottle containing paraffin.

I was up at 5.00, determined to get on the road to Kafue before it got too hot. Sarah insisted on bringing me soft mealie-meal porridge, with no milk of course, because all Daniel's cows are dead and gone. I had to shout our morning prayers together, but even so the sick old man, who had once been in the forefront of the Green Revolution, knew no more than that we had knelt together.

I set off on the bike, and as I cycled along the road, people who had heard the rumour of my arrival ran out from their houses to greet me. One of them was the man who long ago brought his lantern through the darkness to help us to see where to cut the umbilical cord of a child who was born in the back of our pick-up, on the way to hospital. They had called her Mukwakwa, the one who is born on the road. Unhappily she was not there to greet me, as she died when she was only five years old.

Lost in the Bush

The Gwembe Valley: 26 to 28 November

I HAD PROMISED that I would be at the Kafue bridge by 6.00am, as my friend Andrew Dale had agreed to drive me in his Mercedes down into the Gwembe Valley. We were approaching Lake Kariba at Siavonga when Andrew signalled to his son to turn off, saying he wanted to show me a plot by the lake where his son is building an eighty-bed motel, with restaurant and bar. He told me that this was the site of the Eagle's Rest chalets, where we used to come for family holidays, but, like everything else in Siavonga, they had to close down while the guerrilla war in Zimbabwe was going on.

Andrew drove me to the quay where the boats come in. At first I thought I was in luck, because there was a boat waiting, but it turned out to be the boat belonging to the Siavonga Nutrition Project.

At 5.00 p.m. a young man called David walked in from the mission. He said that if I knew how to handle an outboard motor, there was just time before sunset to get back to Munyama. The lake was calm, but the waves come up with the breeze at sunset.

I had not used an outboard motor for thirty years, but was quite prepared to have a go. David said he would start the engine, but I must not let it stop as it was a beggar to get going when hot. Then there was the little problem of how to find the way. However, two young men from Munyama, who happened to be sitting on the quay, said they would show me the way if I carried their sacks of mealie-meal in the boat. We loaded up and set off at full throttle. The sun went down, the wind got up, and soon I was soaked with spray. I dared not slow down lest there be no light in the

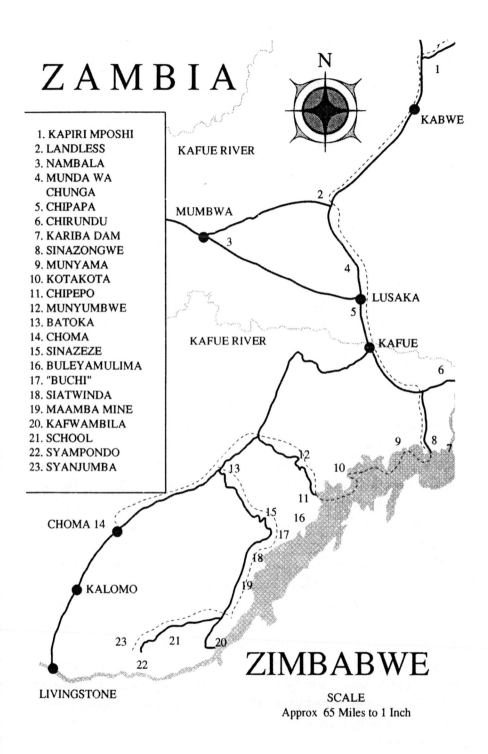

ZAMBIA

1. KAPIRI MPOSHI
2. LANDLESS
3. NAMBALA
4. MUNDA WA CHUNGA
5. CHIPAPA
6. CHIRUNDU
7. KARIBA DAM
8. SINAZONGWE
9. MUNYAMA
10. KOTAKOTA
11. CHIPEPO
12. MUNYUMBWE
13. BATOKA
14. CHOMA
15. SINAZEZE
16. BULEYAMULIMA
17. "BUCHI"
18. SIATWINDA
19. MAAMBA MINE
20. KAFWAMBILA
21. SCHOOL
22. SYAMPONDO
23. SYANJUMBA

N

KAFUE RIVER

KABWE

MUMBWA

LUSAKA

KAFUE

KAFUE RIVER

CHOMA 14

KALOMO

ZIMBABWE

LIVINGSTONE

SCALE
Approx 65 Miles to 1 Inch

sky to land by. We just made it, dodging tree-stumps in the twilight. I was glad to hear the sandy beach grating on the keel. The guest house where I slept was right on the edge of the lake, under a solitary baobab tree.

I woke as dawn was breaking over the Zimbabwe hills. The wind had died in the night, and the still water reflected back the pale pink, blue and grey clouds of the sunrise. I walked east along the margin of the lake, and the low light made a silhouette of the horned cattle lying contentedly on the soft bed of their own dry manure.

It was only just over four years since Leo and Ginnie Goodfellow had found this lake-shore site. They lived for a while on their boat, while they planted their first trees and made a garden. The air of the Gwembe valley is always warm, and with limitless water from the lake, everything grows with tropical exuberance. Date palms and coconuts, lychees, grapevines and cashew nuts were but a few of the great variety of plants I found growing here. It was Ginnie who was the genius of this agricultural mission, but she and her family could not survive without the infrastructure that Leo provided: not only the engineering shop where the boats were built and maintained, but the massive logistical support that even the simplest idea required if it was to be put into practice.

The first thing that Leo and Ginnie did on arrival was to travel through the villages, and ask the people what they felt their greatest need to be. They were unanimous in their desire for medical assistance, so an African nurse was found, a team of helpers recruited and trained, and a boat was built, because there are no roads through the rocky hills that line the lake. Grass shelters were built at selected centres for the women to gather with their children for the under-five clinic, and for the sick to have their ailments treated.

The next thing needed was a grinding mill for the corn, which would save the women hours of back-breaking work with their wooden pestles and mortars. Small cooperatives were formed to run the mills, and men were chosen and sent to the mission workshop for training in the mechanical maintenance of the diesel engines. Little cooperative shops were opened where salt, soap, matches and safety-pins could be purchased. There were no schools for the children, so the cooperative groups made bricks. The mission helped with nails, frames and corrugated iron sheets. In a matter of only a few months, four schools had been built, which the government supplied with teachers.

The Goodfellows, who were off that morning on a 600-mile journey to collect their three daughters from boarding-school at Kasenje in the North Western Province, handed me over to Alexander for the next stage of my journey. *Silweendo* (Pilgrim), the large boat that Leo had built from steel sheets, plies twice weekly up and down the lake calling at all the little cooperative centres. It had left Siavonga early that morning, but would not call at the mission. However, a boat was sent out to intercept it with a request to pick me up further down the lake later in the day.

At 8.00am, I went with my bicycle to the jetty, where I found Alexander and the five-woman medical team, dressed in smart brown uniforms, loading up a twin-hulled speedboat. With two 70 hp Yamaha outboard motors it can develop speeds up to 60 mph. My first thought was "what extravagance", until it was explained to me that when they used the old slow boat in the past, the five-woman nursing team spent so long on the water that they had little time to give to the mothers and their babies at the different centres.

I was now about to embark on the hairiest and most uncomfortable part of my journey so far. We put on our orange life-jackets and sat astride the long seat which ran down the centre of the boat. Clutching one another round the waists, we must have looked like a bob-sleigh team, or a line of children on the rocking horse in our local recreation ground. Alexander took the wheel. The wind was getting up and we could see white horses capping the waves beyond the quiet waters of the bay which shelters Munyama's harbour. As we gathered speed I could see rainbows in the walls of spray on either side created by the bow-wave of our boat.

We had tied the bike transversely behind the long saddle seat and as I was last in the line I found the crossbar sticking into the middle of my back. At first it seemed like a good back-rest, but it soon became an instrument of torture as it rode up and down my vertebrae. The waves grew steeper as Alexander revved the engines to top speed to get his craft to plane across their crests. We rose and fell in our long saddle like riders in a rodeo, but we had no bridle to hold, nor any stirrups. All I had was the ample waist of the girl in front and a deep gratitude to God for giving me a rugged constitution and immunity from sea-sickness.

We stopped at one point to see a school at one of the lake cooperative centres, and have a word with the manager who runs the grinding mill and the shop. There was hardly anything on the shelves as they were expecting a drop from the supply boat which services the co-op shops. Devaluation had knocked these little shops for six. A 25 kilo bag of salt which three months ago cost £4.75 now cost £20, and that rate of increase applied to all essential commodities like matches, soap and paraffin.

In order to short circuit this scandalous exploitation of the rural poor by the urban rich, the mission was transporting goats and fish to the towns in their truck, which otherwise would travel empty up to Lusaka for supplies. In this way they enabled the people in the valley to get a fair price for their produce.

Leo and Ginnie, when handing me over to Alexander, had told me how utterly dependent they are on him and his wife Rose, the leader of the medical team, for all the grass-roots development going on amongst the five thousand Tonga. What they had not told me is that Alexander was a passionate organics man.

His interest had started with his own father, who worked as an assistant in the Ministry of Agriculture, loyally implementing their chemical fertilizer policy, but never allowing fertilizer onto his own farm. Then Alexander went to the Roman Catholic school at Chikuni Mission where Father McDonald, an enthusiast for cattle manure, taught organic farming to his pupils. Ginnie, who had run her own organic nursery in Lusaka before she married Leo, found in Alexander a man who seemed to understand, without lengthy explanation, the basic principles that underlie the organic view of life.

Alexander had recently attended a seminar, organised by the Catholic Church, on 'New and Renewable Resources', and found that he was the only person present who had any practical experience of making a compost heap. At that year's district agricultural show, he had set up a demonstration of compost heaps, from the first collection of materials, through construction of the heap, to the final friable material with young fruit trees growing in it. There was great interest amongst the farmers present, who were looking for an alternative to chemical fertilizers because they could see them destroying their land, and because the price of a 50kg bag of fertilizer had risen in a year from £6 to £20. The officials of the Ministry of Agriculture either walked past the demonstration without noticing, or stopped to ridicule it.

Redoubling my tracks

Our arrival at Kota-Kota, where we were expected, was one of the best things I have ever experienced. All the women and children and outpatients had been waiting under the trees that surround the thatched buildings of the clinic, store and co-op headquarters. When they saw us coming they streamed down the gently shelving grass bank of the lake, singing and dancing their welcome. They waded out to the boat, each one taking back a medical box, a baby-scale, a collapsible table, a chair or a basketful of record cards. First they all gathered for a session of health education— today the subject was weaning—then they divided into groups for antenatal care, the under-fives clinic, and the outpatients. Two health-helpers live at the centre treating day-to-day ailments, but they keep the difficult cases for Rose to treat when she comes on her monthly visit.

However I was told that there was no public transport down the lake, so I would have to return to the plateau, eighty miles up the road at Choma.

The next day I set off on my bike, and eventually came to a village store. I waited for a while outside the store and then a fish lorry drove by. He gladly offered me a lift, but half an hour later the differential broke down. It would take a week to get a spare part from Lusaka. Sadly I set off once again to climb the escarpment on my bike. As I approached the foothills that skirt the mountains of the escarpment, the sand gave way to gravel and stone. The hills, like those in Devon and Cornwall, are steep and sharp, and the surface of the road too dangerous to ride down at speed to get momentum to climb up the other side. Since I was climbing out of the valley, there was a great deal more to go up than down. All the trees on either side had been cut down when the road was made, so there was no shade. I dared not take the bike off the road, because of the thorns. A three-inch thorn had pierced the sole of my sandal when I turned off into the bush for a moment.

No one else was travelling in the heat. If there were any villages they must have been far off in the bush, away from the road. What reason would there be for anyone to live amongst these rocky hills? I began to regret bitterly my lack of foresight in not obtaining a water-bottle in Lusaka. I had intended to do so, but in the excitement of all that happened there, I had quite forgotten this essential piece of equipment. The heat was intense and the energy required to push the bike up the hills made me sweat profusely.

I was nearing the top of a long steep hill and had fallen into a routine of four minutes walking then two minutes rest. My two minutes of rest were up, but I could not make myself go on. There was a big stone at the side of the road, so I lent the bike against the bank and sat down on it with my head in my hands. Suddenly I heard the sound of an engine coming from the direction in which I was going.

Through the dust I saw the red lights of the brakes go on. It was a rerun of what had happened on the desert road in Tanzania. A young man got out and ran back up the hill towards me. "You must be Merfyn Temple," he said.

"For sure I am," I replied, "and who are you? Ought I to know you?"

"I'm Malcolm Oliver, the Methodist minister in charge of the United Church in Choma. I recently read a piece about you in our Methodist Recorder. I have never seen you before, and I'm not the driver of this vehicle, but when I saw a white man with his bicycle right down here in the valley I thought it could be no one else but you."

Malcolm took me in his pickup with the bicycle along the Great North Road, to drop me at Batoka, which used to be the railhead for the heavy trucks bringing coal from the Maamba colliery in the valley to the plateau. The front brakes on my bicycle had given me constant trouble, so I took them off. I made the journey of thirty miles to the Gossner Mission at Sinazeze in two hours, as the road surface was good and there were not too many deep pot-holes to dodge.

I spent the night with another old friend, Reverend Mark Malyenkuku. He was a 'big man' in the area and sat all day long, with a stream of people coming and going, seeking his advice and carrying out his instructions. He had quite a large farm and a shop. Even though he was retired, the current minister of the Kanchindu church, who was a woman, did nothing without first consulting him. The congregation had steadily grown under his fatherly care over the years.

Mark and his wife were model organic farmers. All the rubbish was heaped in the cattle kraal, where the cows and oxen trampled it. It was allowed to rot down for a year before they used it in their fields. They had also discovered how to breed a flock of tame guinea fowl. They are not prone to disease and thrive on a diet of locally grown sorghum and millet.

On my way to Livingstone: 6 to 12 December

At 9.30am Pastor Luig of the Gossner Mission team picked me up and took me on the next stage of my journey. It had rained heavily in this part of the valley last week, and it was only due to Luig's superb driving and the ruggedness of his Japanese vehicle that we reached the last river at Syampondo by 1.00pm. At first we had been told that the only way to get out of the valley at this point would be on a very rough track to a mission station at Kabanga, on the edge of the escarpment on the Batoka plateau. However as we approached the last river, we were told that pack-donkeys regularly pass through from Syampondo to Livingstone. I myself had passed through with a bike in 1962, so felt confident I could do it again. Luig left me at the river and returned home.

I had done the journey before and I would do it again. What I did not know, was that on my first journey the villages had been strung out along the valley floor, but the people had since moved up into the hills below the escarpment, perhaps as a result of the ZAPU guerrilla war. I knew in which direction I had to go and I could see the donkey spoor and the marks of their round hooves, here and there. I found myself crossing deep ravines with sandy dried-up river beds below. Sometimes I had to offload my bag, take it up the far bank, then return and carry my bike up the slope.

Syampondo is not one compact village, but clusters of families living in small groups of houses scattered over a wide area. I finally came to a cluster of huts and saw an old woman who was tending the fire under a blackened forty-four gallon drum of simmering Tonga beer. I sat down in the shade of a hut and she brought me a cup of water. I asked the way to Livingstone. A young woman with a baby came out of one of the huts and said she would go and find the men.

An hour later two teenage boys arrived and taking charge of the bike, marched off through the trees, where I could see no path at all. I was very grateful for their help in manhandling the bike through the ravines and after another hour we arrived at the headman's house. He offered to take me on to the last group of houses in Syampondo, which he said was on the way to Livingstone. Again I was very glad of his help, especially to pump the tyre when I had a puncture.

After a while I found myself walking along a short stretch of disused road running up to Kalomo. Before it climbed away into the hills of the

SOWING SE

Missionary's amazing pilgrimage to Africa

MERFYN TEMPLE thought he was going to die. Lost in a desolate region of Africa, his hand stung by a scorpion, the 70-year-old missionary's chances seemed bleak.

After three days alone in the hills, he wrote in his diary: "I have a growing feeling that God is not going to deliver me from the mess I have got myself into . . ."

But he was wrong — the next day he was spotted by a hunter who put him on the right road to the nearest village.

That was five months ago. Since then, Temple has completed a trek around Zambia, much of it by bicycle, and has shed tears of joy with his "old friend" Kenneth Kaunda.

© Reading Evening Post, 13 April 1990

escarpment the path turned west and he handed over the bicycle, pointing to where the path disappeared into the rocks. The front wheel had punctured again, but as I could not ride I left it flat. The path grew steeper and rockier and I was afraid the outer cover would fracture, so decided to do a repair. My water was nearly finished. I stopped for a rest and chewed a piece of dried hippo meat.

As darkness fell I reached a small cluster of houses. A woman came out and brought me a drink, then led me to the house of a senior villager, named Anderson Mudenda. I told him I was going through the villages to see how much had changed since I was last in this area. There was a large herd of cattle and a number of goats. They all looked fit and well, but Anderson told me that there was no school for the children, no clinic when they were sick, no well for clean water, no shop to buy soap, salt and matches, and there was no access road. Anything they wanted had to be brought in by pack donkey from Livingstone, fifty miles away, or from

:DS OF FAITH

Kalomo up the escarpment. Later the villagers spread out a reed mat for me to sleep on under the platform of a grain-bin built on stilts of mopani poles. They gave me a blanket to lie on and another to put over me. It was too hot for that, so I rolled one up and made a pillow of it.

I woke at dawn, determined to make an early start and break the back of my journey before the sun became too hot. I packed quickly and asked someone to put me on the path to Syanjumba, the next village along my route. I felt in my bag for money to give my host a small reward, but the 1,000 Kwacha I had with me had all gone, stolen by some men who had been talking at the house and left in the darkness.

My young guide helped me for a mile or so along the way. We crossed a dry river bed and on the other side he said that the path would lead straight on. Finally I would come to a cattle-camp with two huts and the people there would show me the way to Syanjumba's village. The way was even more rugged than the day before, and I had no one to help me up the steep sides of the rocky ravines. Sometimes the path split into half a dozen trails and I had to cast about to find the one with the donkey spoor. There was no sign of any wildlife on the hillsides, though once I met a very large tortoise and had to pull the bike to the side of the narrow path to let him walk sedately by. He showed no surprise, just blinked his eyes and kept on course.

My guide had said I should keep right on until the path crossed a deep gully, with a little water flowing since the recent rains. I was to climb up the steep bank on the other side where I would see a couple of shelters and a cattle kraal. I found the shelters, but there were no people.

Lost

It was a hot and uncomfortable wait of five hours, but still no one came. I then thought I would cast about and find another path and hoped it was the right one, though I could see no donkey spoor. I pushed on for another hour, then crossed a small river with a little water in sandy pools. Try as I might, I could find no sign of a path on the other side. I should have turned back, but I had come a long way through a lot of rocks. The village of Syanjumba could not be far away. At a bend in the river I caught a glimpse of some animal moving in the bush. It was a cow and her calf. Cattle mean people, I said to myself. All I need to do is to join them. I shall follow and find a village.

The cow and calf joined a small herd of about twenty-five, which seemed to be led by an old black cow with a cow-bell strapped to her neck. Wherever she went I followed, over the rocks, round the boulders and underneath the thorn trees. I had a puncture and hardly dare stop to mend it lest the old girl escape out of sight and sound. I did a hasty repair and lost the cow, but found her again on the other side of a little hill. I began to laugh because the whole episode was so absurd, an old man of seventy chasing an old cow round and round in circles in the middle of the bush. Twilight came, then the night was lit by a brilliant half-moon, but no one came from the village to find the herd.

Before going to bed I sat down with my back to a tree, to think out what my next move should be. I put my right hand on the ground and something stung me. I yelled with the pain—I had never known pain like that. It must have been a scorpion, because it paralysed my hand. It was a long miserable night. I found a tube of Anthisan cream in my bag, but although I smeared it liberally over my hand, it made no difference at all. My water was long since finished and there was not enough saliva to swallow an aspirin.

I got off the hard ground as soon as it was light enough to pack my bag. I made a sling from my spare pair of khaki trousers to support my right forearm and aching hand. There was no way I could manage the bike with only my left hand, so I decided to abandon it. The essential thing was to find water while I still had some strength. I found a dry creek which must have poured its water into a bigger river and followed it down hill. I found the water just as I began to wobble at the knees. I scrambled slowly up-stream hoping that I might find a path, or a place where the people of Syanjumba came down to draw water. I did find a path that ran for a while along the banks, and to my amazement saw the tracks of a bicycle; I must have come along here yesterday.

Although it was only 8 am, the sun was intensely hot. I dared not take the risk again and leave the water. I left a note on the path by the bicycle track which read: *To anyone who has followed my spoor thus far, I am camped further downstream, waiting your arrival.* I had decided that the best thing to do was to conserve my strength near water and wait for rescue.

I had noticed on my way up-stream an ideal place. On a sweeping right-angled bend the river-bed was twenty-five yards across, and water was trickling through between two great boulders, which must make a spectacular little waterfall when the river was in spate. There were a number of pools among the rocks, some big enough for me to bathe in. In order to prevent myself becoming dehydrated I submerged myself fully clothed in the water and the evaporation cooled me down.

By 5 pm I had summoned up enough energy to go looking for fire-wood. As I passed a shallow pool that ran alongside the flat face of a massive rock, there was a great commotion in the water. I thought at first it was a three-foot monitor lizard, but then I realized it was a very large catfish wriggling its way into the sand along the rock. I rushed to catch it, but was too late; however, I was just in time to grab a much smaller fish about a foot long. By the time I had gutted it and grilled it over the fire, I got about two tablespoons of tasty meat from this skinny fish. I ate the skin, bones and all—it was delicious.

I went to bed a much happier man than the night before, for although I had no friendly cattle to keep me company, I had plenty of water and some food in my belly. I made a large fire along the side of a fallen tree on a sandbank, dug a hole for my hip and went to bed early. It was a magical night. The moon with a soft halo shone bright in the sky and the stars were brilliant beyond belief. I lay with my back to the glowing embers of the fire and looked up straight into Orion's Belt. The Southern Cross was low on the horizon and the six stars of the Great Dipper were on my right. Tiny specks of fool's gold sparkled like sequins on the banks of silver sand. The bark of a single tall *mugongo* tree glowed white in the light of the moon. I decided to get up early and dig out the catfish and have a breakfast fit for a king.

As soon as it was light I began to dig, mostly with my left hand because my right was still numb from the scorpion sting and sometimes if I used it too much it became very painful. I did not find my big catfish; he must have squirmed deep under the rock or dug himself into the sand somewhere else. I wandered off downstream. The low rays of the rising sun shone through the leaves of the trees which at this time of the year are every shade of green, from pale to deepest emerald.

I did not now have the strength to walk more than half a mile, and I knew I must stay close to water, not only to quench my thirst, but to wash my clothes and clean my teeth. More than anything else the water boosts my morale. Under these conditions cleanliness seemed more important than godliness. I found that like Spencer Chapman, in his book *The Jungle is Neutral*, my New Testament had no attraction for me. I think it must be that hunger brings lethargy to the soul as well as to the mind and body.

In the far distance, I sometimes heard the tinkle of the black cow's bell. I wondered if she took her docile herd to guard my bike at night. Perhaps a troupe of baboons or monkeys was playing with it. I never heard any human sounds, no voice, no clunk of axe or beat of distant drum. If there was a village near, I had no way of finding it, as there were no footpaths amongst the cattle tracks.

Suddenly I became aware of someone standing behind and above me on the jutting rock. He was a tall man with a spear in his hand and at his heels were four lean hunting dogs.

"*Wabonwa*," I said, using the familiar Tonga greeting, which means "You are seen." "*Ndabonwa* – I am seen," he replied. Then in my stumbling

Chitonga I said, "My God, I am glad to see you. I have not seen another human being for four days."

I told him my story but he did not believe it, especially the bit about the abandoned bicycle. As we talked I realised that he thought that the Nkomo War had never ended and that I was a white Rhodesian spy.

I asked him to lead me to the road. He took me two hundred yards to the river crossing and said, "There is the road," pointing to the donkey track down which I had come.

"But I want you to take me to the main road. I am very tired. I would like you to carry my bag. If you find my bicycle, you can keep it for yourself."

"It is a long way to Syampondo. I have to find the cattle I am looking for. I might never find your bicycle, and anyway what good would it do me if I did? You can't use a bicycle in these hills; only donkeys are any good."

I told him that the President would be very pleased when he heard how a Mutonga hunter had rescued his friend Merfyn Temple. He was not impressed, and I realised that the President meant nothing to him, and a letter from a strange white man, promising a reward, was not worth the paper it was written on. I was scared to go on alone through waterless country.

There was nothing for it, but to go back along the donkey path, though the rain had obliterated any of the tyre marks in the sandy places. After an hour of trudging through the heat, I stopped to eat the last half of my emergency orange and chew the last stick of hippo meat. That kept me going for another hour. It was very hot in the midday sun, so I decided to rest in the shade of a tree till it was cooler. An inquisitive kakelaar bird found me and called his little flock of friends. Ten of them came, beautiful slim black birds, who hopped round excitedly in the branches of the tree above my head. The sun shone through their transparent orange bills as their white-barred tails flicked back and forth on the slender twigs above.

I do not know what kept me going. Perhaps it was desperation. Perhaps it was the prayers of my ancestors in heaven, or perhaps it was the prayers of all my children. Anyway, what strength I needed came from somewhere outside me, or from very deep down inside me, from some fountain I had never tapped before. By nightfall I was back in the village where I had slept four days ago. Full of sympathy, the people gave me some thin gruel of maize, some sour milk and three hard-boiled eggs.

If it was true that I had been acting a part in a play which was written for me before I left home, then this was the *dénouement* in the last act. It ended not with a dramatic rescue by the President's private helicopter, but with this tired old dog with his tail between his legs, stumbling back along the donkey track, which had led him, not to Livingstone, but to Anderson Mudenda and his family. It taught me two very salutary lessons which I knew to be true, but with my usual Western arrogance, had refused to heed. Firstly, before taking a journey into the unknown, you should consult local opinion. Anyone who lives amongst these hills could have told me the only way to travel is with a donkey and not a mountain bike. Secondly, you should never try to find your way alone. A guide who knows the path is the only guarantee you will not get lost.

At 3.45 am I heard the thump, thump of women pounding grain in their wooden mortars, then the grating of stone on stone, as they ground their finger millet on their stone querns. Three cocks vied with one another to shout their greetings to the rising sun, the grey and white pigeons began to coo in the village dovecot, and a flappet lark mounted into the clouds. Mudenda's head appeared over the top of the metal drum that blocked the entrance of the visitors' hut and he asked me if I had slept well and how were my poor sore feet? Mudenda's first wife—he has four—brought me thin porridge and sour milk.

Anderson Mudenda's younger brother Kembo was detailed to show me the road and to carry my bag for the first mile or two. The path was very stony and I was glad of the thick soles of my leather shoes. Kembo was wearing sandals made from tread-bare motor tyres. He had bought them at an exorbitant price from a trader who had carried them in a donkey pack from Livingstone. He said he knew how to make his own if he had some way of purchasing an old tyre or two. I am sure that the sandal makers of Livingstone have cornered that market. When we parted, all he asked for was a box of matches. Hoping that I would never have to light a fire in the bush again, I gave him my little book of cardboard matches. I had to show him how to tear them off the pack and strike them, as he had never seen that kind before.

By midday I was back where Pastor Luig had left me last Wednesday. I found a great tree on the river bank, and as it was getting very hot I rested until 3 pm. I thought I should press on to the school that night and I might somehow get the teacher to send someone with a message to rescue me. I reached the school at 4.30 pm. It was holiday time and the teacher was away drinking beer in a neighbouring village, so a schoolboy was sent to find him and I sat on a stool to wait.

I heard the sound of a car. It was a beautiful white Toyota twin-cab with a power-winch mounted on the front bumper. In it were two young Zambians doing a follow-up immunisation survey for World Vision. They had not intended to come as far as the school, but a woman to whom they gave a lift begged them to come on a further ten miles. At first they did not believe me when I told them that I was Merfyn Temple, co-author with Kenneth Kaunda of *Zambia shall be Free*. They told me later that they thought I was an impostor. In the end it was the fact that I could speak Chitonga that finally convinced them that I was indeed the person I claimed to be.

I felt a strange reluctance to leave this valley of burning heat and rocky hills. How genuine and courteous all the people were! For a week it had been my home and filled my life with an intensity of feeling which I have seldom experienced before. Saint Paul wrote in his letters that sometimes we get a foretaste of the Kingdom of Heaven. I think this is what I had just experienced. After this everything will seem like anticlimax—just an epilogue to the drama.

Back to Lusaka: 13 to 17 December

When I reached Lusaka I found that no one had missed me. I seemed to be the only person in Zambia who knew that I had been lost.

On Sunday I preached in the Cathedral:

"Your young men will have visions, and your old men will dream dreams."

"On 9 July 1962, two young men stood together on the black rock of Mulungushi in a country then known as Northern Rhodesia. It was an historic occasion, because on that day the decision was taken to reject a constitution imposed from outside. The United National Independence Party decided to seek a new constitution giving Africans majority rule.

"One of those men was black and one was white. Kenneth Kaunda and I shared the same vision, a vision of our country free for ever from colonial rule. The vision we had twenty-seven years ago has become a political reality. Zambia is free from political oppression; however, we have exchanged political oppression for economic bondage to the Western world. Today Kaunda and I stand on another rock, the rock of a fisherman's faith. We are too old now to have visions, but not too old to dream our dreams of a Zambia that shall be free forever from the chains that shackle us to the economic values of the Western world.

"Together we look back to the days of the struggle and ask 'How did we manage when we were so weak and inexperienced, political babes in the wood, to send our colonial masters scuttling back across the sea to the Mother of parliaments in Westminster?' We did it because we knew exactly what we wanted; we knew our cause was a just cause. We knew we had the Old Testament prophets on our side and we were following Jesus in his way of non-violence.

"So must it be today if our dream is ever to come true. Our cause is just. It is a struggle alongside the poor whom our Jesus came to save. With them we shall bring down the mighty multi-nationals from their seats. Together we shall send the gnomes of Zurich scuttling back to their vaults of gold, deep hidden in the caves of Switzerland. First we must analyse our economic situation as bond-servants to the west. What is the root cause of our slavery? We are bound because we have allowed ourselves to be bound.

"Twenty-five years ago, at our independence, we thought we were rich, but we have squandered the riches from our copper mines. In order to strut like peacocks on the international stage, we have borrowed far beyond our ability to repay. What we have failed to do is to understand that the only way to economic salvation is to develop our own great natural resources. This we must do with our own strength and our own traditional skills. Instead of using our axes and our hoes to create wealth, we have used them to destroy our land and our trees. We are doing this so cruelly that I can hear our Father in Heaven crying out in pain.

"The earth is not ours to rape and pillage at our will. We shall be free when we understand once and for all that the economic revolution and the ecological revolution and the organic revolution are one and the same revolution. The disregard of the sanctity of the soil and the holiness of the trees is leading us not only to ecological disaster, but also economic disaster. But God is not only a God of judgement; He is a God of mercy. It is not too late to repent of our blindness, our folly and our violence.

"Now is the time for us all, rich and poor alike, to work together as one nation in true community of spirit. We must work on the land again to restore the soil's fertility. We must spread over it the rich manure of our cattle kraals and replant the trees whose leaves protect the soil from the lashing rain. Only by this can the poor escape from the chains of their poverty, and the rich find release from the heavy burden of their riches."

I went from the Cathedral to have lunch with Kaunda at State House. He was delighted to hear about the plans for an Agro-Ecology Training Centre for the Southern Province on land given by Chief Mapanza. He was shocked to hear about the isolation of the people in the hills between Syampondo and the Victoria Falls. Although I had failed to reach Living-stone, Kaunda told me he had recently been there himself. He was so impressed with the work of Mr Fikoloma, the principal at the David Livingstone Teacher Training College, that he bestowed on him an honour and told the Ministry of Education to send staff from all Zambian Teacher Training Colleges to see how a college can become self-sufficient for its food from an organic farm. My dream of a teacher trained in organic farming in every Zambian school could become a reality sooner than I dared hope.

Blowing on the Organic Embers, 1992

ON MY JOURNEY through Kenya, Uganda, Tanzania and Zambia, I had seen how modern methods of agriculture were destroying the environment and throwing rural people into poverty. An agricultural revolution was needed, that would enable people to develop their own resources in their own organic way. Self-reliance, not dependence on overseas aid, had to be the way to freedom.

Between 1989 and 1998 I went back to Zambia eight times, always to encourage rural people in the development of forms of sustainable agriculture that would break their dependency on foreign aid.

After two years without news, I decided to go back and follow up some of the projects initiated on that previous visit, and to enquire for news of my abandoned cycle. In 1992 I returned. En route to the Gwembe Valley I reutrned to Chipapa, as my diary records:

A 'brigadier-general' picks me up and takes me to Chipapa

The minor road to Chipapa which leaves the main road at this point serves only the villages and a few farms. I set off to walk the seven miles to the village. As there was no one about and the midday sun was blazing hot, I put on my ridiculous hat. I had gone no more than a couple of hundred yards and was standing at the roadside, when I saw a big saloon car coming slowly up behind me. There was one man in the driving seat and no passengers.

The car was a highly polished silver-grey Mercedes-Benz with red plush seats, and the driver was a pleasant-looking man of about forty. He wore a khaki shirt of fine Egyptian cotton with something embroidered in gold thread on the pocket. He said that he would be glad to give me a lift, but he had only a mile to go to his house, and he had not heard of Chipapa. He told me that he had retired last December from the post of Brigadier-General of the Zambia National Youth Service after twenty years of honourable service. I did not tell him that I had been one of the founders of the service in 1963, but in those days I was not called a Brigadier, I was simply called the Deputy Director. I had not retired taking with me my personal Mercedes-Benz; I had been sacked with no pension because I had dared to suggest that the only future for the young men in the service was to get them back to the land.

We came to his house which was surrounded by a ten-foot concrete wall with a capping of vicious-looking jagged glass. We drove through the massive iron gates, up the concrete drive lined with orange trees, to the front of the house where two other sleek saloon cars were parked. He offered me a comfortable chair on the spacious veranda and went inside to get me a bottle of iced Coca-Cola. I peeped through the glass doors into the lounge and dining room. Two free-standing electric fans played back and forth ruffling the edges of the embroidered antimacassars along two rows of lavishly upholstered settees and armchairs.

He kindly offered to run me out to the village if I would show him the way. We had to change into the other Mercedes which had a higher clearance to lift it over the obstacles along the village road.

The Brigadier had never been along the road before, and exclaimed with surprise as we passed the cluster of whitewashed school buildings. We left the car at the roadside and walked the last hundred yards through the tall grass to my old house. Through the trees we saw Sarah sitting by the kitchen fire with two young women. We announced our arrival with the call, *"Odi! Odi!"* They came over to welcome us, and when Sarah saw that it was me, her face lit up and I gathered her into my arms.

I think the Brigadier was not only surprised but also embarrassed when he saw the house I had lived in. Compared with his, it is indeed a shanty, but this man has cut himself off from his own people by adopting his affluent lifestyle. He did not stay long because we had little in common to talk about.

Rebuilding the dam

Daniel was asleep in the house when we arrived. He is now so deaf that only shouting into his ear can get a message through, but his wrinkled smile showed how pleased he was that I had come back. The two other women who came to welcome me were young and beautiful, Sarah's granddaughter and her niece. One of them went off to the house behind the mango trees to call John Zumbwa, the man in the village whom above all others I wanted to see.

On my last visit, in my despair for Chipapa, it was John and the five young men with him who gave me hope. He is twenty years younger than I, clean-limbed, spare and alert. We sat on the open veranda of my old house under the purple bougainvillea which I had planted. Through the trees we could see the sparkling water of the dam.

John had wanted to help his people get the water flowing again from the dam, so he persuaded someone from the Department of Water Affairs to come and see the situation. They said they could do nothing, so he went to a white farmer in the area to ask for advice. This man said if the people would clear the bush around the blocked valve he would come to see, but in spite of repeated requests he never came.

Since my last visit, John had stood for election as councillor for the Chipapa ward of the District Council. During the election campaign he visited everyone including the local farmers who live between the railway line and the main road. One was a successful black South African woman farmer married to a Dane called Jansson, who owns an engineering works in Lusaka. John outlined his proposals for the development of his ward, which included repair of the irrigation scheme. Jansson offered to go to Chipapa to see if there was anything he could do to help. As soon as he saw the situation, he realised that the dam had silted up over the years and that to unblock the pipe would be a major operation. He said to John,

"I know what needs to be done and I believe if everyone in the village is prepared to work, we can get the irrigation system going again. I'll give you one week to mobilize the people with their axes and hoes, to clear all the bush round the dam wall and along the furrow into the garden. When I come back, if I see you are serious about getting the dam repaired, I'll tell you what we have to do next."

When he returned he could hardly believe his eyes. All the land had been laid bare, as though a bulldozer had scraped it clean. He went to his drawing board and designed a new system of pipes which would allow for the blocked pipe to be cleared. He said that if the people would provide all the labour, he would give his services free to supervise the job. The cost of materials would be £50,000.

"So where can our village find that kind of money?" said John.

"You could always try the Danish Embassy," said Jansson.

Together they drew up a request for aid, and a fortnight later came the good news that the money had been given. Then began weeks of work with gangs of men and women working with hoes and buckets. They cleared the silt and Jansson dismantled the old system and supervised the whole operation. Everything was completed by the end of the dry season of 1990. The dam began to fill during the 90/91 rains, and by January this year there was enough water in the dam to start irrigation in March. John Zumbwa said that my arrival was most opportune because he would be able to take me down to turn the taps to see how the first water would flow.

We set off with John carrying a sack over his shoulders containing the spanners and turning wheels. Daniel tapping the path with his stick followed along behind. We waded through the tall green grass that had overgrown the concrete channel where the large pipe ran. As soon as we had parted the grass, John knew that something was wrong. The dome of cast iron covering the valve was all askew on its setting. The six strong bolts which secured the flanges of the stopcock had been removed and it tilted drunkenly, held only by the central brass screw. A thief had come in the night and stolen them. John was sick at heart and kept saying over and over again,

"Who has done this thing? How could they destroy all the work we have done? How can I face Jansson when I tell him what has happened?"

Daniel shuffled forward feeling the damage with his hands, his face almost touching the pipe as his glazed eyes peered close to the stopcock. He said, "This has been done by a man who needs bolts to mend a plough or harrow or the broken shaft of an ox cart."

John agreed and tried to think of anyone he knew who had a spanner strong enough to have loosened the nuts and stolen the bolts. Fortunately the damage was not irreparable, and as we walked back to the house we discussed the question of where to obtain replacements for the missing bolts. It would all take time but once Jansson got over the shock he would probably help again.

Tamed guinea fowl are roosting in John's trees

We went to John's house and he introduced me to his wife Charity, who is a teacher in the Chipapa school. She was squatting next to the fire in the round kitchen shelter, a simple structure of six upright poles supporting a low thatched roof. He showed me the little orchard which he had planted on the land which slopes down from the house to the lake. There were of course mangoes, guavas and pawpaws (papaya), but he had also grown bananas and a couple of pomegranate trees.

We sat on a couple of stools as he told me more of the triumphs and failures of the last two years. As the sun went down and the light faded from the sky, the chickens came to roost in the tree. They had only recently been taught to do this by helping them to climb up the tree on long poles which sloped upwards from the ground propped against the lowest branches.

In another tree, John's little flock of tame guinea fowl had come to roost. In my time at Chipapa we never saw guinea fowl in the villages because they do not seem to breed well in captivity. Now I find them everywhere, and John told me that by feeding them, a flock of cocks and hens can be sufficiently domesticated for the female birds to lay their eggs in nests on the ground in the bush round the house.

Six of John's precious cattle had been stolen and four had died from black-leg disease, but still he had managed to plough, and he had proved to his own satisfaction that a green crop of sunn hemp ploughed into the soil was just as good, if not better, than growing the maize with an under-dressing of Compound D chemical fertilizer.

Over the years most of the things had been stolen from my house, but somewhere a bed was found for me and was made up in the little room which we had built for my son Robin, when he came to spend a few months with me in 1969 before he went to university. It took me a while to get to sleep because the rain had enticed a thousand frogs to come out of the mud on the margin of the lake to mate and fill the night with raucous song. A family of rats chased one another up and down the sloping rafters of the roof, and from a mile away on the other side of the lake at the foot of the Mpande Hills came the urgent beat of drums.

The church on the hill

The next morning Sarah brought me a bowl of warm water to wash in, then made me a cup of 'tea' from *masamba* leaves. I found I enjoyed it better than tea and wished I could take some home with me. There was no sugar nor milk, so I had to eat the bowl of thin maize-meal porridge as best I could.

At nine o'clock I walked the half mile to the little white-washed church on the hill beyond the school. It was built in 1965 with help from the Methodist missionaries at Kafue Mission seventeen miles away, although it was the people themselves who made the bricks and burnt them in a kiln.

When I preached there in the 'sixties, the congregation was seldom more than a dozen souls. Today the church was full, with more than eighty people sitting on the wooden benches made by the village carpenter. There was a choir of twenty-seven young men and women, all but one in white-collared pale green gowns. The conductor, a youth of seventeen, was distinguished by the black collar of his gown. And how they sang! What rhythmical movement of their bodies and their hands! During one song all but the three drummers moved out of the choir stall and danced in the aisle. With all the praying and preaching, the singing and reading in three languages, the service went on for two hours. Then there was another two hours of the annual church meeting when officers were elected: chairman, deputy chairman, secretary and treasurer, not only of the church council but of the choir, the women's group, the stewards, the discipline committee etc. I am sure that the orderly manner in which Zambia conducted the democratic election of its new President owes much to the example set by the churches.

I spent the evening with John Zumbwa and Gilbert Shachikwa, the son of one of the four men who built the church here. These two men explained to me their ideas for Chipapa's long-term development. The re-establishment of irrigation below the dam will benefit perhaps fifty families. But the population is growing, and if young men and women are to be encouraged to see farming as a way of life they will need to have part of their farm irrigated, even if it is only a small plot for growing their fruit trees and vegetables and for making their fish ponds. There is underground water if wells and boreholes can be sunk.

For me this has been a high point in my journey, because I see the new green shoots springing out of the wasteland of our past failures. Many of our concepts were right, but we had only old men and women to work with; all the young men and girls had gone off to look for work in the towns.

It was this competent management that was so lacking in the past and it is our hope that John Zumbwa will provide this in the future, for he is not only a well-trained agriculturalist, but has worked as an administrative officer at Mount Makulu agriculture station.

After my return in 1992 we sent parcels of good second-hand clothing to John and Charity Zumbwa, which they promised to sell, using the money to fund the various projects which the Young Farmers' Club had started, but we did not hear whether the parcels were arriving safely. Then Charity wrote to say that her husband was very unwell and although he went to see the doctors in the university teaching hospital in Lusaka, the medicines they prescribed did not seem to do any good. At the end of the year we received a letter to say that he had been taken to a Salvation Army Mission hospital where he died.

27 February 1993: A sad visit

I had somehow made myself believe that Charity, John's widow, would step into his shoes and keep things together until a new leader could be found. But I had forgotten what cruel things happen here when a man with property dies. In Tonga custom a man's wife is his property, and in the past would have been inherited along with his children by a brother for whom she would become another wife.

When Charity married John Zumbwa ten years ago, he had two children of his own aged four and two, from his previous wife. Charity brought them up as her own and herself bore two, a boy and a girl. After John's death his relatives took everything from her including her two step-children. All she kept were her clothes and blankets which she took, along with her own son and daughter, when she fled to live with her widowed sister in Matero, one of Lusaka's oldest and poorest suburbs.

I was taken to see what John had managed to do with his band of helpers before he died. They had built and burned a kiln of bricks, excavated two thirty yard long fish tanks, and prepared the fields for planting. All the time John had been feeling very unwell, but none of the doctors he consulted were able to tell him what was wrong. A week before he died, the Salvation Army doctors at Chikankata found a tumour in the bowel, but it was too late to operate.

John's right-hand man is Obert aged 25, with nine years of education but a minimal understanding of English. As well as working on the development project, he spends a couple of days a week going round the village as an agent of the Planned Parenthood Association. He is supposed to give talks on health education and AIDS, but I think that means not much more than distributing condoms. He had been promised some 'allowances' for this service but so far has not received anything. Everyone says he is a hard worker and they want him to be their new leader.

It is twenty-five years since I first set foot in Chipapa, and on the surface so little seems to have changed. In spite of the good rains, many of the fields have not been cultivated, and those that have show little sign of yielding much of a crop. But there is more water in the dam than there has been for 20 years, and the irrigated garden land which has lain fallow for three years can be revived when the dry season comes, so there is still hope.

Millions of Small Holdings[1]

Merfyn Temple
10 March 1996

Preamble

The hunger and poverty of Africa's rural people is increasing in spite of all efforts made to alleviate it by governments and non-government organisations. Yet it should not be beyond the wit of man to make a **radical change** in the situation, because Africa has all the material resources and all the human power to enable the mass of the people who are predominantly rural to live full, carefree lives undaunted by the threat of hunger and poverty.

The causes of hunger may be complex, but at the root of them all is the failure of rural people to produce and store enough to feed themselves throughout the year. This failure is almost certainly due to the **introduction into Africa of Western agricultural systems,** which are not merely inappropriate but downright dangerous because they threaten the survival of the human population and their natural environment.

Western systems are based on high cost, high risk, high output, high profit, advanced technology, and low use of labour. In contrast, what Africa needs to increase food production is a system which is low cost, low risk, low output, low profit, simple technology and high in labour usage.

The present **need is to concentrate resources on improving the productivity of the small family farm** enabling it to provide enough food, fuel and employment to reduce migration to the towns. This must start with teaching an increased **respect for the soil,** not regarding it as just a mass of mineral matter but as a dynamic entity, containing organic matter and living organisms, which needs protection, feeding and careful management if it is to be productive.

The most rewarding method of increasing agricultural output is by **raising the level of soil fertility,** both by improving the long-term structural stability and moisture retention of the soil and by increasing the supply of plant nutrients.

The only way forward at present must come from "greater concern for the soil, improved husbandry and increased recycling of organic waste back to the growing of crops on **millions of small holdings."** (FAO Soils Bulletin No 56)

---

1 One of Merfyn's broadsheets circulated among his friends and contacts. See also p. 69.

A Nation of Small Farmers

If we agree that the way forward in Zambia is to establish millions of small holdings then we must address ourselves to the practicalities of how this is to be done.

An Action Plan   One Man, One Axe
                      One Woman, One Hoe

1. **Select one or two farms in each district** of Zambia as demonstration small holdings to show how by adopting an organic system of low cost, simple technology and high use of labour, a family can feed itself and provide an income to meet basic needs of water, housing, clothing, health and education.

2. **Give instruction, training and support** to the men and women who are selected to run these farms. Initially it will be necessary to set up a training centre somewhere in Zambia.

3. Enable demonstration farms, once established, to become places to which local farmers can come for **short courses to learn how to become organic smallholders themselves.**

4. **Organic collaboration** in each District between government and NGOs.

A shining example of how this is being done is the cooperation between the Zambian Government and the British NGO[2] *Harvest Help* in the Gwembe Valley, the Luano Valley, and at Ipongo in the Kabwe Rural District.

Start-up finance will be required from a consortium of Aid Agencies and NGOs while Zambian staff are being trained in the principles and practice of organic agriculture. It may be necessary to engage overseas staff with African experience at the national training centre.

---

2 Non-government organisation. This has become the commonly used term to describe voluntary agencies working in global development, peace, justice, environment and related fields.

Back to Zambia with family, 1997

On my 1997 visit, I invited my daughter Jane and grandson Jonathan to come with me. Jonathan had been raising funds for Harvest Help, and I felt it was important to give him the chance to see their work at first hand. We decided to go and see the work at Ipongo, and also to show him the house in Chipapa where I had lived for seven years.

Kitwe church service

Preached in the big church in Kitwe, which when Colin Morris went there in 1956 was for 'Europeans only'. Now amongst the sea of black faces which looked up eagerly from the crowded pews there was not a single white one. The black minister who led the worship has as many letters after his name as did the young Colin Morris when he was the Methodist minister there. At a time when apartheid was practised as rigorously on the Copperbelt of Northern Rhodesia as in South Africa, it was he who erected the placard outside the church with the startling message: THIS CHURCH IS COLOURBLIND.

It was a joyful occasion, with choirs singing, drums beating and dancing down the aisle. The only threads still connecting this congregation of the United Church of Zambia with its Methodist past were the few tattered copies of the 1932 edition of the Methodist Hymn Book. None still had its hard cover on and you were lucky if you had one which started before hymn no. 42.

Here the gospel has taken root and this urbanised African church is flourishing.

Dinner with an organic farmer

At dinner I met Samuel Kaluba whose story is so interesting and so relevant to the purpose of my visit that I must relate it here:

Fifty years ago Sir Stewart Gore Brown's 'garden boy' at Shiwa Ng'andu in the Northern Province of Northern Rhodesia (now Zambia) bore a son named Samuel.

He was a bright boy and soon became the favourite of the local school's headmaster, Mr Kashoki, who ruled his children with a rod of iron, believing in the old dictum "spare the rod and spoil the child".

When Samuel completed his secondary education he went to the Kitwe Training College. There students were allowed to cultivate small plots to grow vegetables and sell them to earn a little pocket-money. Samuel and his friend Chileshe started gathering waste from the college kitchens and throwing it into a compost pit. Amongst the waste was a good quantity of *nshima* (maize porridge) left over after college dinners. All this went into the pit, and after six months of decomposition, the two friends found a rich black friable soil in their compost pit. They spread it on the ground and began to produce vegetables which were the envy of all the other students. Indeed in 1962 they won first prize at the Kitwe Agriculture Show with a cabbage bigger than a football, weighing over seven pounds.

This was the beginning of a life-long interest in organic gardening. After a successful career first as a teacher then as a salesman, he rented a twenty-five-acre farm, twelve kilometres south-east of Ndola. There for the past three years he has been producing amazing crops of maize using only chicken manure, composted grass, and collected nshima waste.

He has become convinced that the use of chemical fertilizers is detrimental to the development of rich fertile soil and that crops produced by applying chemicals are less nutritious and healthy than organically grown crops.

Breakfast on an organic farm

5 am: collected by Samuel in his old Isuzu pick-up and taken out to his farm. What a glorious sight it was in the soft light of the early morning sun. The tall stalks of maize with their heavy crop of golden grain had not yet been harvested, and down in the dambo, where two young men were working the damp soil with their broad bladed hoes, a thousand dew drops sparkled like diamonds on cabbages, tomato plants and rape.

Samuel showed us the secret of his success. It was the deep pit he had excavated ten feet wide, five feet deep and twenty feet long. He was filling it up during the last month of the rains, while waiting for the ripening of his corn, with great bundles of green elephant grass and barrowload after barrowload of chicken manure, and of course the daily drums of kitchen waste which he collected from colleges in town. By the time he plants his maize seed in November it will all have rotted down into a rich black compost, which he will lovingly apply a handful at a time to each of his growing plants in his ten-acre field.

Merfyn and his grandson Jonathan, with Obert Kayaya in Chipapa

Samuel and his wife are saving to build themselves a four-bedroomed house on their farm. They purchase 250 day-old chicks and can get £3 per broiler bird at the end of six weeks, making a clear profit of £2 x 250 birds and an annual income from their poultry of £8500. He pays his workers £15 per month plus food ration, which gives them as much spending money as an Ndola taxi driver who has to buy his food at highly inflated urban prices. If given the chance to work the land, small-scale organic farmers could grow all the food that is needed to feed the population of the Copperbelt towns of Ndola, Chingola, Kitwe, Luanshya, Mufulira, Kalulushi and Chililabombwe. In fact given time and encouragement, these Copperbelt farmers could produce all the food which is presently grown by the large commercial farmers in the south using chemical fertilizers, hybrid seed and the heavy imported machinery which consumes huge quantities of diesel fuel at a high cost from the Middle East.

24 April: Chipapa to Kankotula

We set off on our bicycles along the track which leads to the village of Kankotula, where Filipo and his family live at the foot of the escarpment. I had visited his place in the 'sixties, and wanted to see whether this remarkable man's experiment in self-help sustainable agriculture had survived.

Jane, Jonathan and I were probably the first 'outsiders' to have been to Kankotula since I went there in 1970; indeed no one from any government ministry had ever thought it necessary to visit this inaccessible place. We arrived hot, tired and thirsty, as the deeply rutted track forced us not only to push the bicycles uphill but also walk beside them rather than ride them downhill.

There was no one in the village because they were out working in the fields; however after a while one of Filipo's sons appeared and took us to see the furrow. The original spring high up on the escarpment had dried up, but Filipo and his sons had found another source of perennial water, which they had brought in a second furrow to a small earth dam half-way down the escarpment. This filled up overnight, then during the day they directed the water into the inter-connecting irrigation channels which watered the carefully contoured vegetable beds. It was an amazing feat of engineering, but the villagers were running into a number of problems:

- As the gradient levelled out in the valley bottom, the furrow had to be made deeper and deeper,
- Where the soil was soft, the sides of the furrow kept caving in,
- They were losing a great deal of water through seepage along the length of the furrow,
- Some species of crab or crayfish was boring holes into the earth dam, causing it to collapse.

I was not able to ascertain how the people here have been able to sustain the soils' fertility over thirty years, but I do know that they never bring in chemical fertilizers and they have used quantities of bat guano, dug out from a cave which we saw high up on the hillside above the village. Perhaps Samuel Kaluba could come down from the Copperbelt for a week or two to show them how to make deep compost pits and rear broiler chickens?

The high point of our visit came when I talked to one of Filipo's grandchildren whom I found irrigating his own field of rape. There he was, stripped to the waist in the heat of the day, carefully flooding the water onto the narrow terraced beds which his father had shown him how to contour along the sloping ground. Later he showed us in the village, the small thatched house which his mother had helped him build and shown him how to decorate with traditional designs painted with mud in soft colours of black and grey, brick red and chocolate brown.

Transport

On our return journey we met two young men pushing their bicycles, each with two large grain sacks stuffed full of green rape, which had been grown by women in the irrigated garden below Chipapa's dam. I don't know how much the women pay them for their hard day's slog through the hills and up the escarpment, nor how long it will take them to repay the capital they have invested in their bicycles, but this way of transporting vegetables to market makes no economic sense. Surely this huge expenditure of youthful human energy for taking food from countryside to town should go not into food distribution but into food production.

In trying to solve this problem of transport, the people of Kankotula had made a rough road up the escarpment, then they had bought an old pick-up truck and one of them had learned to drive. It had saved them hundreds of sweltering cycle-pushing man-hours, but they found that they had to sell an awful lot of vegetables to pay for petrol, repairs, tax, insurance and replacement. Near the house where we left our bicycles before climbing up to the little storage dam, we saw the empty shells of two battered pick-ups and another on chocks which we were told was waiting until the owner could accumulate enough money from the sale of his vegetables to buy a new engine.

Ever since the Chipapa dam was made half a century ago, the people have been trying to solve the 'transport' problem, and they are no nearer a satisfactory solution than they were fifty years ago. Looking back over the years, I now see where I made the mistake of encouraging the people of Chipapa to think that their 'transport' problem can be solved by a road and some form of motorised vehicle.

I should have paid more attention to observing how the Ba-Tonga of the Zambezi Valley, who live at the foot of the Batoka escarpment, have dealt with their 'transport' problem. They have used donkeys as pack animals—sure-footed donkeys who do not need a road, only a footpath. Hardy donkeys which cost nothing to feed and which cost nothing to replace; indeed a young man who invests his money in a donkey rather than a bicycle will see his capital grow, and donkeys are inflation proof.

Charcoal burning

In the early days, when Lusaka was little more than a clearing in the Northern Rhodesia bush, the cooking fires of Africans and Europeans were fuelled with firewood cut from the surrounding forest. But as the population increased, and the people had to go further and further into the forest to get their fuel supplies, the cost of transporting heavy loads of firewood became prohibitive. Then people discovered that charcoal is a more efficient source of heat than firewood: it is light and can be transported long distances at a fraction of the cost of carrying fresh firewood. One man can carry on his bicycle, enough charcoal to keep the cooking fires of ten urban families burning for a month, whereas it would take ten men and ten bicycles to transport the equivalent heat energy if the fuel was firewood.

There is no substitute for charcoal as a cheap fuel for cooking the food of millions of urban families in Zambia today. The demand for it is irresistible, and for unemployed men who see no other way of earning a living, charcoal burning and charcoal transportation has become a way of life. The legitimate need of Zambia's exploding urban population to have enough charcoal to cook its daily ration of maize meal, is having a disastrous consequence in the short term for the forest, and in the long term for the climate.

The Mpande hills form the plateau between the valley of Nabwale and the Kafue Gorge. When I lived in Chipapa thirty years ago I would sit in the evening on the open veranda of my mud-brick house looking out across these hills, at that time covered with forest trees as far as the eye could see. Nobody lived on the plateau in those days, but sometimes in the rains, when it was necessary to keep the cattle out of the maize fields, some people would take their herds to graze there. Also it was there that they went to cut the straight poles which were used to make the walls and roof structures of their houses. They thought then that this natural supply of building materials was inexhaustible, but they had not foreseen, nor had I, the results of Lusaka's population explosion.

Obert leads the cycles into the Mpande Hills

We set off in the morning with our bicycles along the track which climbs up the escarpment to the Mpande plateau. Last year's rains had cut a deep gully through the stony soil where the charcoal transporters' trucks had worn away the surface of the rough road. I was completely exhausted by the time I had manhandled my bicycle to the top, so we rested for a while in the homestead of Mr Moonga before he took us for a long walk to see the devastation of the forest wrought by a great number of migrants who have moved into this area from all parts of Zambia, and from as far away as Tanzania, Malawi and Zaire. We had met a gang of sixty or seventy of them on the way up, trying to fill the gullied road with rocks so that the transporters could get through to buy their charcoal.

In some places where they have made homesteads, they have left a few trees to provide shade, but over the past thirty years nearly all the forest has been cut down, and the time is not far off when there will be no trees left to bum for charcoal.

Mr Moonga told us that there are some places on the plateau where people have developed small subsistence farms. He himself has a herd of goats and a few cattle. Sadly he once had more cattle, but thieves from Lusaka stole his big oxen, so now he just keeps a few cows and their calves which he sells off as yearlings before they are big enough to be worth the trouble of stealing. One of his neighbours used to breed donkeys which he used to pull a homemade cart. They were theft-proof, because no one in Lusaka eats donkey meat, but his friend had moved away and he did not know what became of the donkeys.

The motley group of people who have come to live on the Mpande plateau fall under the jurisdiction of Chieftainess Nkomesha, who is doing her best to keep the charcoal burners under some kind of control by insisting that they obtain licences for their activities from the government Department of Forestry. But it is an impossible task. Nothing she can ever say or do will turn back the tide of deforestation. When all the trees have gone, some of the charcoal burners will leave, but most will remain in the Mpande hills somehow eking out a precarious living from their goats, their chickens and subsistence gardens of millet, maize, and sorghum.

Chipapa: Visit to Obert Kayaya's farm

Obert's project to provide land and dig a well for the Chipapa Young Women's Organic Gardening Club has been held up because of last year's heavy rains but the well has been dug, the concrete well liners have been purchased, and there is still money in the bank to pay for the barbed wire needed to protect the garden from cattle and goats.

Meanwhile Obert has been planning ahead to develop a poultry project which he hopes will encourage the young women to make their club economically viable. Last year he made a contract with Mimosa Farm Shop near Lusaka to supply them twice weekly with green beans. From this he made enough money to purchase a small second-hand diesel-driven hammer mill which he will use in the preparation of chicken feed. He also obtained a hand-operated hydraulic oil press to produce cooking oil from sunflower seed and groundnuts, using the residue to make a balanced diet for the chickens.

Obert is setting a fine example on his own farm of how to produce organically grown food and cash crops. He is well known and trusted in the community, and in spite of his physical disability he is able to get round on his ladies' bicycle. He covers a wide area as a voluntary family planning visitor travelling down the Nabwale valley and into the Kankotula hills and up the Mpande escarpment.

Lusaka to Mumbwa

Jane, Jonathan and I decided that we would have to abandon our bicycles, because our experience in the Mpande Hills had finally forced me to admit that I am not as young as I used to be. We therefore decided to go by bus to Mumbwa, and then by whatever means we could, to travel the last 70 km to Ipongo on the edge of the Lukanga swamps where I had planned to visit the organic farming project sponsored by Harvest Help.

The long-distance bus station in Lusaka is at the centre of the notorious Soweto market, where Jonathan had been roughed up by a gang of youths on the day of his arrival, so we took a taxi to drive us through the seething throng of marketeers, waiting passengers and shouting hawkers. Then clutching closely to our tummies our wads of dirty kwacha notes and our hold-alls, and with the taxi driver carrying our bedding roll, we dived through the crowd into the comparative safety of the waiting bus. All along the first 140 kilometres of the Great West Road there were huge potholes, which the driver of our ramshackle vehicle made little attempt to avoid, so we arrived in Mumbwa four bone-jangling hours later, glad to take refuge in the District Government rest house.

Mumbwa to Ipongo

When I tried to find a 'taxi man' to take me to Ipongo, I encountered a curious reluctance. Then we had a stroke of luck. A young woman from whom we had bought some oranges in the market befriended us and put us in touch with a young taxi man of her acquaintance, named Godfrey, who agreed a price of £25 a day for three days to take us in his pick-up to Ipongo and bring us back using the short route.

His vehicle had obviously had a misspent youth, but he assured us that the engine was as good as new. All the tyres were completely bald, but why should we worry? he carried a spare. There was no upholstery on the front seat, so in the market we bought a cushion stuffed with kapok. I agreed that as the self-starter had packed up some while ago, we should carry two men behind with Jonathan to bump-start it each time it stopped and we needed to get going again.

Long ago this road had been made, but no one had ever bothered to keep it up, with the result that it has become deeply eroded by the rain. However Godfrey, with years of experience in coaxing his ancient Isuzu along similar tracks, and with the help of his human-starters when things got really rough, covered the 70 kilometres in just over four hours, which is about the same time it takes on a bicycle when the farmers go to collect payment for their cotton crop.

Next day over breakfast, one member of the project team told us the story of the Ipongo project. Some four years ago, the Harvest Help development team in Zambia was looking for opportunities to replicate the experience it had gained in the Gwembe Valley. They were taken to the area south of Lukanga swamps, where there was endemic famine every year because the people were failing to keep sufficient grain after harvest to feed themselves over the hunger months, and in seasons of drought were forced to eat their own seed corn.

With financial support from Harvest Help, an agriculturalist and a community development worker went to live in the area. After careful consultation with the local community, and in cooperation with government agencies, they encouraged the people to set up their own autonomous farmers' clubs whose first task was to build a central grain store. When this had been done each farmer was given 10 kilos of good open pollinated seed in exchange for a 90 kilo bag of their own grain, which was kept in the grain store for distribution to the farmers and their families during the hunger months.

The project team is helping farmers to obtain sunn hemp seed which they are planting as a green manure crop, and already there is active discussion going on about the possibility of creating a revolving loan fund to assist farmers to purchase oxen so that they can extend the land under production of food crops and obtain manure. Fortunately chemical fertilizers have become so expensive and so costly to transport the long distance from the line of rail, that by force of circumstance rather than by choice, all the 375 farmers are practising organic and therefore sustainable agriculture.

As I heard this story, it seemed that all the things we had been saying in theory about self-sustainable grassroots development were happening on the ground. It all sounded rather too good to be true, so when our host went off on his bicycle to collect his colleague from Chiyuni we went on a walk-about to see for ourselves.

However, this walk raised many questions. Why had so many forest trees been cut down to make gardens? Why were there such large areas covered by those tell-tale weeds which show that the soil has been over-cropped and mono-cropped, thereby losing its natural fertility? And what was the clearing in the bush with a board nailed to a tree which simply read 'Lonrho Depot'? Then I heard a different story, one which is becoming all too familiar throughout the African continent, of how a big multi-national company has come crashing in to exploit the land, leaving in its wake devastated forest, ruined soil, and people whom they have forced to become poor cotton pickers in their own impoverished fields.

On the road to Ipongo

Lonrho now owns the modern ginnery built by the Japanese in Mumbwa and has taken over the out-growers who provide it with the raw cotton. Lonrho has a complete monopoly and arbitrarily fixes prices. It bears no responsibility for how the growers live, nor for how they use or misuse their land. Every year more and more trees are chopped down, as farmers clear the fields which after two years of intensive cropping have lost all their fertility. When all the forest has gone and all the good land has been destroyed, Lonrho will move somewhere else to find more trees to cut down and more peasant communities to wreck.

Kamesi Matafeni, man of dignity

We left Ipongo before 6 a.m., packing up our bags and bedding rolls by candlelight. We hoped to complete the return journey to Mumbwa before the heat of the midday sun burned up Jonathan in the back of the open pick-up.

We passed through the *matala nzovu* (the grain bins of the elephants) where the tall elephant grass heavy with morning dew swept our cracked windscreen clean from yesterday's dust. Then we came to an open field where on the right, the ripening maize stalks had been gathered into tall stooks so that the grain could dry out before harvesting, and on the left were crops of sunflower, groundnut, beans and cotton. I had seen no other farm like this in Ipongo, so we stopped in the hope that we might meet the farmer.

He came to greet us; his name was Kamesi Matafeni and he had emigrated from Zimbabwe to settle here in 1978. He knew all about the Harvest Help project and had helped the members of one of the clubs to transport bricks from the kiln which they had made, to the site where they were building their grain store. He spoke with that quiet dignity which seems to be the hallmark of all good farmers anywhere in the world, and if anyone needs proof that agriculture in Zambia can be sustainable, let them meet Mr Matafeni who has been farming here for twenty years, with soil as fertile now as when he started.

At 10.00 a.m. we heard an ominous sound coming from below the chassis of our trusty Isuzu. We stopped, Godfrey slithered underneath with screwdriver, hammer and spanner, and after a while came out with a piece of fractured metal in his hand and announced that the universal joint had cracked apart. We estimated that we were about twenty kilometres from Mumbwa, so we set out to walk, arriving four hours later very thirsty, dirty, and tired. It had taken all that time because we needed to keep stopping to find villages where we could get a drink of water, and also I needed ever-lengthening rest pauses to restore the spring in my ageing step.

Sunday at Nambala church

At 11.30 hrs on Sunday, we attended the Sunday Service at Nambala Mission. The church which Reverend Will Harrison built in 1945 (he was a builder and carpenter by trade before entering the ministry), still stands

four square and strong. There were more than one hundred and fifty people, singing and clapping to the beat of drums and dancing up the aisle with their gifts. The black-robed minister thundered through a lengthy diatribe, and administered communion to the forty or so full members who stayed behind for the third hour of the service.

Then I spent another hour getting down to business and answering questions:

- No, it was not true that I had been sent out by the President of the Methodist Church in Britain to give support to the 'UCZ splitters' who had recently registered a new 'Methodist Church of Zambia'. On the contrary, I regarded them as 'thieves and robbers' who had not 'entered through the gate' but rather, like hyenas climbed over the fence of the kraal.

- No, the government has no right to claim UCZ church property in Mumbwa just because there are no title deeds to the land. No deeds were given when the church and manse were built. In those days the District Commissioner had the authority to grant land to the church. The District Commissioner at that time was Ian Dinwiddie. He is still alive. I will ask him to write a letter to the government.

- No, the Methodist Church in Great Britain will not take back the old mission schools and send money for new buildings, equipment and employ white missionaries to run them.

At 16.00 Godfrey arrived bringing our luggage. He had borrowed a bicycle, cycled to Mumbwa, found somewhere an old universal joint, took it out to his stranded vehicle, fixed it and driven home.

An organic 'network'?

Returned by bus to Lusaka where I spent the next four days tying up loose ends and making useful contacts, the most important being with the central office of HODI, the local NGO formed by Harvest Help U.K.

I heard that HODI has taken the initiative in encouraging the setting up of a network of local NGOs who have a common interest in the development of training for sustainable agriculture programmes. Already five organisations are interested, including the Gwembe South Development Committee. Part of the plan is to establish a resource centre which is accessible on the internet. One of the things that needs urgently to be done is to produce in Zambia for Zambians a simple hand book for farmers on the principles and practices of organic farming, such as the one produced for Kenya by John Ngorogi. I therefore visited Multimedia Zambia. I met their publishing director, Reverend Gideon Simwinga, who showed me samples of some of their books.

My dear Frank,
I think you will be interested in part of the report of my recent visit to Zambia.

In my old age I become ever more certain that we Western developers have got it wrong. We have made the mistake of making Africans believe that our Western, 20th Century Christian 'civilisation' is 'better' than their traditional culture. We have made them jump through the hoop labelled 'EDUCATION' from their healthy (whole) world into our ersatz tacky world. Like Jacob [sic] they have sold their birthright—their land, their trees, their rivers – for the mess of pottage that is the mess of our urban can of worms.

It is time we went to sit at the feet of Filipo and his sons and grandsons, daughters and granddaughters and let him tell us how with no education, and no Bazungu offering aid, he has created a self-sufficient community in the hills below the Lusaka escarpment.

It is clear to me that we should get some donkeys from Siameja with their Ba-Tonga drivers to demonstrate to the people of Chipapa and Kankotula and the Mpande plateau that far far better than the Chiloto bus and clapped-out Nissan pick-ups is the despised donkey.

When Christ comes to Chipapa he will be riding not in a Mercedes truck nor even on a bicycle but on "a colt, the foal of a donkey".

As ever, Merfyn

To Valentine Banda, Bulawayo, Zimbabwe

My dear Valentine,

I am very touched that the story of Chipapa and Daniel and Sarah and Chipo moved you so much that even tears dropped onto the pages of that little book. Perhaps it is the spirit of Our Lord who is speaking to us both and saying that the lost ones and the little ones and those who are very poor and feel forgotten and lonely, are the ones whom He specially loves and is calling us to care for with tender loving care.

It is good to hear that you are looking ahead to the future and that you are building a place for your family in the communal lands. As far back as 1995 you were demonstrating to the people that "Organic farming is cheap, healthy and economic . ." Only our Lord Himself can have revealed to you the secret of His coming down from Heaven to live amongst us on this daily earth. I know you mean it when you pray "Thy kingdom come on earth as it is in heaven" because you say "I know that if I live with them I will win them." There is no other way. There is no easy way. The only way that God could find was to "become flesh and dwell amongst us".

I am being encouraged by my family and some of my friends to write my autobiography, but I am hesitant to do so. It may be that there is another book which I need to write which tries to analyse the causes of failure. Why did I fail as a young man to persuade school drop-outs to stay on the land? Why did the Chiloto bus fail? Why did my friend Kaunda not leave politics when de-selected as President and go back to his farm in Lubwa as I advised him to do? Why is Christ's church becoming strong and wealthy in Harare and Bulawayo but does not seem to care that there are still many children, for example, who never even get a primary education and will live in poverty all their lives in the Binga District?

Those early pioneer missionaries like Moffat and Livingstone and John White, for all their faults, still believed in the power of Christ's Holy Spirit to redeem the life of the amaNdebele and the Mashona. We must believe that too, and we must have faith even as small as a mustard seed that this is still God's holy purpose. When your girls pray, let them pray earnestly and believingly for the transformation of the bodies, minds and spirits of all who live in Zimbabwe's villages.

Audrey and Patricia send their warm greetings as do I
Ndime Muluti, Merfyn Temple

Small Miracles, 1998

My 1998 JOURNEY was a response to Fergal Keane's plea that a way should be found to report on "the numerous small miracles of African life in such a way that they provide an antidote to the inevitable mulch of crying and dying about Africa, which defies understanding and solution." Yes, I discovered hunger, poverty and corruption in high places but, more importantly, I also found 'small miracles' happening everywhere; and in them lay the hope of Africa's salvation. What follows are excerpts from a diary I wrote on that journey.

Chipapa and the Mpande Hills

Before going out to Zambia I had written asking for an audience with Chieftainess Nkomesha, so that I could explain the purpose of my mission and gain her support.

We meet the Chieftainess

We walked to the palace and sat at one of the tables under the trees waiting for the chief to call us. Half an hour later her *kapasu* (personal assistant) took us through into her inner sanctum. Under the tall mangoes outside her colonial house, on the newly swept ground, two white-painted chairs had been set, with another one fifteen feet away. The *kapasu* said we were to sit down and then when the chief came we were to stand up, wait for her to be seated, then we too would sit down.

Again we waited; then the chief appeared, walking towards us with open arms. "Welcome, welcome Muluti. How delighted I am to see you. It must be over thirty years since we last met." Don't ask me what she was wearing, but she had a blue scarf tied above her sweet and kindly face. I took to her immediately. No, she had never received any letter from me and knew nothing of my coming. But she was deeply appreciative of the present which Audrey had sent her; indeed she had already used the soap and body lotion!

Everything was arranged satisfactorily. I am to travel to Chipapa tomorrow and report to her again in a few days' time, when she will lend me a *kapasu* to go round the villages.

We arrive in Chipapa

When we reached Chipapa, Sarah was the only one to greet us. All smiles, we fell on each other's necks. Sarah went off to find her granddaughter Fanny and sent someone to call Obert Kayaya, who was working on his farm on the hill behind the house. While Sarah and Fanny cooked our evening meal of nshima and cabbage, Obert brought me up to date with all the news.

We discussed the problem of Obert's cattle which he uses for ploughing. Two years ago he lost by theft four cattle from his small herd. Two were partially trained (value £100 each) and two fully trained (£180 each). Keeping cattle so near to Lusaka is a constant hazard. Tractors are out of the question and it may well be that donkeys are the answer, for no other reason than that Zambians don't eat donkeys.

Sunday service in the village chapel

The service in the little church half a mile down the road is supposed to start at 10.00, so I set off at about 10.15. I passed five bicycles in a matter of ten minutes; this is what I call modernisation. I was turning over in my mind what I was going to say during my sermon. It was going to start with Genesis and the creation when God looked upon all he had made and said "It is good." I walked past the entrance to the school and was rejoicing in the long avenue of mango trees which were planted thirty years ago, and now form a high canopy of thick branches right up to the main school building.

As I suspected, the congregation numbered only two when I arrived at the church. They had lit a small fire outside, and sitting on their drums they were heating the beeswax on the stretched drum-heads to make them more sonorous. Bit by bit the rest of the congregation arrived, and by

11.00 there was a youthful choir of nine boys and five girls and two drum-mers, about thirty men and women, and a dozen small children. At every point in the creation story I got the congregation to repeat the refrain *"And God said this is good."* We had just completed the herbs and the trees and I was coming up to lions, elephants, etc. when there was a commotion amongst the women on the back three benches who all came tumbling forward. They had found a small black snake which had to be dealt with before I went on. When I got to snakes and all creeping things they simply said *"And God said they are bad."* I tried to explain about the snakes in the sugar-cane fields of Jamaica, which had been dispatched by the workers, only to be replaced by a plague of rats which ate all the sugar cane, but of course they didn't believe me. Finally, I came to the problem of how you say sorry to God for cutting down his precious trees and despoiling his land with pests and fertilizers. It was quite a problem, because when we say "forgive us our sins as we forgive those who sin against us," who is to blame when a desperate man cuts down trees to make charcoal for the city-dwellers who have no other way to cook their food?

So if Chipapa is going to forgive us, it will need a lot more than a few brief words. It means that we, the transgressors, must help the people of Chipapa, against whom we have transgressed, to rebuild their despoiled land.

New gowns for the Choir?

As I left the church, the Choir chairman approached and said that the choir would like to come to my house to talk about some of their prob-lems. In due course they arrived and sat solemnly on a rug we spread on the floor; the boys of course found stools to sit on. The great spread-ing bougainvillea always provides welcome shade on the verandah of my house. I discovered that only a few of the choir—38 in all, twenty boys and eighteen girls—are full members of the church. They meet every Tuesday and Saturday for choir practice, but there is no one there to instruct them in the Bible. I hope to send them some simple books of instruction and make sure that each one has a New Testament.

Their next problem was their uniforms which they have had for five years, and which have lost most of their lime-green colour. They have tried to raise money by working on local farms, but they get paid such a pittance, which they need for food, that they have no chance of succeeding. If you are hungry, the chance of raising £4 for your own choir gown seems impossible. Finally, if they are going to compete with the other town churches in choir festivals, there is the question of how to raise the bus fare to get there. They can "go footing" (walk) as far as Chilanga, but then there is the 50p fare to Lusaka and back.

We set off for the Mpande Hills

At 7.30 the next day, Obert arrived with the bicycles. He gave me the Japanese machine which had been provided for him by one of the supporters of the Planned Parenthood Association. It is a splendid ladies' bike with everything: chain guard, skirt protector, dynamo lamps and wire basket attached to the elegantly sculptured handlebars. Obert had the stripped-down 1950 all-steel Raleigh, which I had brought out for him last year. These two bikes are brilliant, knocking spots off the modern cheap imitations now exclusively imported from India.

It was easy going from Chipapa up to the foot of the escarpment, then the climb begins onto the Mpande plateau. The road is just a boulder-strewn, stony track only negotiable by large tractors, 4 x 4s, or ox-wagons. It is not an official road, but is maintained by the people who want to encourage charcoal transporters to have access to their precious product. At one point on the ascent I had to stop and rest in the shade of a tree. Obert went on to the top where he left his bike and blankets, returning to collect mine while I scrambled slowly up on foot. In spite of his lameness Obert is astonishingly tough for his thirty years, and walks behind his ox plough for long hours in the rain when the ground is soft enough to till. He is also extremely good with his hands, managing to maintain and repair not only his own but also the women's hammer mill.

The whole journey took only about two hours, and we were glad when we came to the home of the indomitable Mr Moonga, who is the self-appointed and now officially recognised headman of the area. He brought us large mugs of *chibwantu*, the sweet drink they concoct from lightly boiled maize and a root called *munkoyo* which somehow holds the grain in suspension. This milky white fluid provides both food and drink in one go. People take it with them when they go to work in their gardens and it is perfect for their needs.

Mr Moonga's story

Mr Moonga had done a number of things including being a mission medical orderly and the last driver of the Chiloto bus. In 1974, being a man still full of energy, he felt too hemmed in at Chipapa, so climbed to the top of the Mpande Hills fifteen kilometres away and staked his claim in the forest there. Year by year this was being decimated by charcoal burners from many tribes, especially the Eastern Province, 600 km away, across the Luangwa River. He never bothered to build a brick house, but his pole and wattle mud house under its wide thatched roof must have been something of a palace in its heyday.

Almost single-handedly Mr Moonga and his wife Esther have built up the grass-walled United Church of Zambia (UCZ) church here. There are now about fifty members but no one has ever visited them from either Kafue or Lusaka—what minister would ever sweat up the escarpment to bring them Holy Communion?

As we rested in the shade of Mr Moonga's 'village meeting house', I began to ask him some questions which puzzled me:

Why do people leave their villages to live in towns?
"It all started when Europeans came to live here. These white people did not want to live in villages. They preferred the towns from which they came. They needed Africans to help them, first in their houses as houseboys and cookboys, and then they needed workers on their farms and on the mines. At first Europeans did not want their workers to be educated because that made them 'cheeky'. It was missionaries who said Africans must be educated, because one day they would have to take charge of their own country.

"The development of towns gave Africans the chance to earn money and buy the things they wanted. In rural areas they had no opportunity to earn a living. That is the reason why they left villages and came flocking into town. Parents send their children to school to get an education, because that is the way to earn money. They are prepared to send their children to school, in the hope that when they get old, they will have the support of children to care for them and look after them. In Zambia today there is no social security for old people, so education is therefore important."

What is going to happen in the future?
"We do not know but two things are becoming clear to us:

1. The cost of living in towns is becoming more and more expensive and it is hard to find a job. There you can only get very low paid jobs, even if you have Grade 10 or 12. The cost of housing, water, fuel and food makes staying in town too costly. The temptation to enter a life of crime is becoming too attractive and girls are becoming prostitutes.

2. The attraction of rural areas which are near towns is becoming obvious, if ways can be found for people to earn enough to live comfortably and have some money for other things. Before, in Chipapa not one single boy or girl wanted to stay; now boys and girls with better education are willing to stay as farmers. They have made up their minds not to go to towns in search of work. This is a new thing, and younger people are taking the leadership."

We walk around the village

When the sun had passed its zenith we went for a short walk to see the UCZ church and school. We came first to the church, a grass-walled building erected some four years ago complete with rough hewn benches supported on forked legs. I thought of the people meeting here every Sunday with no leadership except Mr Moonga, who never regarded himself as a preacher; he has always been the practical man. Nearby we saw a tiny hut with a few bundles of grass thrown on top to keep out the rain. Mr Moonga said the church hoped to build a new hut for the widow from Tanzania who lives here with her three children. Last November he and his two strong sons had come with a pair of oxen and a plough to cultivate the little garden behind her house. She herself had planted the maize seed and kept it weeded, growing a few pumpkins and melons in the shade of the tall maize plants. Good for you Mr Moonga, you have the right idea in your tiny church where the rich are taking care of the poor.

The self-help school

We went on to see the self-help school which the people built a couple of years ago. Like the church, it is built from poles and thatch with open sides to let the light in. At one end is quite a large plastered room where the equipment is kept. It is not used much because there isn't any equipment apart from an ad hoc blackboard at the far end propped against the teacher's 'lectern'. As the people have to raise their own money from the proceeds of charcoal to pay any 'teacher' who happens to be available, and as no charcoal is being cut because everyone is harvesting maize, the school has closed. The reason why the school was built is quite understandable, as children as young as 8 and 9 have to walk fifteen kilometres to Chipapa school, a journey which Obert and I managed in a couple of hours each way, and that with bicycles.

An uncomfortable pillow

We slept that night on the ground, and though I had brought a blanket and sleeping bag with me I had no pillow, so I asked Mr Moonga to bring me one. He came back with the seat of his best chair, which unfortunately for me had seen better days, the springs just about to herniate from its innards. All I had to lay my head on was a jumble of coiled springs. In the end I made do with my shorts and shirt rolled up in a towel.

I got up at 2.30 am and went outside into the bright moonlight. The night was still except for the stamping of the cattle. Two little kids slept for warmth on the dying coals of our fire. All the other goats had been penned up but the nanny and her kids had been allowed to run free. At 4.30am I heard the guinea fowl making a great commotion. They had flown down from the tree as they had seen a hawk in the sky so were warning all the chickens to take cover under the bushes.

Kankotula

Obert and I cycled to Kankotula, the village which made a furrow through the hills where Filipo and his family live, at the foot of the escarpment of the Lusaka plateau. Last year I sent them £100 to see if they could do something about the crayfish. Before climbing up the hill to see their little dam we met three of the seven men who are all part of Filipo's family. One of them produced from his pocket a receipt showing the amount they had spent on cement (plus VAT) and the money they had paid for transport from the cement works at Chilanga.

The cement was dumped at the top of the escarpment, then the seven workers, all young men, managed to cannibalise two wheelbarrows from six old wrecks and barrow the cement down a path that they had hacked through the bush, to the dam site. On the lower side of the dam they dug a deep narrow trench about six feet into the mud until they reached hard rock. They filled this with boulders, sand and cement, until they were half way up the earth wall of the dam. This prevented the dam collapsing as it had done when the crayfish riddled it with holes.

As we walked up the steep hillside, I heard what I thought was the wind rustling the leaves of the banana trees, but I was wrong. It was the rushing water as it tumbled down the furrow to the garden at the bottom of the valley. When we reached the site, it was about half full of water because they had been irrigating since first light. They had raised the weir with an earth rampart to contain more water during the rains. We sat together on this wall discussing plans for further construction. I asked them to tell me what difference it had made. They said, "See for yourself, water is gushing down the hill twice as fast as it did last year and we can irrigate our gardens much better, keeping the crops greener and more valuable for sale."

Donor countries are beginning to change

On this journey I have become aware that overseas governments are indeed slowly beginning to change. The Germans have a small-scale programme for the support of local NGOs, and so do the British and the Swedes. However, there is still something missing. They do not listen at the grass roots. Instead of providing large sums of money for single projects, which usually include mechanical transport, they could spend funds on intermediate technology, such as bicycles and donkey carts not cars, village sewing machines not factories, widespread training of farmers in organic methods, not supplies of fertilisers.

Rather than providing a diesel pump to lift water from a weir, they could provide fifteen treadle pumps. In the end the diesel pump will need to be replaced with another one from South Africa, and who knows what will happen to the price of diesel when the oil wells dry up? But the treadle pump needs only a couple of leather washers once a year and a piece of rope and some pulleys every five years, the whole thing easily manufactured by an illiterate worker at Kasisi. Even should Zambia's economy crumble beyond repair, treadle pumps and donkey carts will go on and on.

All that governments need to do is to *listen*. Most people are not very interested in their rights, as long as they are not oppressed by rapacious landlords and corrupt politicians, but they do get angry when no one listens to what they have to say.

One woman's view of the Church in Zambia

I went to visit Violet Sampa Bredt at Makeni. Seven years ago I was in Lusaka when she was installed as the first clergywoman to become the Secretary of an African Christian Council. She soon made her mark in the World Council of Churches (WCC), where she chairs the Committee of African States.

At breakfast this morning we had a long discussion about aid from donor countries and Violet expressed her views with some force. "The basic issue is that the Western world runs a system which uses sophisticated accountancy methods with plenty of checks and balances. They have to, because if they take gifts for 'distribution to the poor' they need to assure their donors that their gifts have been properly and wisely spent.

"The poor however, operate on a different system, in which relatives, friends and relations expect to share in any windfall that might come as an aid gift to one of their number. They have little idea of accountability to some far distant donor agency and very little idea of record keeping and accounts." (I think I was lucky with the Watchtower people of Kakontula because they are traditionally honest. The gift of money for the dam was a grant for a specific purpose for a limited time.)

"Projects which include large sums for motor vehicles, staff allowances etc. often fail because, although they are given with the best intentions, they are given on the assumption that 'Africans ought to learn to be like us'. Nearly all aid is given in the belief that development means 'modernisation and improvement'". Violet as a member of the WCC is deeply involved in aid management, and stated quite categorically that "modernisation is a myth". It is a global concept which exists in the minds of the West, but is meaningless to three-quarters of the people of Africa who are unlikely ever to use an e-mail or touch a computer.

We go together to the tiny church in Makeni

It was already long past 9 am when we hurriedly got ready for church. Most of Makeni's wealthier inhabitants jump into their cars and drive off to Trinity or St Paul's, but we set off for the ten-minute walk across Makeni's windswept plain, where the poor of this place have begun to build their own church. They erected twelve stout poles, across which they have supported ten asbestos sheets to give shade from the blazing sun, and to offer limited protection from heavy rain. All is surrounded by a three-foot high breeze block wall, and from somewhere they have found sufficient pews to seat fifty-odd people. There were seven red-bloused women and half-a-dozen old men and women, but all the rest were young, at least seven with tiny babies.

As we were late, Violet and I sat on the back pew, and when mothers held their babies on their shoulders I could see their wide-eyed faces as they peered across at the strange white man seated on the back pew. We sometimes sang from tattered Bemba hymn books, but most of the songs they knew by heart. At one point a man stood up and sang one of his own compositions in a kind of tuneful African plainsong. It was cold, and a strong wind swept across the dusty ground, rustling the leaves of the tall mango trees on the northern side of the church. At any moment I expected an ox or an ass to put its head over the wall to join in our celebrations.

Jubilee demonstration from Britain

This evening we watched the churches joining hands round Birmingham for the Jubilee Debt Forgiveness Programme. Violet said, "This business of forgiving Zambia's huge debts is necessary because of what happened after Independence, when Kaunda took over 120 private companies and turned them into government 'parastatals'. I worked as an accountant in many of them and they all began to behave in the same way. First a politician was appointed as managing director. He promptly ordered a company car for himself, another for his wife to take his children to school, and a third to run around on small household errands. Other heads of departments, sales managers, finance directors, personnel managers, overseas buyers etc. all did the same. They gave jobs to a plethora of relatives and friends, so that you couldn't get a job unless you knew somebody, and it was not long before they employed three times as many people as the company needed. The extravagance and mismanagement was unbelievable. When a parastatal found itself in financial difficulty, all it had to do was to go cap in hand to the Minister of Finance who would arrange a loan with a foreign government. The world at that time was awash with 'petro-dollars' and countries, particularly in the Middle East, were only too happy to oblige."

Who was to blame? Was it the irresponsible borrowers or the money-gathering lenders? Zambia's present debt is in excess of seven billion dollars, and I went to bed that night with my head reeling, for I'm no economist and I would like someone to explain to me how Zambia can ever escape from the 'aid trap'. Political independence was achieved in 1964, but what does it mean? Kaunda used to talk confidently of "reclaiming the economic heights of the economy" but now we are lucky if we can scrape up the dregs at the bottom of the barrel.

A trip into the Zambezi Valley: Rose's AIDS programme

The bus driver was magnificent, sweeping us fast and safely from Lusaka down the two-thousand-foot drop into the Zambezi Valley. We were there by 1.30 pm, about seven hours after I had boarded another bus for what should have been a two-hour journey. At the Harvest Help HQ I found Alexander Kasenzi, the programme director, and we returned in his car to Siavonga where his wife Rose, who runs the medical programme, was conducting a two-day seminar on AIDS.

I asked Rose how she first became aware of HIV and AIDS, and she told me that ever since she started her medical work in 1986 she knew that she was facing a problem. Villagers were aware that some people were losing weight and developing other symptoms which did not respond to treatment. Because of their condition, they nearly all died fairly quickly.

In 1995 Rose decided to divide the end of the lake on the north bank into three zones, one for the Sinazongwe area and the other two along the lake shore. There are about 6,000 people living in this area, most of whom are grouped into seven centres. Key women in the villages were gathered into groups and Rose taught them about AIDS. This went on for over a year, and gradually Rose began to pick out women who formed 'peer education groups'. These peers were then gathered into a larger group which met to discuss the question "What shall we do?" Of course the awareness training had to continue until every man, woman and child was made fully conscious of AIDS with all its devastating consequences. At this point all the peer women formed an association of women's groups with four to six in each, with their own officers and stringent by-laws.

Each group would decide what particular economic activity they wished to embark on, such as poultry keeping, grocery, weaving or machining. They borrowed capital to set up their enterprises and repaid money to a revolving fund at a fixed rate of interest.

When I arrived yesterday, we found fifty or more of Rose's peer women gathered under the mango trees on the Rest House lawn. They were being addressed by a young man from the Department of Trade, Industry and Marketing. When he finished there followed an hilarious play conducted by a local drama group.

A man sat on a chair while his wife sat on the mat at his side. He had lost his job and there was no money in the house, so his wife was encouraging him to go out to find 'piecework'. After a good deal of argument, he left, and a young man in a flashy suit with brush-cut hair appeared, to be greeted by the wife with great passion. He felt sure she would like to buy a chicken and something extra for herself, so produced the necessary money which she hid in the folds of her dress. More love-making followed as they took their pleasure on the mat, to the huge delight of the audience. There was a knock on the door and the couple's daughter arrived. The mother introduced her to "the nephew of your uncle, who left many years ago to live on the Copperbelt".

After a while we heard in the distance the noisy arrival of the drunken husband. The boy friend, much to the amazement of the daughter, slid quickly behind the chair on which the husband was sitting.

"Did you find some piecework, dear?" asked the wife. "No, this is my piecework," he said, holding up his bottle. The daughter meanwhile was trying to explain to her father that he must meet his long-lost nephew from the Copperbelt, but he was too sozzled to understand. In spite of the mother's frantic gesticulations, the daughter began to shout to her cousin to come out of hiding. The two women began to fight. At last the drunken husband, realising he had a quarrel on his hands, took his daughter by the scruff of her neck and threw her out of the house, thus giving the boyfriend time to slip away unnoticed.

Meanwhile, Rose's assistant Catherine had prepared on two large sheets of cartridge paper the progress of the clubs, showing how in nearly every case the 1997 results were even better than those in 1996. The top club had already accumulated sufficient capital to buy a fully electric sewing machine (power is available from Kariba). Then there was quite a long debate about many internal issues in which the members shared their problems. Sometimes they would appeal to Rose for a decision, but she always handed back the argument to the women themselves.

Afterwards Alexander told me that over the years he had organised a number of co-operative societies, always run by men, which invariably failed. Perhaps women are used to handling small amounts of money and they are very careful about where the money goes. Everyone knows, even the men, that women are the best managers.

What of small miracles?

No one could claim that the organic revolution is sweeping like wildfire through the African bush, but it smoulders almost everywhere, and little fires are waiting to burst into flame. When I set out I thought it was my job to light the fire, but I have found it already burning. I realized that all I had to do was to bend down and blow on the sparks wherever I could find them.

My dear Obert,

I hope you are all well in Chipapa and making preparations for the coming of the rains at the end of October.

I think that every day you are too busy, because you have so many things to do. You have your farm and the grinding mill and the water harvest club and the building of Fanny's house. You are indeed a leader of the people and you need an assistant to write letters, run messages, and do so many things which take up your valuable time.

Many things are happening here as a result of people reading 'Small Miracles'. Money raised has been handed over to the Methodist Relief and Development Fund, who will be handing it on to you for the purposes you have decided. I have asked that it be sent in two amounts in your name to your bank in Kafue. It will be sent in dollars, one amount for £300 and one for £350.

Please will you send a letter to Lewis and Nyelet at Shantumbu, telling them that you have received £300 to help them to buy cement for their dam and pipes to carry water in deep places. Let them work out what they need and bring the pro-forma invoices to you so that you can release money to them.

Mpande Hills: When reading my report, a certain lady who worships in a nearby church rang me up and asked me if she could supply the little school on Mpande with books. I had to explain that in grade I and II they do not use English books, but if she would give me the money I could send it to Mr Moonga. Under separate cover I am sending a copy of *Small Miracles* to Mr Moonga and Job Banda.

Many thanks for sending that excellent photo of the dam building. I have now had it printed on the front cover of *Small Miracles*. I am sending you another copy so that you can hand it round to your fellow members in S.D.A and others.

There is very little I can do here in UK because you are so far away. The only thing I can do is to pray for you all believing that God will send the power of His Holy Spirit into your hearts and minds. Chipapa has so many problems, but 'all things are possible to God'. May He work His miracles in your hearts.

Ndime Muluti, Merfyn Temple

My dear Obert,

Thank you for your letter of July 27 which arrived on August 4 1998.

I am glad to hear that you are all well, but indeed sorry to hear of the death of the old man Mr Robinson Kapaipi.

1. Sending Money

a) I left £100 with Mrs Sureya Mwanza. At today's rates that is worth 100 x 3210 = K321000. I shall tell Mrs. Mwanza that you should let her know in good time (at least 14 days) before you need it, so that you can go to Lusaka to collect it for any purpose such as cement for the Water Harvest dam or for repairs to Lumuno House.

b) I hesitate to send money to your bank a/c because I do not know what rate of interest they pay on your Kwacha. Please let me know.

2. Fanny Njobvu

Please tell Fanny that I was very pleased to receive her good letter. I like to hear about the people of Chipapa. How is Sarah getting on with her chickens? Please thank her for the estimates for building a house. Perhaps you can help her to design the house. Does she want it to be like her grandfather Daniel's old house? Much depends on whether Fanny intends to marry again.

3. *Football Jerseys*

I will do my best to find these jerseys. First you need to give me a rough measurement of size. You can start right away by getting the team to appoint a committee. You should fix an hourly rate so that each boy keeps a record of the hours he works either repairing Lumuno House or making bricks for Fanny or helping widows in the community.

I hope you have planted seeds of the 'relish tree' which we obtained from the old man Mulendema. Patricia is going to plant some here, but our climate is too cold in the UK.

With warm greetings to you all and may God bless the work you are doing for the people of Chipapa.

Ndime Muluti, Merfyn Temple

My dear Ennias,

I was delighted to receive a copy of your letter to Bob Mann of 18 July with all the encouraging reports.

Most encouraging of all was to hear that you have established with your colleagues an organic network and data-base. It is wonderful to know about the work being done in the Southern Province and by Kasisi near Lusaka.

It is clear to me that the Roman Catholic Church is taking the lead in advocating organic agriculture as the only hope of sustainability in rural areas. My question is how are you going to develop the **rapid spread** or the organic movement through every province? The key must be something like a Zambian Fambidzanai for the training of trainers.

You will see from my report that I was able to visit Kasisi. Really excellent work is being done there. But being a European I am impatient with our British aid organisation, because they are not giving you the money you need so desperately to expand a hundredfold the work you are all doing so admirably. Should you not have a full-time organizer for **all** Zambia? Who for example is organizing in the North-Western Province? That place could supply the whole of the Copperbelt with all the maize it can ever need from now until Kingdom Come.

Ndime Muluti, Merfyn Temple

Dear Maurice,

How lovely it was to receive your lovely letter of 18 Oct from Mongu. Was it so long ago? it seems like yesterday when we stood beside your well with Robin and Ruth—now both well with Abigail at sixth form college writing poetry, and Rachel at 13 a stunning beauty.

David my brother is well and happy, running a "charity shop" with his wife in Chislehurst; in the past four years they have raised £100,000 for charities—all from other people's junk! Their daughter Elizabeth is now in the Methodist ministry with three bonny children of her own. Please pass his warm greetings to any now still in education, who remember him in those halcyon Livingstone years.

I was so sorry to hear how the terrible scourge of AIDS is decimating youth and young adults. So hard when you have poured so much life force and energy into the young people who begin to take up positions of responsibility in the community. Just when the older generation feel that they can sit back and let the young look after them, they have to take on all over again the task of caring for them. Today I go to Rye to preach to a tiny congregation there about the need to care and love the people of wounded Africa. All we can do is to pray for you—I shall take your letter with me—and ask that God in his infinite goodness and love will comfort you and shine brightly in your eyes when all those people keep coming to ask for your help. Is it not an amazing thing that they need you and trust you? Can anything be more wonderful than that?

I was so delighted to hear from you all, and I shall not expect to hear again until the year 2000. I like your quote from Mother Teresa; indeed we in the West must make sure that Africa has all the wells they need, and all the small wee dams they need, to conserve all the water that God pours down on you out there in the Western Province.

Audrey sends her love, Merfyn

My dear Valentine,

I was the one who wrote the last Psalm, because of my anger with the rich people in Zambia and Zimbabwe who care only for themselves, and take no heed for the poor who increase every day in poverty and suffering. But we do not need to spend much time in anger. Jesus was only once really angry, when he cast the money-changers out of the Temple. For most of his time on earth, he prayed for the poor; he had compassion on them and washed their feet (John 13).

I was very interested to see that you have picked up in the Harvest Help pamphlet that Alexander Kasenzi was asking the basic question: How does true education equip children to stand on their own feet and take their rightful place in the modern world? Your grandparents, long before the white men came to Africa, taught the children how to behave and take a full part in the life of the community.

Of course in our modern world all children have a right to read and write. Some will go on to University and take their place in a modern state, but the majority must learn—as their grandparents did—how to live in harmony with one another and with the environment in which they live. The time must come when people like yourself and Alexander, who are thinking clearly and realistically about the true meaning of education, get together and ask yourselves "What does true education mean for Africa in the 21st Century?" Western forms of so-called 'education' have taken African people into a deep pit from which they must escape.

My grand-daughter Abigail is preparing for her great adventure in Zimbabwe with Student Partnerships Worldwide. They do not tell her until she arrives where she will be stationed, Mashonaland or Matabeleland. I enclose a copy of the brochure she has prepared for her family and friends in this country, which I am sure you will find interesting.

The days of the 'missionary' are long past, because the church in Zimbabwe is learning how to stand on its own and evangelise the people of Zimbabwe. But this does not mean that we must cut off Zimbabwe's relationships with the rest of the world. Student Partnerships Worldwide seems to be a good way of involving the youth of Zimbabwe with other youth worldwide.

It seems to me that in the third millennium Africa will be facing huge new problems: environmental destruction, educational limitation, decimation by AIDS and malaria, which should make us all, you in Zimbabwe, me in UK, face up to the great opportunities which God holds out to us. Jesus taught us to pray 'Thy kingdom come'. We do not have to wait for His Kingdom to come in the year 2000, for He is working His small miracles all around us as we sing His praises and wash one another's feet.

May God bless you all, Merfyn Temple

A Dream of Donkeys, 1999

In the summer of 1999 I went back to Zambia one last time as part of a trip with Ruth, Patricia and her husband Robin, to collect granddaughter Abigail from seven months of volunteering in Zimbabwe. Once again I kept a diary, and what follows are extracts from the time spent in Zambia.

My dream begins: Chipapa, 16 August

Before sunrise I climbed Chipapa's little hill to watch the dawn break over the Mpande Hills. At 6.30 the first rim of the sun appeared above the horizon, and within a few moments its brilliant orb flooded the whole world with light. It was here that my dream of donkeys began. I looked down to the east along the road which winds down the valley of the Funzwe River. I dreamed that it was Good Friday in AD 2000 and I saw a child driving a donkey. The figure appeared over the brow of the hill and was followed by many others singing as they waved fronds of borassus palm in the warm sunshine of the morning air. They came towards our little hill, and many other donkeys followed, big sturdy jacks that could pull a plough by themselves, and smaller jennies. Everyone was singing James Ngewa's Ci-Ila lyric.

He was Nambala's Francis of Assisi, putting words to the ancient tunes of his Ba-Ila ancestors. This is one of only two indigenous hymns printed in the book, as most of the others are rather bad translations of Western hymns which were brought here eighty years ago by the missionaries themselves. This one is in praise of God, our Creator.

Its verses sing of the Almighty who made the hills, the sun, the moon, the stars, the animals and birds, the flowers, the crickets and the frogs.

The verse I love best, which I sometimes teach with actions in place of the children's address, goes:

Mayoba ngatuma	The rain which He sends
Maila ngutulima	The grain which we cultivate
Mulilo ngutuzota	The night fire we sit around
Walumba namakungwe	They all thank the Father
Keemba mwami wesu	Our Creator

On the top of the hill above Chipapa I saw a single cross, but no man hanging on it, for He lives down amongst the people in the village. The face of the cross was covered with burnished aluminium so that the light of the sun shone back on the patient faces of the donkeys, the anxious faces of the people and the eager faces of the children.

Later that day Gideon Muyangana came with his nephew, who is now a private doctor in Lusaka. We talked about his ideas for a rural community school which would not just prepare the children for an academic career, but teach them all the skills of life in the village.

We then all set off for a walk to the dam. We saw the six-inch pipe that siphons the water onto the irrigated land. People were already hard at work planting out their tomatoes, peas, beans, and rape. Over 120 people have small plots of land in the garden, and they have not only enough to feed the family, but also to grow a cash crop for sale in Chilanga or Lusaka.

There are far more people in Chipapa than can find a place to make a garden below the dam, so Obert Kayaya has formed the Water Harvest Club and they have begun to make a weir. Their first attempt was not successful because they did not reach down to the bedrock beneath the stream bed. However, on the second attempt they dug a trench 3 metres deep and filled it with rock, stone and cement. Now the stream above the weir has begun to fill and throw the water back along the stream. This is true conservation. When they have a stirrup pump they will be in business because the water will flood back onto their organic vegetable gardens during the seven-month dry season, thus effectively extending the five-month wet season throughout the whole year.

All through the evening and on into the night, people kept coming with their small schemes and plans for developing the great resources of this area.

The Funzwe river valley: 19 August

The story of this river valley is worth telling. In 1944 the people who had been evicted from Chipapa in the 1920s were allowed to move back to their ancestral homes. The colonial administration at that time built a dam at Chipapa and a weir with a ram pump at Nabwale. In the 1970s Nabwale's people were once again evicted by the Kaunda government to make it available to the Chinese for train-ing Joshua Nkomo's guerrillas. The army destroyed their homes, killed the game with AK rifles and stole the ram pump. People were 'resettled' in swampy land on the banks of the Kafue. Many died and were buried there. In the 1990s the people began to trickle back into the Funzwe Valley.

Today we followed the badly eroded track which once a year is 'scuffled' by villagers desperately seeking a weekly food ration from the NGO, Programme Against Malnutrition (PAM). At one point we crossed a thirty-yard culvert. The waters are still flowing strongly five months after the rains stopped. The potential for weirs along the Funzwe is enormous.

When we reached the Nabwale weir we found only one old man whom I had known in the seventies. He and his family were irrigating a small patch of land by lugging buckets of water up the slopes, using their hands to sprinkle their wilting crops. What a difference a treadle pump would make, and how many more people could earn a living if the ram pump was to be replaced. The real problem for those at Nabwale is the high cost of transporting their vegetables to market in Lusaka 60 km away. No vehicle apart from a costly 4x4 could brave that eroded road. As with Shantumbu and Kankotula, the answer must lie in the development of solar-dried fruit and vegetables—Roma tomatoes, guavas, bananas and, in ten years' time, dried mangoes. With a string of pack donkeys to carry their produce, they could achieve the cash income which they so desperately need. The donkey versus the engine is no idle dream, and indeed goats, for milk, meat and hides, are better than cattle on these steep hill-sides. Hungry men do not make good farmers, so the primary task of sustainable agriculture is to grow food and thus eradicate malnutrition.

I visit the Zambezi valley: 22 August

We left in good time for Siavonga and the Kariba Dam, dropping down the 100ft escarpment of the Tonga Plateau to the Zambezi Valley.

At the junction of the Chirundu/Kariba road we were stopped at a police road block, no doubt established at this point to stop smuggled cars entering Zimbabwe. Having shown the officer that all our papers were correct, he looked down his long list of 'first offences' and, selecting one that might have a good chance of success, he said politely "Do you mind showing me your accident triangles?" We searched under the rear seats where the tools are kept, then had to admit that our vehicle hirer had omitted to include them. The policeman shook his head disapprovingly and said that it would be necessary to fill in a long, complicated form. We sat under a tree, providing every detail from chassis number, tax number, driver's full name, date of birth etc. We assumed he would ask us to report to the police headquarters in Siavonga, but he said casually, "If you prefer to give me the K58,000 (£14.50), then I won't need to give you a receipt, will I? And we can use the form for rolling our cigarettes." We paid up and left, praising God and thanking Him for allowing us to submit to this corrupt policeman.

Soon we began to pass through the terribly eroded lands of Lusitu, where in 1950 the colonial government had evacuated the Batonga at the time of the great resettlement. Colonial officers had been forced to settle three times as many people as were recommended in the development schemes, which had been so meticulously drawn up by the land-use planners. Many people died from a mysterious disease which appeared to have no medical cause, but which we suspect was psychosomatic, as the Batonga pined sorrowfully for the loss of their ancestors, whose graves lie drowned beneath the rising waters of Lake Kariba.

Six years ago, I visited Berlin to encourage closer liaison between the Gossner Mission and the Methodist Relief and Development Fund (MRDF). I was sitting in the Director's office when the door opened and a missionary from the Valley, who had stepped off the plane the previous day, walked into the room. With little more than a greeting, he said:

"Last month, some of us from the Valley went to see the condition of the people in Lusitu. Ever since the dam was made years ago, the Batonga have been destroying their habitat and subsist on aid handouts. We went back to our own people in Zambezi South and said that if they carried on there as they are doing now, in ten years' time they too will all be living on permanent aid."

The director and the missionary discussed the problem and came to the conclusion that only a massive programme of sustainable agriculture could possibly save the people. But the Gossner Mission had no such people to deliver the programme. Now it was my turn to intervene. "In the Methodist Church in the UK, we have an agro-forestry consultant called Bob Mann. He is not only a skilled water engineer and convinced agro-ecologist, but a dedicated Christian who has spent his whole life serving the needs of village people from the Gambia and Ghana to Kenya and Malawi. He is your man."

Since then Bob has become a passionate advocate of the Batonga, visiting their valley every year and building up, with his colleague Bazak Lungu in Muzio, a programme of community agricultural workers, which is the envy of both governments and NGOs.

At one point along the badly pot-holed road, we saw a large group of ragged men with hoes and wheelbarrows dumping gravel into these gaping holes. I guessed the government must have run out of money for repairing this main road to Siavonga with tarmac, so they had decided to bail out the Batonga using food provided by PAM. In exchange for these poor rations, the people are expected to repair the road. What other way is open to a cash-starved government than to feed the Valley Tonga in this degrading way? Long ago, they gave up all hope of restoring to fertility Lusitu's tragically eroded land. Rather than let them die, they have turned the people and their children into permanent paupers. Why can't the faceless director of the World Food Programme see that his policies are on a hiding to nothing? By dumping America's genetically modified maize on the Third World, he has found yet another way to keep Africa in poverty. Monsanto, the architect of the genetically modified food racket, has seen its shares plummet dramatically on the stock exchange. This has happened since Europe decided to ban their products. However this may only be a minor problem for them, as they are targeting Zambia and the rest of the Third World's hungry people with their 'Terminator' seed.

Why can't you, Mr Director, use your vast stocks of relief food—and God knows the Batonga need it—not for subsidising a self-seeking Zambian government with mindless road repairs, but with something imaginative to exercise your tiny mind? What is the purpose of this tarmacadam road other than to transport the government's office-bound executives to visit, like any other tourist, the glory of Kariba, this inland miracle? Why Mr Director, didn't you use your food aid to do something creative and sustainable, like building dams and weirs and fishponds? Why don't you, bit by bit, initiate a plan to replant with forest, the deserts now appearing where charcoal burners have chopped down every tree and the naked earth cries out for covering? You ought to know by now that there is a way to help the Batonga climb out of their wretched poverty. They can rediscover a dignity which was theirs before the white man came. It was he who taught them how to destroy their habitat and wreak vengeance on their sacred land. In your heart you know it, but riches have paralysed your hands.

Munyama: Alexander, Rose and the Apostles' Church

We had time to spare on our arrival at Siavonga so we went down to the lake shore to look out across its shining waters. It was like a vast and endless sea, for we couldn't distinguish the mountains over on the Zimbabwean side. Under the mango trees which line the edge of the Council Rest House, we drank Coke and played Scrabble.

We wanted to visit Alexander Kasenzi and his wife Rose at Munyama. They sent a boat for us, which we boarded at Harvest Help's private harbour which lies three kilometres south of the town. It was the first time my daughter Ruth and I had been together on our own since leaving England. All her childhood experiences of sailing on the lake and swimming out to the little island in the bay came flooding back to her. Of course, in those days we all swam more because the dreaded Bilharzia snail had not yet arrived. We set off with the wind in our hair as the little boat slapped over the white horses on the lake. We had a lot to talk about, because as a social worker, Ruth's experience with the parents and children of the poor, living in Luton's backstreets, has given her a unique understanding of village people here.

I told her how Leo Goodfellow had died four years ago when flying his microlight, only 100 feet above Munyama. When the Batonga heard of it, a great cry of pain went up from all of them on the lake shore. Thousands came to his funeral when he was buried in a blanket beside his only son. He lies in the garden which his wife Ginnie planted when they came to settle here twelve years ago. The grass is always green around the grave. The coconut trees and flowering shrubs are kept fresh by water pumped from the lake.

At first there had been darkness and anger in the Batonga when they remembered how they were driven from their ancient homes on the banks of the Zambezi River. But as the years roll on and new generations are born, they are beginning to understand that, in their hot valley with its erratic rainfall and frost-free climate, they have an opportunity not matched anywhere else in Zambia, for the sweet waters of the lake can be pumped onto the richly composted soil and almost anything can grow

Alexander took us to see his extensive gardens. Unfortunately his most productive area—what he calls his 'golden garden'—onto which he has forked hundreds of tons of rich manure from his cattle kraal, was flooded this year by an unprecedented rise in the level of the lake. This year it reached its highest point for thirty-three years. His problem now is how to keep the hippos from trampling his crops. A couple of them have grazed bare his onion fields, spitting out the half-chewed residue when they found the taste unpalatable.

Since I was last here, a beautiful new clinic has been built, but the floodwaters have already lapped round the foundations of one well-built staff house. The first rise in the level of the lake comes with the heavy rains in November and December, but the lake really begins to fill up in January and February when the waters surge down from the vast plains of the Zambezi in the Western Province, where the Ba-Lozi live with their great herds of cattle.

For the first time in all our journey, we discovered the truth in that trenchant phrase "Europeans have watches, Africans have time". Alexander took us to his house where Rose, his wife, had prepared lunch for us and where we could talk and talk. In Alexander and Rose, Leo and Ginnie had found two Batonga who have taken on board all their own belief in the basic dignity of these people who live along the lake. Over our leisurely meal, Ruth and I listened intently, because I wanted my daughter to hear for herself a story which I have heard before, but which only a tiny handful of people in Britain either hear or understand.

About five years ago, Rose and Alexander, two faithful Salvation Army members, became aware of two things:

- In two of the co-operative shops there was no sign of dishonesty, because all the committee members were 'Apostles'.
- When Rose found herself unable to cure certain diseases in her clinic, people would go to the Apostles Church to be prayed over, and often they were healed.

They both decided to investigate the Apostles, and in the end joined this church, much to the alarm of the local Salvationists, and some of their European friends. The Apostles started in South Africa many years ago, and when *apartheid* came, the whites said that the time had come to separate into Apostles and African Apostles. When apartheid collapsed they all became the Apostles once again. No one seems to know when they appeared in the Zambezi Valley, but there are now large numbers here. When Rose and Alexander joined, they found themselves committed to paying one-tenth of their combined income and one-tenth of their crops and their cattle to the church. This made quite a difference to the local church, as all the other members are very poor. These two Harvest Help leaders were the first educated people to join the Apostles, but now two university lecturers and some students have also joined. Rose put it well:

"All healing comes from God, and when He thinks it necessary He uses modern medicine to heal the sick. At other times He heals through prayer. Particularly in African society demonic elements are at play and sometimes the *basangu* (spirits) use witchcraft to pursue their ends. Jesus came to heal the sick and commanded his disciples to cast out demons, so that is what we do. When someone is very sick we ask two or three of our elders to go and pray with them. We say that we ourselves have no power, but God is all-powerful and we pray that He sends His healing. Sometimes this happens quickly, especially when they are possessed with demons. Sometimes it may take three days of praying. Sometimes nothing happens so we close the prayers, then maybe a week or so later that person is healed.

"We have a friend who lives near the Salvation Army Hospital at Chikankata on the plateau. For two years she had been very sick with a serious liver complaint. The doctors said she should go to Zimbabwe for treatment but she could not find the bus fare. We went to visit her and

188

prayed. In only one week the swellings subsided and she could cook in her kitchen again. She is the head nurse at the hospital and her husband is headmaster of the school. He had been away for some weeks and when he returned he expected to find that his wife had died. 'No, she did not die, she is cooking your food in the kitchen,' we said. He was so overwhelmed that he fell on his knees, and had his friends not been there he would have fallen to the ground, as the old people used to do in villages.

We know that the power of the *basangu* is very near to everyone in the valley, but Christ is the conqueror of all our fears so it is always right to pray to Him for healing. Witch doctors sometimes try to harm us, but they always fail and sometimes their charms turn back on themselves."

We had finished lunch and Alexander had gone off to look for a lift. Rose began to share with me her dream of a little home for orphans at Munyama. She wants to give up all her other work, which she has now so successfully handed over to others, and become a foster mother to children under five who have been abandoned by their parents and for whom no other "parents" can be found. Some of these children may be infected with AIDS. Rose will continue to live in her own house but she will need an assistant to look after them at night. To accommodate about twenty children they will need two dormitories with ablution blocks and toilets, a dining room, a kitchen and a place to play together. The land is available and there is plenty of water in the lake to irrigate their gardens. This is one of the most productive areas in the country, as everything along the margin of the lake burgeons and grows rapidly. In addition to their staple diet of maize and vegetables, the children would have their own chickens for the pot, and there is always plenty of fish in Kariba. All manner of fruit grows here: coconuts, cashews, mangoes, avocado pears, passion fruit, guavas, bananas, lychees, and pawpaw all the year round.

We talked on late into the afternoon before returning to Siavonga. Half-way across the lake we met Ginnie returning to her Munyama home in the yellow boat she calls 'Banana Split'. How sorry we were to miss her because, of all the Europeans I ever met in Zambia, Leo and Ginnie are the most exceptional, perhaps because they came to share with the people both their tragedy and their hope. As Ginnie sped away towards Munyama, she stood up and waved goodbye. I knew then that her Quaker faith will never let her give up.

Looking back: Merfyn talks with John Pritchard

John　It's now over 60 years since you first went to Zambia. What is the most exciting thing that has happened to you since then?

Merfyn　Well, I went out as a dyed-in-the-wool colonialist. And I came in the society of other colonialists who saw their mission in life was to bring education—civilization—to Africa. For my first years as a missionary I was deeply involved with all the other European developers and the District Commissioner. And then I realized that my fellow-missionaries hadn't begun to get the message at all, they were still colonialists. Tom Beetham came from Mission House and was not allowed to talk to the Africans—only to the missionaries.

The most important thing about my life was that I moved into a new world of African nationalism. I became a friend of Kaunda and that was the experience of my whole life, as I moved from the dominance of colonialism to be part of the new African nationalist situation. At the same time I was also having serious doubts about [whether] our mission policy was going in the right direction.

John　Disappointments?

Merfyn　I had attempted to become part of the African world by living in this village. I'd done everything in my power to try and make myself part of that world. But in a sense I hadn't. I could not change the fact that I was born in a Western community, I came to Africa with all these Western ideas, and though some of them began to change, in the final analysis I was still a foreigner. I was not accepted as one of them. I did know one or two people who had [tried to integrate], and had married African wives, and lived there, but for myself, I still knew that I was part, and my family was part, of another world. And I knew that my children had done the right thing by not coming back to Africa, because they were finding their life in a world which was familiar to them, which was never possible in my African world.

I know in a sense, that when I went down to Chipapa, I was trying to prove something to Kaunda, to show him that I could take an African villager and make him an economic man by using fertilizers, and it was a totally wrong thing to do. I look back and realize 'You don't do development in one year. You don't bring people out of their primitive situation and suddenly make them affluent. It was an illusion that I was living, and that illusion has gone.

John   You've learned a lesson, and you've been able to apply it.

Merfyn   I think so, yes. I think the only future for the African villager is the organic way. I'm convinced of that in this country and I'm so glad that now it is happening in the place I've loved so much, which is Chipapa.[1]

December 2005

Dear Friends

It hardly seems possible that almost sixty years have passed since I first sat outside my mud brick house in Nambala, Zambia, two hours west of the capital, and watched the sun rise over the virgin forest. This was to be my home as the newly installed Methodist missionary for the district.

But time passes and I cannot escape the fact that I am now 86 and the time has come to take a step back from my life's work with the people of Africa.

I am writing to tell you of my decision to retire and ask you to continue to support the good work through the auspices of my friends at Harvest Help.

Over the more than thirty years I lived and worked in Zambia, there were dramatic changes. In Chipapa the forest has all but disappeared, felled for charcoal to feed the cooking stoves of Lusaka. Soil erosion and degraded soils followed and the area, when I left, was a shadow of its former pristine glory. Poor rains in recent years have made the situation worse, and a land that once fed its people and supported abundant wildlife is now too often home to hungry families, desperate for emergency food aid from the west.

But there is hope. Since I returned from Zambia to Devon, I have been involved with Harvest Help, who are working quietly and effec-

1 Interview with Rev Merfyn Temple by John Pritchard, 2006, Methodist Church Oral Archive project, British Library reference C640/146 tape 5 side B © Trustees for Methodist Church Purposes on behalf of the Methodist Church Oral Archive project.

tively with thousands of families to put an end to hunger and restore the land through sustainable use. I was personally thrilled when they began a project at Chipapa, but they work throughout Zambia and beyond.

The enclosed leaflet will tell you more about Harvest Help, but I am writing to launch an appeal they have been kind enough to call the Merfyn Temple Zambia Fund to mark my retirement. I hope you will feel able to join with me in continuing to support my beloved Zambian people through this fund.

In Chipapa now the trees are growing again, the fields are more fertile and the animals are coming back - there is hope!

Most sincerely yours, Merfyn Temple

PS: Please send all replies to Harvest Help. They have promised to keep me informed of the progress of the fund and I have promised my family that I really will retire!

News Release from Harvest Help
sowing the seeds of self-reliance in rural Africa
Wednesday May 24, 2006

Missionary's Retirement Fund Rakes In £5,000 For Africa Charity

A Methodist Minister who launched a special fund to mark his retirement from 50 years of active service has raised thousands of pounds to help poor Zambian families out of poverty.

Rev Merfyn Temple launched a fund with overseas development charity Harvest Help to continue his work in his beloved Zambia when he retired at the beginning of this year.

So far generous friends, family and colleagues have raised over £5,000 which will go towards projects run by Harvest Help in Zambia where Merfyn worked for many years.

Merfyn, who is 86 and now lives in Honiton, Devon, devoted much of his life to the people of Africa, where he served as a missionary minister for 31 years, travelling extensively on a bicycle and gaining the trust and love of many local people.

After returning to the UK, Merfyn continued his association with Africa.

In 1989, he travelled 3,000 miles from Nairobi in Kenya to the shores of Lake Kariba in Zambia on a mission to promote organic farming. In 2003 he travelled to Zimbabwe, to deliver a letter of protest to Robert Mugabe and was imprisoned and deported by the Zimbabwean regime for his stance.

He also worked on the Abingdon circuit in Oxfordshire serving Methodist churches in the area from 1976 to 1982, and on the Reading Circuit from 1983 to 2001. Rev Temple is now writing his autobiography charting the story of his fascinating life.

Harvest Help's Head of Fundraising Kevin Lawrence said: "We have been staggered by the generosity of Merfyn's friends from many parts of the country who have raised a fantastic sum to allow us to help even more families in Zambia out of poverty.

"The *Merfyn Temple Zambia Fund* is a testament to Merfyn's lifelong passion for Africa and the high regard in which he is held by many. It means his contribution to the world fight against poverty will long be recognised. We will use the money, in accordance with Merfyn's wishes, to develop, amongst other things, farmer training and tree planting in Zambia."

Part Four

Resurgam

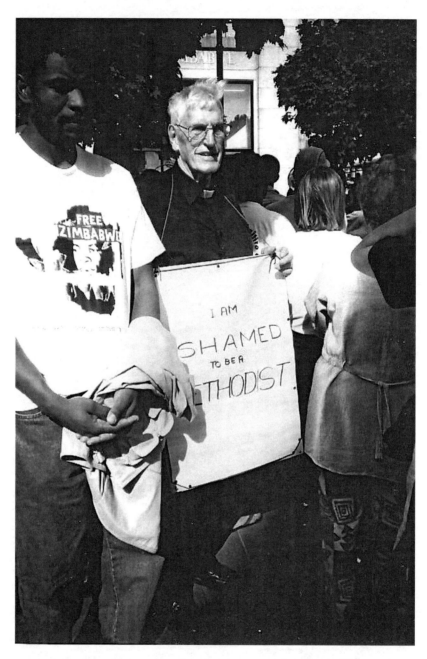

Protesting against the Mugabe regime, London 2004

A guest of Mr. Mugabe, 2003

ONE THURSDAY IN JULY 2003, in the Honiton Methodist Church for our weekly Bible study, I was having a dialogue with God about the worsening situation in Zimbabwe.[1] I was saying to God, "Why don't you do something about that man Mugabe who is a worse dictator than ever Hitler was?"

Then something rather surprising happened. God said, "I want you, Merfyn, to go and tell Mugabe yourself."

I began to make excuses such as, "This is not a British problem, it is an African problem. My friend Kenneth Kaunda should tell him. Anyway, where am I going to find the money? I am 83 years old. I daren't tell anyone here because they will try to stop me … "

Ten days later, I was on a plane to Harare.

We arrived on Saturday evening, and on Sunday I went to the big Methodist church in the High Street. In the vestry, I saw a wall plaque to my father-in-law the Rev. Douglas Gray, 1910-1912. I asked the preacher if I could have a word to the congregation at the end of the service. I stood in the pulpit and read the letter I was taking to the President:

Dear Mr Mugabe,
The sufferings of the people of Zimbabwe are an abomination in the sight of the Lord. I am praying that the British Government arrest you and charge you with crimes against humanity.
    Yours faithfully, Merfyn Temple.

---

1 Zimbabwe was suffering from declining living standards, rampant inflation, and forced expropriations of white-owned farms. The situation in 2012 shows little if any improvement. President Mugabe and his Zanu PF party remain in complete control.

I left all my possessions in the church, and carried only a small canvas shopping bag. It was quite a long walk and I saw nobody, as the streets were empty at that time of day. Finally I saw a European man and his African partner, so I asked the way.

"Keep going and on the right you will see the road leading up to State House." Then laughing, he went on, "But you won't get anywhere near it, it is surrounded by the army."

I walked a little further and saw another soldier who called out, "What are you doing? Come over here." When he asked me what I wanted, I said, holding out the letter in its white envelope,

"I want to give this letter to your President."

"Why didn't you post it?"

"Because when you post a letter you can never be sure it will arrive, so I thought I would deliver it by hand."

"You should have made an appointment. There are notices everywhere saying you should make an appointment."

"But I am also a busy man, and anyway I only want to deliver this letter."

There were now three soldiers surrounding me at bayonet point. One of them went off to find a senior officer. I was glad of the shade of the banana trees, as it was getting towards noon, which was the time I had written on my letter.

More senior police officers arrived in a Land-Rover. More discussions, more questions; then the security man said, "We would never deliver a letter like this to the President himself without opening it first to read it ourselves." Everyone crowded around as he ceremoniously unfolded it. He did not read it out loud, he just passed it round for all to see. It took time for the contents to sink in, then suddenly all hell was let loose as they shouted,

"Who do you think you are, delivering this letter to State House?"

"We don't want you here, white man."

"Go back to Blair!"

Perhaps one of the senior police officers saw that things might get out of hand. Within moments a police pickup truck arrived and I was bundled into the back and we drove off at high speed along a very bumpy road. There were two others in the back, a young man and a young woman. "She says I raped her," said the man, "but it is not true."

Zimbabwe cell ordeal fails to weaken retired Methodist minister's resolve

Protester, 83, vows to oppose Mugabe

LOUISE THOMAS

A WESTCOUNTRY minister will today take to the streets to publicise suffering in Zimbabwe after being imprisoned in squalor by Mugabe's regime.

In an exclusive interview with the WMN, retired Methodist minister Rev Merfyn Temple, described his imprisonment in an overcrowded, flea-ridden cell at Zimbabwe's central police station in the capital, Harare.

Mr Temple, who lives in Honiton, has spent 50 years of his life living in different African countries. He said that as he approached State House with a letter for the president, he was surrounded by Mugabe's armed militia but kept his nerve.

He said: "This was something I knew I had to do – I did not feel scared as I approached State House because I knew what I was doing was right and I knew I would be protected by my British

He was arrested and bundled into a six-man cell inhabited by 18 men where he was kept for nearly three days before being given access to a lawyer.

His family were oblivious to his arrest and the conditions in which he was being kept. Mr Temple said: "We had to sleep two to a bed and on the floor – when one turned we all had to turn, space was so tight."

© *West Country News, 20 August 2003*

"Oh, yes you did," said the woman.

None of us knew where we were going. I tried to sit on the spare tyre, but I kept being bumped off onto the floor. Finally we came to a group of houses somewhere in the bush. The security man got out of the front and disappeared. We just waited, wondering what was going to happen next. Finally he returned. More bumping over atrocious bush roads until finally we were on tarmac again for the long, smooth drive to Harare's Central Police Station.

The prison cell

With a policeman grasping my arm, I was marched into a room with 150 numbered kit bags hanging on the wall. One was allotted to me, number 137.

Into this I had to put my shoes and socks, my clerical collar and my watch. I was allowed to exchange my clerical black shirt for a grey pullover. The other things in the shopping bag were hung by the kit bag on the wall.

From an old exercise book they tore out a piece of paper the size of a large postage stamp on which was written my name and number. 'Temple' is a difficult word to pronounce in Shona so they called me Tembo. Someone had made a note that I should take my medicines every evening, so once a day I would go with my piece of paper downstairs to the 'locker' room and take my pills.

I found myself on the ground floor of a four-storey building, centred around an extensive courtyard about 80 yards square. They marched me up and down innumerable concrete stairs and along interminable corridors until we came to the Department of Law and Order.

I stood in front of a desk, at which sat a genial fellow in a cloth cap. On the wall were ten cup hooks, but only two carried police revolvers. There were four or five other policemen there and one policewoman. They seemed to spend most of the time chatting and drinking bottles of Coca-Cola, but they all carried notebooks and wrote down meticulously all my replies.

"What is your name? Spell it out please, slowly."

"Where do you live?"

"Honiton, Devon, UK."

"Why did you come here?"

"To deliver a letter to your President."

"Why didn't you post it?"

"Because it is always safer to deliver a letter by hand than to post it."

"Who sent you?"

"Nobody, I just came by myself."

"We don't believe you." They looked at my passport. "How can a man of 83 just get on a plane in UK and fly to Harare? Who paid you to come?"

"Nobody. I just bought the ticket myself."

"How did you get through immigration at the airport?"

"I had my visa and said I was a tourist on holiday in your beautiful country."

"But that was a lie. You should have shown them the letter."

The interrogation went on and on and my feet got colder and colder on the cement floors. The police, of course, all wore brown shoes. Finally they said that more senior officers would interrogate me the next day, and I was marched upstairs to my cell.

When I arrived at the barred gate of the cell I was met by a sea of black faces, all peering at me. The iron gate opened inwards, so the other inmates had to step back to let me in. The gate clanged shut and the warder, taking out a large bunch of keys, locked us in.

The cell was designed for six people. On either side were three bunks, each with a flimsy cotton mattress and a red cotton blanket. The first bunk started two feet from the ground, then two-foot spaces between the bunks and to the ceiling, which was truly filthy. It was covered with smears of blood where the inmates had squashed the bedbugs and the lice. Someone had found a piece of chalk and written graffiti over the blood stains, but it was all in Shona, so I could not understand the writing.

There were two concrete benches on either side, with room for three to sit during the day, as there was no room to sit on the bunks. In the corner by the door was a shit-hole. Long ago the lid had gone missing so someone had torn off the corner of a mattress to cover the hole, but that itself was soaked in foul-smelling urine. There was a brass tap from which we could drink, but sometimes the whole prison had no water.

We were eighteen men in the cell. The man nearest the door was a big man, as tall as myself, but stronger. He wore a khaki shirt and shorts and his head was as bald as a coot. He never smiled but with his eyes. Everyone recognized him as boss in the cell, and it was he who decided where we slept, two top-and-tail to a bunk and six on the floor. He seemed to take a shine to me, and just before we bedded down for the night he said, "I am a Roman Catholic and my name is Emmanuel."

"Good," I said, "that means 'God is with us' even in this shit-hole."

"Will you bless me, father?" he said.

"Of course," I replied, as he knelt down at my feet. "May the Lord bless you and keep you and make His face shine upon you and give you peace." For a moment I wondered whether a Roman Catholic priest would have said something different, but I doubt that God was too bothered.

Emmanuel said, "You can sleep next to me on the floor by the gate." I lay down beside him with another man as big as he on the other side of me.

We couldn't move unless we all moved. After a while I couldn't bear it so I said to Emmanuel, "It isn't working, is it? We are all too big for this tiny space."

A small man on the second bunk overheard our conversation, and without a word gave up his place to me, and lay down beside Emmanuel. My real problem was that I had no pillow for my head, but it seemed to be no problem for my African companions, who simply tucked their hands under their heads and slept. When the cell door was open during the day, air came in from the corridor, but at night when the door was closed, the only ventilation was through a tiny grille one foot square, high up in the corner above the top bunk.

The next day our jailer unlocked the cell door and we all trooped out into the corridor. Emmanuel signalled to me to stand beside him in the line, and I felt comforted by this small sign of his friendship. Back in the cell again, everyone seemed to be talking at once, in Shona of course, so I sat hunched up in one corner of the seat and waited to see what would happen next. Apart from the tiny shaft of light from the grill, our cell was lit night and day by a neon strip light in the ceiling above the barred gate, so since no one had a watch we never knew what time of day or night it was.

I heard a warder shouting above the sound of conversation "Tembo! Tembo!" The cell grew silent for a moment, and a warder came to unlock the gate. He was a tall thin man with an entirely expressionless face. He wore a cap on his head, which made him seem even taller, and he always carried a leather strap in his hand. I followed him downstairs to the charge office, and waited with six others on a wide concrete bench. We watched while the police brought in the people whom they had arrested during the night.

One man lay on the floor, crying out in pain. He was shouting and shouting something in Shona, which I did not understand, but after a while he crawled across the floor and sobbing, lifted himself beside me on the bench. I put my arm around his shoulder to comfort him but he brushed it off. Barefooted prisoners seemed to be coming and going all the time, and one quickly shoved a large bundle of notes into my hand. I had no idea what he was doing, but not wanting to incriminate myself, I shook my head and he went off to plant his Zim dollars somewhere else.

They brought in a man in handcuffs and made him squat down on the floor. They kept shouting at him and kicking his ankles. Finally they took off the handcuffs, twisting them ruthlessly as they did so. He came whimpering to sit beside me, rubbing his swollen arms. He told me he had been in handcuffs for three days. I never saw my warder beat anyone with his strap, but if he found a new prisoner in a leather jacket he would take him round the corner and the 'thwack', 'thwack' of his belt would reverberate along the corridors. Everyone would suddenly fall silent.

Interrogation

Another warder came and said "Tembo, follow me." Again we climbed up and down the stairs, and cut diagonally across the wide courtyard to the Department of Law and Order.

I was ushered into a small conference room. There was a plush blue carpet on the floor, and a long table which could seat about six people on either side. At the head of the table sat a policeman in full regalia. On either side of him were two other officers in smart mufti. They asked me to sit down on an upholstered chair at the end. They said they had been trained by the FBI in methods of interrogation, so we might as well be friends.

"Tell me about yourself, Mr Temple. Where do you live in the UK, and who are your friends?"

"I live in the small Devonshire town of Honiton."

"May we have your address please?"

"36 Orchard Way, Honiton, EX14 1 Hotel, Hotel."

They exchanged knowing glances, and I wondered what was significant for them about Honiton.

"Have you ever been to Africa before, especially Zimbabwe?"

"Oh yes. I lived in Zambia for 31 years from 1943 to 1974, and I sometimes visited Zimbabwe."

"Now please tell us exactly the dates and the places you visited."

"The first time was in 1946 when I came to Umtare, for my honeymoon. I am a member of the Methodist Church and during the next few years I used to attend our Inter-District Committee. Sometime in the nineties I went to Binga to visit Dr Peta Jones to talk about donkeys and - oh yes, in 1999 I came with my daughters to visit my granddaughter, who was teaching at a school near Bulawayo."

They faithfully wrote all this down in their bulky notebooks and then said, "How did you get from the airport into the town?"

"I met an African man on the plane, who said his wife was coming to meet him and he would give me a lift."

"What was his name?"

"I can't remember." This was true, because I can't remember anyone's name until I have heard it a dozen times or more.

"Where did he take you?"

"First to the Trinity Church to deliver 15 kilos of flour and then to a hotel."

"Which hotel?"

"I can't remember, but if you go to the Methodist Church where I left my suitcase which is unlocked you will find the receipt."

CAMPAIGNER AND RETIRED MINISTER FOLLOWS HIS CONSCIENCE

Merfyn is a martyr to causes

MAN WITH A MISSION: Methodist Minister Merfyn Temple spent much of his life in Africa

RETIRED Methodist minister Merfyn Temple knew the risks when he decided to try to personally deliver a letter to Zimbabwean president Robert Mugabe accusing him of crimes against humanity.

True to form, he was slung into a Zimbabwean police cell for three days.

But the 83-year-old, a missionary for much of his life, had not told his family about his courier duty and it was only when he was incarcerated that he realised no one would know where to find him. Instead of being at his Honiton home, he

PEACE campaigner Merfyn Temple is not afraid of confrontation and told **Anita Smith** his latest stand saw him infuriate Robert Mugabe

Real Lives

was with 17 other inmates in a filthy cell signed to accommodate six.

Merfyn is not afraid to stand up for causes he believes in. During the Falklands War he tried get a fishing boat to sail into the war zone.

© Express & Echo, 11 September 2003

"You may think you know a bit about Zambia and yet you know nothing at all except by hearsay about Zimbabwe. You talk in your letter to our President about 'the sufferings of the people of Zimbabwe . . .'; what are these 'sufferings' which you are so concerned about?"

"First, you have an inflation rate of about 300%, and ordinary people cannot even get enough bank notes to buy food. Second, three years ago Zimbabwe was a net exporter of food, today it is a net importer."

"Where do you get this information from?"

"Mostly from the Guardian newspaper."

They laughed. "Nobody here believes a word that is written in the Guardian. We know it is all rubbish. Who paid for your ticket? You say nobody sent you, it was all a personal matter. We just don't believe you. You expect us to believe that an old man of 83, who knows practically nothing about Zimbabwe, would walk out of his house in Honiton, go to Heathrow and catch a plane for Harare without telling anybody that you were coming, neither in the UK nor here? It is just too crazy for us to take seriously. You are a spy for Bush or Blair."

"Why do you think I am a spy?"

NO MATTER WHAT DANGERS AND INCONVENIENCE HE FACES

PROTEST: Merfyn Temple outside the Houses of Parliament calling for the arrest of Zimbabwe president Robert Mugabe

Though deciding while still in short trouse on mission work as a career, Merfyn did n become a devoted Christian until he was 19.

It was 1940 and Merfyn had gone to Trafalg Square in London calling for peace. It was on then that he started believing what he had bed taught during his very religious upbringing.

He said: "You know it all in your mind but un it's in your heart it makes no difference."

Merfyn trained for the ministry at Richmo College before sailing to Africa in 1943 to beg his missionary work.

By 1962, then married with children, he h met Kenneth Kaunda, leader of the Zambi United National Independence Party, and t came the first white man to join the party.

At the time, because of his views, he became social outcast to many Europeans and an e barrassment to some of his missionary c leagues.

After the independence of Zambia, Kaun appointed him secretary of the Land Settleme Board in 1966.

He chose to give up the comfortable house th had been provided for him in Lusaka to live in mud hut in the village of Chipapa 17 miles aw; and stayed there for five years.

He said: "You can't develop a country from tl air — you start on the ground with the people

About eight years ago he introduced donke after all the cattle died from a disease called Ea Coast Fever. The donkeys pull the ploughs ar are the main means of transport. He sai "Whenever people say what can I do for tl Africans, I tell them to give money for do keys."

In 1974, Merfyn returned to the UK, havii spent 31 years of his life in different Afric countries, and became minister of a church Abingdon, Oxfordshire.

He said: "It took me a year to come down earth and I had eight wonderful years until came to retire."

On retirement, Merfyn took off on a thre

He has also fasted on numerous occasions in protest against various issues and has set off for three months at a time on his bicycle in England and Africa on different missions.

He said: "I want to get people to recognise the real discrimination there is in Zimbabwe. But the general impression is that Britain doesn't care."

Being a Methodist minister is something that

They left China to return to England when Merfyn was three.

Later his father was appointed to St Mary's Methodist Church in Truro and it was there Merfyn met a great influence in his life, Douglas Gray, known as the the modern Livingstone of Africa. Later Mr Gray's daughter, Audrey, was to become Merfyn's wife.

Merfyn said: "Livingstone was mauled by a

"We have to believe you are 83 years old because your passport says you were born in 1919. But we believe nothing else. We think you are a spy for three reasons:

1. You are tall and you look like a retired brigadier.
2. Your arms are very brown so you must have spent many years in Africa.
3. When you gave us your coded address in Honiton you said Hotel, Hotel. That is the kind of language the army uses when it relays messages."

I didn't say anything but I wanted to burst out laughing.

"We have wasted a lot of time interrogating you and we find you increasingly provocative. You had better go back to your cell and we shall see you again tomorrow." They never did.

At midday and in the evening, relatives were allowed to come to the prison gates to pass food through the bars to their relatives inside. Some cell doors were open, and it was a kind of communal hour when you could wander about a bit. I went along to the cell next to ours, which also had eighteen to twenty people in it. They called me over and asked what my charge was. There was no warder about so I said,

205

"No one has told me what I am being charged with but I guess it is because I said something which Mr Mugabe didn't like to hear."

"What did you say?"

"I tried to deliver a letter to State House which said the people of Zimbabwe are suffering and I think the British Government should arrest him and charge him with crimes against humanity."

It took time for my words to sink in. Somebody said, "There is an MP on the top bunk." He waved to me and everyone was grinning.

I said "I think Mugabe is shit."

They laughed and stretched out their hands through the bars for me to shake, but I saw a warder coming, so I skedaddled.

Once, when walking behind a warder along an endless corridor, I asked him if he liked his job in the police force.

"Yes."

"How much do you get paid?"

"Enough," he answered smugly.

The lawyer

Someone, I think it was Emmanuel, said if you don't get a lawyer quickly you don't stand a chance. The next time a warder passed our cell gate I asked him to arrange for me to have a lawyer. He said he would do so. Some time later, how long I do not know, Emmanuel said that the warder had gone off duty. For some reason the cell gate was unlocked so I went downstairs to find another warder. He was chasing a couple of prisoners down the corridor back to their cell. I said to him very politely,

"Please will you get me a lawyer and let me see you write it down in your book."

"You don't need to see a lawyer."

"But I do."

He took no notice, so I shouted, "I want to see a lawyer! I want to see a lawyer! I want—"

"Shut up!" he said. "You are being provocative. If you are not careful I'll start hassling you." I guessed he might be serious, so I joined the two other prisoners and we fled in panic up the stairs to our cell.

I sat panting on the edge of the bunk while the warder locked the gate. I said to myself, *You are in a right pickle now, Merfyn. No one knows you are*

*here, no one has been to visit you or brought you any food, and no one has told you
what you are being charged with. You don't know what to do.*

A warder unlocked the gate and said that all the prisoners were to go
up to the fourth floor for their daily food, which was a lump of maize porridge and a spoonful of beans. Although I had eaten nothing since breakfast in the hotel the previous day, I didn't feel hungry, so thought I would
add a bit of fasting as a protest.

When the other prisoners returned, they could not understand why I
had not taken food with them. I explained that it was not that I didn't like
maize meal and beans, but unlike many of them who seldom have enough
to eat, I came from an affluent world, where there is always plenty of food
for three meals a day and no problem about money to buy it. I needed to
lose some weight, so they need not worry that I was going to fade away
and die.

Suddenly I heard the man with the strap shouting "Tembo! Tembo!"
He led me over to the Law and Order Office, and there was a young black
woman from a private local law office called Susan, who began to take
down my details. I said to her, "Please, I want two things. First that you
get in touch with my family; my daughter's phone number is in the suitcase which I have left in Trinity Church. Second, please find out what is
the charge against me." I then dictated from memory the exact words of
my letter to Mr Mugabe.

She had with her a document which contained legislation passed only last
year, making it an offence to speak disrespectfully of the Head of State.

She said "If you plead guilty, and undoubtedly you are, they will make
you pay a large fine or put you in gaol."

I said I would plead not guilty, because I wanted my lawyer to say in
court exactly what are "the sufferings of the people of Zimbabwe" under
the dictatorship of Mr Mugabe.

Before we went to sleep that night Emmanuel asked me to bless him
and all the others in our cell. Everyone knelt down, because in Zimbabwe
everyone is either a Roman Catholic, a Protestant, or one of the 'also
rans.' I said "Shall we all say the Lord's Prayer in or own language: English, or Shona, or Sindebele or Liberian." I said it in Zambian Chi-Tonga,
which they enjoyed.

That night I was thinking about the Lord's Prayer, which we had just
prayed together. Had we prayed it only by rote, or had it expressed some

sense of the comradeship we shared together? We had asked God to forgive us our sins but had we forgiven Mugabe for what he was doing to
us? I think I was not clear in my own mind about the difference between
forgiveness and justice.

Second interrogation

I was called for another interrogation, this time by a group of police officers who crowded round the table where I was sitting. One I remember
in particular, for he towered menacingly over me. They began to ask the
same old question over and over again.

I said, "Gentlemen, I am sick and tired of your questions. In future
I shall answer nothing except in the presence of my lawyer." I held my
finger to my lips and shook my head each time a question was asked. This
seemed to infuriate them.

The big man said, "Here we know how to get our questions answered."
I continued to hold my finger to my lips and shake my head.

"Do I have to say it again? In this prison we have methods of getting
people to talk."

"Well, you'd better have a go," I said, calling his bluff. They took me
back to my cell.

That evening I went downstairs to get my medicines, but when I asked
for a cup of water to swallow my pills, I was told that all the water in the
prison had been cut off. I happened to be with Papi, my Liberian friend,
who had come down to the prison gate to get some food from a friend.
He saw I was upset and said "Don't worry, Tembo, I'll get you some spring
water. Just wait."

Within twenty minutes he was back with a half-litre bottle of spring
water. I think he must have asked his friend who came to bring him food
to get it for me from a shop. The mains tap water did not come back until
about 10 am the next day. How I treasured that sweet spring water!

As we prepared for bed that night, the hum of conversation through
the prison died down and a wonderful thing happened. In the cell next
door they began to sing. First the cantor, then the deep rich voices of the
men. Cell by cell they joined in and then from far away, from the corridor
upstairs, came the sound of women's voices taking up the refrain. When
they sang all the men stopped singing. For a moment it was like being
with the shepherds on the hills above Bethlehem.

The next day, all the cell gates were opened and we trooped upstairs to the big Assembly Room. Down two sides, high up on the wall, were about thirty narrow spaces like arrow slits in a castle wall, through which the sun streamed, making a bright pattern on the concrete floor. Most men stood or sat with their backs to the wall. The only furniture was two upright, very rickety, dining room chairs. Papi was sitting on one of them, and when he saw me come in, he offered me his seat. It was indeed a flimsy perch but better than the floor. Suddenly it collapsed and I was spread-eagled on the concrete. No one laughed, but there was a chorus of voices saying "Sorry, Tembo, sorry."

A warder told us all to stand to attention, because the Senior Police Officer, the Chief Superintendent, would speak to us. Of course he spoke in Shona and I had not the faintest idea what he said. But Emmanuel said it was the day when the judges would be sitting. No one was allowed paper or pen, but he had scribbled a telephone number on the flap of a cigarette packet. He said "Tembo, I know you don't have any money, but I need to pay a lawyer, so when you get out please send something to this number."

The release

We all sat in the cell waiting for a warder to call our names. Everyone else was talking but I heard a voice say "We shall miss you, Tembo". That gave me a warm feeling, as I sat waiting to be called. Everyone knew, except me, that I would never come back. They repeatedly told me that I would be OK.

I was wondering how my lawyer was getting on with the preparation of my case. She had said that when the judge asked why I had come to Zimbabwe, I should simply say that I had come to deliver a letter to the President, because I was concerned for the sufferings of the people. Then it would be her turn to describe those sufferings. I expected them to put me back in a regular gaol.

Above the chatter we heard the warder shout "Tembo! Tembo!". Everyone in the cell stopped talking but they were looking at me with smiling eyes. They nodded. The man with the strap arrived and, after going through his keys one by one, opened the gate and led me up and down stairs to the Department of Law and Order.

Two people were standing by the prosecutors' desk. One was Susan, my lawyer, and the other was a white man. The only other white man I had seen since my arrival was the man I had spoken to on my way to State

My fight for Zimbabwe

● **CRUSADER:** Retired Methodist minister Merfyn Temple, who has published a book telling of the excesses of Robert Mugabe's Zimbabwe

House. At first I did not recognize him, but gradually the truth dawned. It was Bob, an old Zimbabwean friend from long ago, and he had brought me a bag of food, which his wife Beryl had prepared for me. While Susan talked with the prosecuting officer, I asked Bob how he had found me.

He said, "Beryl and I had no idea that you had come to Zimbabwe!" —of course I had not told them, lest they be accused of supporting me. "However, on Monday evening your daughter, Patricia, phoned me to say that she had heard nothing from you since you called her on Saturday from the Bronte Hotel, telling her that you would be attending the morning service at Trinity Methodist Church." (I had asked the presiding bishop to call her but he had not done so).

"I immediately rang the Church, but was told that the presiding bishop had gone to a funeral in the south of the country, and a white man was seen to be accompanying him. That put me off the scent. However, later Patricia rang again to say she thought you were in prison, so I made further enquiries and heard that you were in custody in the Central Prison.

"What I cannot understand is that 300 people in the church on Sunday morning knew that you had gone to State House, taking the letter which you had read from the pulpit. But it appears that no one came to visit you, no one brought you any food, and no attempt was made to get you a lawyer. I didn't know you had a lawyer until I met her just now. Anyway, have some food."

"Sorry, Bob, I have vowed not to eat anything until I know the final result of my case."

At that moment Susan came over, and said they had withdrawn the case and decided to deport me. I would be charged under a 'miscellaneous law' and the fine would be US$5,000. Why I was deported I still don't know.

"OK," said Bob, "you can eat your food now." I know from long experience that you have to be careful when you are breaking a fast. The very best thing is a few spoonfuls of honey. I found in Beryl's bag two bananas, two oranges, half a bar of chocolate, and some peanut butter and Marmite sandwiches. I ate the bananas and oranges and gave the rest to the warder, who reluctantly gave me back my shoes.

Somehow Bob and Susan and the tired immigration official got my ticket changed from Thursday to Wednesday. It seemed to take hours, rushing up and down stairs, from corridor to corridor, signing innumerable forms, before I finally emerged through the prison gates.

We only had an hour to spare, so Bob went to the airport to try and hold the plane until I arrived. Fortunately, Susan had come with a male colleague who had a reasonably fast car. He drove it at breakneck speed and arrived as they made the last call for my flight.

When I got to the desk they said that my ticket from Johannesburg to Heathrow was OK but I would have to pay for the flight from Harare to South Africa. Of course, since Mugabe's government was deporting me, they should have paid, but by this time, with the prospect of freedom five minutes away, I took out my own credit card and paid up the £170. Mr Mugabe will have to whistle for his fine of $5,000.

Before and After

I KNEW THAT MY ATTEMPT to change Mugabe had failed. No amount of pressure from the world outside, nor from inside Africa, would halt this murderer in his tracks. Only the people of Zimbabwe can do that. This man with monstrous arrogance has bullied and cowed them into submission, and now he stands like some stupid rooster, crowing on his miserable little anthill. When he has gone, and the clamour and the shouting dies, the people of Zimbabwe will have to face the two greatest issues of our time: How will they begin once again to use their land, and how will they deal with the terrible devastation of HIV/AIDS?

Long gone are the days when I could put my hand to the donkey plough or show village people how to make their own compost. Nor can I sit at the bedside of a young girl dying of AIDS, but there is one thing I can do. I can point them to Zambia where in small ways these things are happening.

I will ask them to take this story of mine, and read how forty years ago I went to live in Chipapa and made all the mistakes in the book. But some things I did get right. When all their cattle died from corridor disease[2], I went to Pocklington near York where they raised enough money to buy twenty donkeys, and the time came when an African organisation called OPAD (Organisation for Promotion of Meaningful Development Through Active Participation) was set up to teach the people to use their land properly.

I have before me OPAD's report for 2007. A few extracts give a flavour of what is happening there now:

---

2 An acute and usually fatal disease of cattle, transmitted by a tick that usually lives on buffalo. Hence its other name, buffalo disease.

1. **Farmers.** Around 467 farmers were trained in various sustainable techniques.
2. **Donkeys.** Around 20 farmers have access to donkeys for draught power. One farmer has this season ploughed 20 fields for 20 clients.
3. **HIV/AIDS.** The members of the Shimababa HIV/AIDS Club have been meeting together for the last year. OPAD has trained the group in sustainable agricultural techniques, and they have already established a demonstration plot and hope to farm all the year round, irrigation permitting. One of the members of the Club said recently, "If anyone had seen us last year, they would not believe where we are now. We are coming back to health. It is good to be able to share our experience openly with people who understand what we are going through. We support and advise each other and help sort out other problems. We talk to others outside the group to try and curb the spread of HIV/AIDS.[3]

One of the most important people in the development of the village of Chipapa was James Sinyangwe, who worked for OPAD. He rented a house in the township of Kafue for his wife and three children who were all at school, and he himself commuted back and forth to Chipapa on his motorcycle. When the plot of land on which he lived came up for sale, I offered to help him buy it. A year later he died. His daughter Mwanga was in her last year at the secondary school, so I asked my friends to help with the school fees. She wanted to become a doctor.

I am told that there are 300 orphans in the little town of Kafue, and not one of them will be in the position to help Zambia through the dark years ahead unless they receive a good education.

In 2007 we were able to raise enough money to send ten boys, for three years, to the single-sex Kafue Secondary School. All the money has been contributed by pensioners who "out of her poverty, put in everything—all she had to live on," as Jesus said of the widow and her mite.

If we have sent ten boys to the Kafue Secondary School, what do we do about the girls? A beginning has been made. My wife Audrey said to me one day, "When I die, I want my money to go to the girls."

I thought, "That's rather odd. Yes, we do have our three girls but we also have a son. Why has she forgotten him?" However I didn't give the matter much thought, for apart from the £10 a month which we invest in our funeral insurance, we had little money.

---

3 OPAD has been the local partner with Self Help Africa, working in Chipapa.

I was aware that the cost of burial goes up annually, so thought I might be able to save on the funeral expenses by making our own coffins. I read in a book called *Before and After* that this was a possibility for anyone with a modicum of carpentry skills. I decided I would make our own coffins, so I went to see my friend Brian who keeps the local DIY shop.

"Of course," said Brian. He would be only too happy, given the right measurements, to cut the chipboard to size.

Halfway through the construction, someone suggested to me that I might like to lie down in the coffin as a sort of try-out. It was much too small; I had made a cock-up of the measurements. Undeterred, I went up to the Care Home to share my story with Audrey.

"No problem," she said. "It will do for me. I'm only 5ft 6ins and shrinking all the time."

Knowing it was for her, I put in even greater effort, planing it, sanding it and rubbing it down with wire wool. Then having stained and varnished it, I bought a set of stencils and covered the whole coffin with red and white roses.

Later on, one of my three daughters when visiting her mother, asked her, "What did you mean when you said you wanted your money to go to the girls?"

She said, "I didn't mean you and your two sisters. You all have good husbands to look after you. I meant the orphaned girls at Chipembi in the school which my father started back in 1920, the year I was born."

When my daughter told me this, I went back to my bench. This time I did not go down to my friend Brian in the DIY shop. I had an even better thought: I would make my own coffin from scrap. In the main street I found a skip full of discarded timber, including two pallets.

"Forget the idea of a coffin," I said. "My little book *Before and After* tells me that all I need is a bier on which to lay my body down, and of course six good handles which I will make from sash cord and bamboo. I will ask the family to take that glorious cotton cloth, all red, green and yellow, emblazoned with a big golden cross, which was given to me by the United Church of Zambia. When my last remains disappear into the ground and everyone has said their final goodbye, they will think it is the end. But I shall know that the money saved from Audrey's coffin and from my bier will be enough to pay the school fees for one orphaned Chipembi girl for three years. What joy such a legacy will give."

A Peace Pole in Honiton?

From: maryjane ciitheroe
Subject: Peace Poles

Dear Pa
Below is the information about Peace Poles from the Internet. Hope it is what you wanted.
Love and hugs
Jane

Peace Poles around the world

The Peace Pole Project is the official Project of The World Peace Prayer Society. It started in Japan in 1955 by Masahisa Goi, who decided to dedicate his life to spreading the message, "May Peace Prevail on Earth" in response to the bombings on Hiroshima and Nagasaki. Peace Poles are handcrafted monuments erected the world over as international symbols of Peace. Their purpose is to spread the message "May Peace Prevail on Earth" in the languages of the world.

Peace Poles can be found in town squares, city halls, schools, places of

How about a Peace Day?

NOW that we have had Armed Forces Day, what about a Peace Day, since this is what all who serve fight for, including the West Country's late, great Harry Patch, the last fighting Tommy?

And, since we have a war memorial, could we also have a peace memorial, like thousands of other towns around the world?

This could take the form of a peace pole or a Hiroshima cherry tree.

© *Midweek Herald, 7 July 2010*

worship, parks, and gardens - any place where the spirit of Peace is embraced by people of good will. Since the beginning of the project over 200,000 Peace Poles have been planted in over 200 countries around the world.

Some of the extraordinary locations include the Pyramids of El Giza in Egypt, the Magnetic North Pole in Canada, Gorky Park in Russia, and Angkor Wat in Cambodia. They are promoting healing of conflict in places like Sarajevo, the Atomic Bomb Dome in Hiroshima, and the Allenby Bridge on the border between Israel and Jordan.

Mayors in many parts of the world have planted Peace Poles to dedicate their cities and towns to world peace. Both political leaders, such as former U.S. President Jimmy Carter, and religious leaders, such as Pope John Paul II, Mother Teresa and the Dalai Lama, have dedicated Peace Poles.

Midweek Herald

Wednesday, October 6, 2010   *Honiton & District's best-read newspaper*   20p where sold   *Jicreg 01/01/09

Town to send out world-wide peace message

A WORLD-WIDE message of peace will be proclaimed at Honiton later this month in languages from around the globe.

As part of the town's first United Nations Day celebrations on Sunday, October 24, organisers will also be putting up a special Peace Pole.

Urging people to "let peace prevail" it will be planted at the entrance to the Baptist Church in the High Street at 1pm.

Afterwards the words of the Peace Prayer will be spoken in as many languages as possible, including English, French, German, Hebrew, Arabic, Polish and Cameroon. Participants are invited to take along a picnic to share in the church after the ceremony.

The event is being organised by retired Methodist Minister Merfyn Temple – a long time peace campaigner, now in his nineties.

My speech on United Nations Day, 24 October 2010, on the planting of the Peace Pole in Honiton

"Why are people across the world planting Peace Poles? Because people of all faiths realise that our world above all, needs peace.

"Today we shall do three things:

1. Plant this Peace Pole which symbolises our shared belief that 'prayer changes things'.

2. Say together the Prayer for Peace.

3. Hear this Universal Prayer for Peace said in Arabic, Hebrew, Welsh, Cameroon, French etc.

> LEAD ME FROM DEATH TO LIFE,
> FROM FALSEHOOD TO TRUTH.
>
> LEAD ME FROM DESPAIR TO HOPE,
> FROM FEAR TO TRUST.
>
> LEAD ME FROM HATE TO LOVE,
> FROM WAR TO PEACE.
>
> LET PEACE FILL OUR HEART,
> OUR WORLD, OUR UNIVERSE.
>
> PEACE · PEACE · PEACE

We end with the words of Hans Kung:

Campaigners peace pole on UN day

3y BEN MIDDLETON
en@findlenews.co.uk

PEACE campaigners in Honiton have celebrated United Nations Day by putting up a peace pole in the town.

United Nations Day was held on Sunday, October 24th, and marks the formation of the United Nations Charter.

Retired methodist minister Merfyn Temple was the man behind the Honiton celebrations and speaking to *Palman's View* he said: "There are thousands of Peace Poles throughout the world but to my knowledge this is the only one in the westcountry. People need to be able to work for peace — at a very basic level to be able to recognise and greet one another in the streets and market places of the world.

"What we have done is a small step but a significant one for world peace."

The event was held at Honiton Baptist Church and more than 60 people attended including Noel Harrower, the chair of the Exeter and District branch of the United Nations Association.

♦ PEACE campaigners in Honiton have erected a Peace Pole in the town

© *Midweek Herald, 31 October 2010*

"There can be no peace between the nations until there is peace between religions. There can be no peace between religions until they dialogue together."

I want to add a third sentence:

"Let us now go into this church and share a meal together."

This event was organised by the Reverend Merfyn Temple, a 90-year-old retired Methodist minister, Ben Drury, Honiton Baptist minister, and other peace sympathisers.

It has already had an impact because members of the Bahá'í Faith, some of whose members are imprisoned for preaching their Faith in Iran, have been heartened by our gathering. Buddhists replied that they would have come, but they also have ceremonies to attend.

2 November 2010
Midweek Herald, Sidmouth.

Dear Sir,

I wanted to share the feeling of joy and excitement I came home with, having attended the Peace Prayer Ceremony at Honiton Baptist Church.

There were between 25 to 30 of us gathered around the Peace Pole, the first of its kind to be 'planted' in the South West (although these very simple white posts bearing the words May Peace Prevail On Earth have become a very popular and prominent international symbol for peace around the world). The church very graciously agreed to have this monument positioned in their grounds as part of a short and very  moving ceremony instigated by retired Methodist minister Rev. Merfyn Temple aged 90, and inspired by his deep belief in the ability of prayer to bring about change.

We began by reciting together The International Peace Prayer on Merfyn's count of three! We then had the privilege of hearing the prayer spoken in several languages including Arabic, Hebrew, Welsh and Cameroon.

It was clear that several of the faiths besides Christian were represented and the mood matched the weather, glorious and uplifting. I had the sense of some kind of new beginning and the words "great oaks from little acorns" popped into my head as we began to speak together.

We were then warmly welcomed into the church for a "bring and share" picnic lunch and had the opportunity to exchange our beliefs, experiences and visions for a common ground and fellowship between people from different faith traditions and beyond them. I had such a strong sense of willingness, open-mindedness and generosity of spirit, right here in Honiton.

Here's hoping and praying that this delightful and simple ceremony will become an annual event, and that other equally effective and heart-opening initiatives will follow.

Very best wishes,

Trudi Farmer. Interfaith Minister.

Controversy prompts removal of peace pole

PEACE pole outside Honiton aptist Church has been taken own amid fears about what it ally stands for.

The pole was taken down after everend Ben Bendrey from Honiton aptist Church received complaints om members of the community ver what the pole symbolised.

He said: "The pole was taken down ecause it was not actually what it as meant to be and we had a lot of omplaints about it.

"We did, basically, think it was illing for peace in the world but, om what we have been told, it is ot and is for peace in all religions id all roads lead to one god.

"We are not against peace – it is hat the pole stands for. We thought was for peace that's what we all ant, but it has given us a battle."

"It has caused a lot of problems with people in the church and people in the town have complained. In the end we just took it down.

"People felt it was not Christian at all and felt it should not be on Christian grounds."

In the past, the church has been targeted by vandals and it was feared further damage could be caused.

Reverend Bendrey said he was surprised at the reaction the peace pole has sparked.

He added: "I didn't think it would cause that reaction at all. It surprised us."

The pole was planted in celebration of the United Nations Day on Sunday, October 24.

During the celebration, the universal prayer was spoken in six languages, including Arabic, Hebrew, English, Welsh, Spanish and Batonga.

Reverend Mervyn Temple, who was a key figure in the planting of the pole, said: "Its subsequen removal and disappearance has come as something of a shock to those of us involved in arranging this event.

"A public commitment to dialogue harmony and peace has been arbi trarily and anonymously denied.

"Those of us who attended the say ing of the Prayer for Peace and the planting of the Peace Pole are work ing out how we can respond.

"It is my own view that in a spirit of peaceful dialogue it would be good to arrange an open meeting so that those who removed the Peace Pole can publicly express their views, together with those who had been hoping to see the saying the Prayer for Peace become an annual event."

The church is currently investigating putting something else in its place and relocating the peace pole.

© *Midweek Herald, 10 November 2010*

From: "Merfyn Temple"
To: "Trudi Farmer"
Sent: 04 November 2010
Subject: Re: removal of Peace Pole

Hi Trudi,

Merfyn is quite excited! The Pole has been taken down by the Baptist Church following considerable opposition from its members (threats of resignation), so the story and opportunity for discussion seems to be growing! He will keep you informed!

I look forward to meeting you again. What a wonderful letter you wrote about the ceremony.

Many blessings to you, Debbie
Merfyn's 'secretary'

From: "H SIMPSON"
To: "Merfyn Temple"
Subject: Peace Pole

The Honiton Peace Pole has been returned to its High Street location at Honiton Baptist Church. The Pole was removed after being ceremonially 'planted' to mark United Nations Day October 24th by a group of local Christian ministers and peace groups.

A number of elders of the Chapel objected to the messages of peace in different languages. Appeals went out to restore the pole from the Rev Merfyn Temple who made it and Pensioners for Peace representative Tony Simpson who wrote to the press appealing for the restoration of the Pole. He said:

"The return of the pole appears to be a triumph of Christian conscience and common sense in the interests of peace. Our High Street now has a War Memorial and a Peace Pole; both bearing witness to the age we live in. Thanks to all concerned."

From: "Merfyn Temple"
To: "H SIMPSON"
Subject: Peace Pole

I was delighted to hear that the Peace Pole has now been returned to its place on the lawn outside the Baptist Church in Honiton. Whoever moved it has had second thoughts. We can work together to ensure that Peace may prevail in this town and throughout the world.

From: "H SIMPSON"
To: "Merfyn Temple"
Subject: Peace Pole

Dear Merfyn,
Thank you and so good to hear you are not defeated by this strange business. I think you know my views but to clarify. Yes we must go forward and assert the primacy of peace and dialogue. But we must know what has happened here and challenge it. If there is misunderstanding, prejudice, religious bigotry or another agenda we cannot let this pass, or we will be faced with it again - be sure.

When I was at Auschwitz last year I wrote down a statement on a hut: 'Those who do not learn from history are destined to repeat it'

Peace and health, Tony

8 November 2010

Dear Ben and Marie,

I have been asked by those who attended the ceremony on United Nations Day to write to thank you for the hospitality of your church on that day. This was truly Faith in Action!

Here are some of the comments I received after the event:

1. Trish in Alexandria, Virginia, USA

    "What an exciting and significant event . . . it was great to meet some of your good friends such as Dermod Knox of the Bahá'is"

2. Trudi Farmer, Upottery

    "We were warmly welcomed into the church for a 'bring and share' picnic lunch . . . I had such a strong sense of willingness, open-mindedness and generosity of spirit, right here in Honiton . . ."

3. Grandson, Exeter

    "You are a true inspiration. Like a good cheese you get better with age!"

    With many thanks to you all
    Merfyn

Epilogue

All Saints Church, Abingdon
February 2011

Dear Merfyn

I have been passed a request from you for information about the current position of work on the Peachcroft estate in Abingdon which I understand you were very involved in instigating. The work is continuing well and has been given a considerable boost in the last three years by the opening of a large extension to the original premises.

Regards, Peter Bennett

Lusaka Province: Zambia

This project in Chipapa, Lusaka Province, aims to improve the lives of 7,200 poor rural people in the area.

We are working to increase household food production in the following ways:

- Establishing local farmers' clubs so that more families will be able to practice sustainable farming techniques, leading to improved crop yields.
- Running behavioural change workshops looking at the miscon-ceptions surrounding the spead and 'cures' for AIDS. The aim is to make people more aware of HIV/AIDS and more able to cope with its impact.
- Training HIV/AIDS community volunteers to provide information to local people about HIV/AIDS prevention and home-based care.
- Improving community care for HIV/AIDS patients.

Our partner organisation in Chipapa is OPAD (Organisation for Promotion of Meaningful Development Through Active Participation). An important part of Self Help Africa's work involves establishing durable community structures. We are working to strengthen the organisational capacity of both OPAD and the local community.[4]

---

4 From the website of Self Help Africa, http://www.selfhelpafrica.org/selfhelp/main/PR-ZAM-lusaka.asp. Funding ceased in 2008 but the work continues locally.
Self Help Africa was formed from a merger of Harvest Help and the Irish NGO Self Help Development International.

Kenneth Kaunda pays respects at Merfyn's graveside,
January 2012

Death of Merfyn Temple at 92 (© Midweek Herald)

Tributes have been paid to retired Methodist minister Merfyn Temple, described as an inspirational member of the community and someone who was never afraid to stand up for what he believed in.

Reverend Temple died in his sleep at Abbeyfield's Hill House care home, Combe Raleigh, near Honiton on Thursday, January 12, following a stroke. He was 92.

During his life, Mr Temple demonstrated a passion for issues of fairness and justice, and played a significant role as a missionary in Zambia for 30 years. He completed an epic cycle across Africa and was featured in a 1950s film about his work in Zambia, where he was affectionately known as Muluti Tempulu.

He was an outspoken critic of dictator Robert Mugabe and was jailed by the tyrant in 2005 after he openly criticised his leadership.

Mr Temple was instrumental in the erection of an international peace pole outside of Honiton Baptist Church, where floral tributes have been gathering.

Mr Temple was the first vice chairman of the Senior Council for Honiton, whose members are saddened by the news of his death.

Tony Simpson and Tony Smith, speaking on behalf of the senior council, said: "Merfyn was a distinguished member of the senior council. He believed in the dignity and worth of each member, but also believed we gained strength from working together for the common good.

"He was passionate about issues of fairness and justice for older people and for our community. He was not afraid to stand up and be counted for what he believed."

The Merfyn Temple Foundation

OUR GRANDPA was an extraordinary man. He was a man of new ideas, tolerance and action, a tireless worker for change, a giant throughout our childhoods who made adventures from generosity and belief. From Zambian independence, to organic farming, interfaith dialogue and rural enterprise, Grandpa cared passionately about making a difference.

Our families, communities, countries and global population face challenges today that didn't exist when Grandpa was born. The Merfyn Temple Foundation has been set up to support a new generation who believe they can change things for the better.

The Foundation will be run as a social enterprise, because Grandpa was a social entrepreneur at a time when the term had not even been invented! He believed in helping people to help themselves, in making a difference that was sustainable, and in doing it in a way that didn't exploit or destroy the world we live in.

We aim to provide seed capital, micro-finance and match funding for young social entrepreneurs who come to us with projects that reflect the spirit and the values of Merfyn:

- Empowering people to have courage and stand up for social justice and peace

- Helping people to help themselves: sustainable change

- Uniting people based on shared humanity: communities, faiths, ethnicities

All the proceeds from this book will go to the Merfyn Temple Foundation. If you would like to support the Foundation's work, please make cheques payable to the **Merfyn Temple Foundation** and send to:

Jonathan Clitheroe
The Merfyn Temple Foundation
Devonport Guildhall
Ker Street, Plymouth PL1 4EL

email: themerfyntemplefoundation@gmx.com

Nicholas, Jonathan, Abi, Rachel
November 2012

Chronology

1919   Born 7 November in Wimbledon, the second of four sons. Travels with mother to China to join missionary father.

1926   Father appointed Methodist minister in Truro, Cornwall. His friend Douglas Gray comes on deputation, and inspires Merfyn with the missionary vocation.

1932-36   Attends The Leys School, Cambridge.

1934   Father appointed General Secretary, British and Foreign Bible Society. Home in Bickley, then Beckenham, Kent.

1938-40   Methodist theological training at Richmond College.

1942   School of Oriental and African Studies. Appointed probationer, Lewisham and Catford Circuits.

1943   October: Sails for Africa. Appointed probationer, Broken Hill Circuit, Northern Rhodesia.

1944   To Kafue Training Institute for language study. First meeting with school boy Gideon Muyangana.

1945   Appointed probationer in Nambala Circuit, an area about the size of Yorkshire, 100 miles northwest of Lusaka. Starts Rural Training Centre for young boys, teaching farming, building and carpentry..

1946   Marries Audrey, daughter of Douglas Gray, and a qualified doctor.

Children:

Ruth Noel born 29 December 1946

Mary Jane 7 June 1949

Robin Gray 19 March 1951

Patricia Margaret 8 October 1952

1947   Appointed superintendent minister of the Nambala and Keembe Circuits.

1955	Leaves Nambala for the sake of the family.
1957	Works for the United Society for Christian Literature.
1958	Moves to Lusaka. Joins Kenneth Kaunda in United National Independence Party. Publishes *Black Government?* and Kenneth Kaunda's autobiography *Zambia Shall be Free*. Threatened with arrest by the authorities.
1962	Stands for election as a U.N.I.P. candidate for Luanshya
1963	After resigning from U.S.C.L., appointed by Kaunda as Deputy Director of the Zambia Youth Service
1964	Northern Rhodesia gains Independence as Zambia, with Kaunda as President.
1965	Appointed by Kaunda to the Land Resettlement Board.
1966	Audrey and family return to UK.
1967	Moves to Chipapa village, 17 miles from Lusaka.
1967	Appointed as Director of Village Development for all Zambia and a lecturer of the staff of the National Institute of Public Administration.
1968	Invited to U.K. by Christian Aid for the World Poverty Campaign. Fasts in Westminster Abbey in protest against the riches of the church in a hungry world. Chairman of The Haslemere Group, which publishes the Haslemere Declaration, an important milestone in the campaign against global poverty and injustice.
1969	Fasts on behalf of the tomato growers of Chipapa, in protest against local government's failure to repair the Chipapa road.
1972	Lecturer in Zambian Christian Humanism at National Institute of Public Administration, Lusaka. National organizer, Village and Ward Development Committees.
1974	Leaves Zambia and returns to UK.
1975-6	'Tent-making' ministry: milk round and allotment in Oxford.

1976	Part-time at Grubb Institute, London, and at All Saints Methodist Church, Abingdon
1977	Tours China with Society for Ango-Chinese Understanding. Appointed full-time to All Saints.
1980	Visits Zambia for the Credit Union Anniversary.
1982	Visits South America during the Falklands War. Publishes *Angelus for Peace in the South Atlantic*.
1983	CCND protests and arrest. Pilgrimage for Peace plan takes shape.
April-June 1984	Pilgrimage for Peace round England by bicycle, saying the Universal Prayer for Peace, calling all faiths to pray for peace at mid-day at each stop on the route.
1985-93	Merfyn and Audrey cultivate an organic market garden at Garlands Farm, Upper Basildon, Berks.
1989	Travels by bicycle from Nairobi to Zambia, to advocate the importance of organic farming. The bicycle is abandoned in the remote Gwembe valley.
1992-2000	Visits Zambia each year to encourage his friends and continue promoting the organic revolution.
2000	Moves to Honiton, Devon.
2003	Visits Zimbabwe and is imprisoned for protesting the regime of President Mugabe.
2005	Gives up further involvement in African organic farming. Harvest Help set up the Merfyn Temple Fund to continue his work.
2008	Audrey dies. Merfyn still active in Honiton promoting inter-faith dialogue.
2010	Plants the Peace Pole in Honiton.
2012	Dies on 12 January.

Lightning Source UK Ltd.
Milton Keynes UK
UKOW051003311212

204248UK00002B/7/P

9 780953 036929